I0901128

IMAGES
of America

AROUND SWANZEY

SWANZEY, ASHUELOT,
WINCHESTER, RICHMOND,
FITZWILLIAM, AND HINSDALE

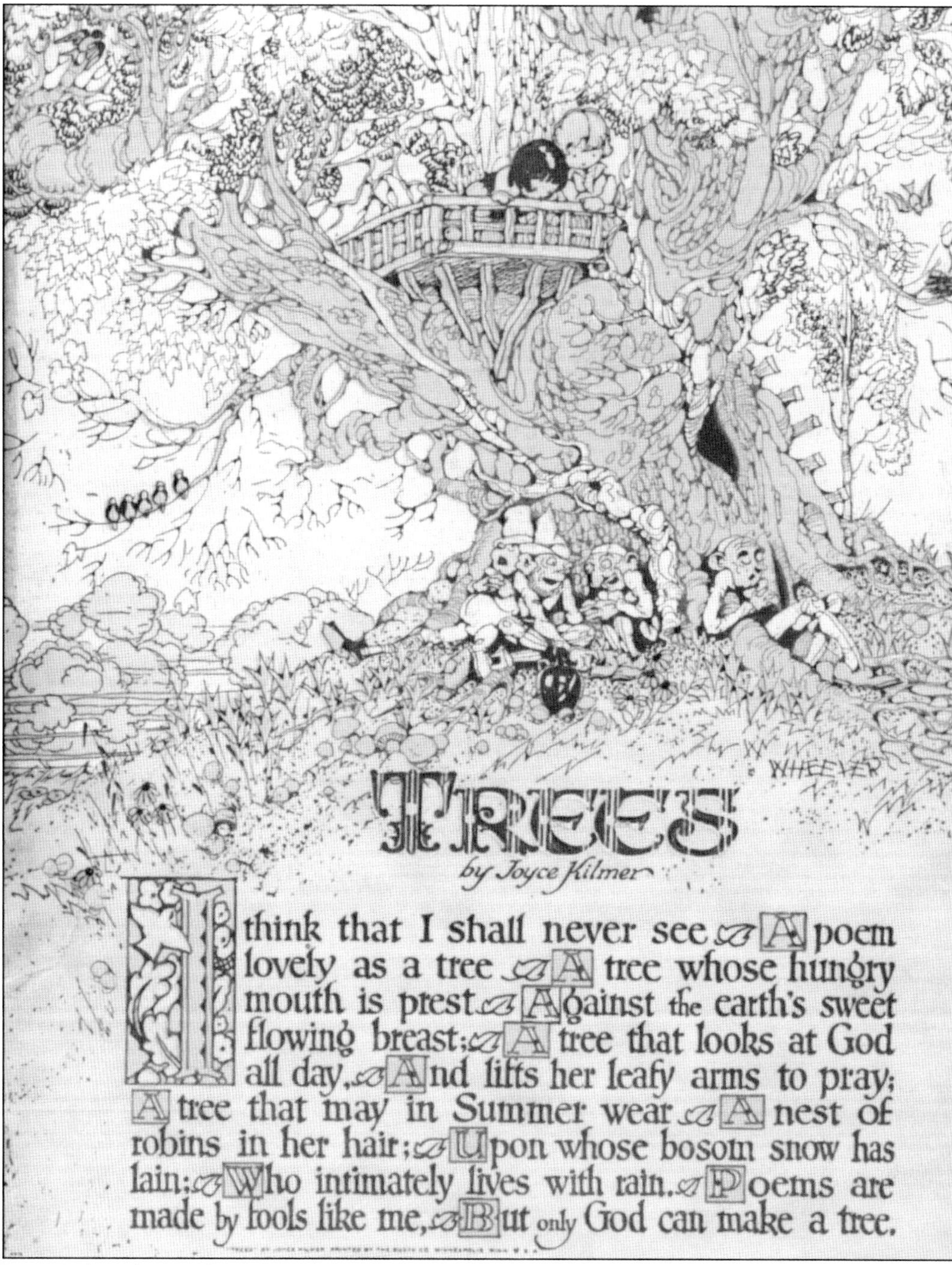

Joyce Kilmer began the poem *Trees* one summer evening in 1914 while sitting on the back porch of the Winch farm awaiting his dinner. The brown paper bag it was written on was thrown away but later rescued by Mrs. Winch. Kilmer finished the poem after dinner, and read it to the other boarders. He felt that it was "good," never realizing his fame would be based on this particular poem. *Trees* was made into a song and recorded; the most famous version was sung by Louis Armstrong. Kilmer was killed in action during World War I, but *Trees* made him immortal.

IMAGES
of America

AROUND SWANZEY

SWANZEY, ASHUELOT, WINCHESTER, RICHMOND, FITZWILLIAM, AND HINSDALE

Pamela Apkarian-Russell

ARCADIA PUBLISHING

ISBN 978-0-7385-8660-1

Published by Arcadia Publishing
Charleston SC, Chicago IL, Portsmouth NH, San Francisco CA

Printed in the United States of America

Library of Congress Catalog Card Number: Data applied for

For all general information contact Arcadia Publishing at:
Telephone 843-853-2070
Fax 843-853-0044
E-mail sales@arcadiapublishing.com
For customer service and orders:
Toll-Free 1-888-313-2665

Visit us on the Internet at www.arcadiapublishing.com

*All images in this book have been taken
from the Swanzey Historical Society archives,
the author's collection,
or the inventory of Chris Russell
and the Halloween Queen Postcards and Antiques
in Winchester, New Hampshire.*

CONTENTS

ACKNOWLEDGMENTS

I wish to thank the Swanzey Historical Society and Charlie Hanrahan for the loan of photographs. A very special thank you goes to Shirley Leonard from the Swanzey Historical Society for all the help she has given me. Her knowledge, generosity, and insight have helped me immeasurably. I also wish to thank Chris Russell, my husband and partner, for his tolerance of my historical excursions! And finally, to all the wonderful people who answered questions and provided dates and clarification, thank you.

INTRODUCTION

Southwest New Hampshire has a flavor and history quite different from that of the rest of the state. There is something quaint and charming about the area, despite its problems, which borders on the theatrical. One of my favorite poems, *Trees*, was written here, and one of the state's most intriguing mysteries involves the area. Langdon Moore—the counterfeiter, bank robber, and prison reformer—spent his last years here, and was an acquaintance of Denman Thompson. Indeed, their lives seem connected in many ways, but their exact relationship has never been determined. Is Thompson the "friend" written about in Moore's autobiography? Why did Thompson support Moore and buy him a house? Why was there such a strong resemblance between Moore and Thompson's son? What happened to all the money Moore stole? How could anyone as high-minded, ethical, clever, and resourceful as Moore have been one of the most wanted criminals of his day? The answers to these questions have intrigued many researchers and historians, and were probably found somewhere in Moore's autobiography, or Thompson wouldn't have bought up every copy he could buy back, as well as the plates, and destroyed them.

The drama of a theatrical giant of his day and a master criminal has turned Swanzey and the surrounding towns into a stage for mystery in my eyes. Despite the fact that the area needs businesses and jobs to up-grade the standard of living of many of its residents, as well as to clean up the industrial debris of years past, it remains hauntingly beautiful, full of potential and untapped resources. As a writer, I can find fantasy and inspiration here, and that in itself was reason enough for me to do this book. Hopefully, others will see the potential in the area and want to become part of it. The Old Homestead is still here, just waiting for others to join the cast of the thousands of residents who are ready for a modern-day revival.

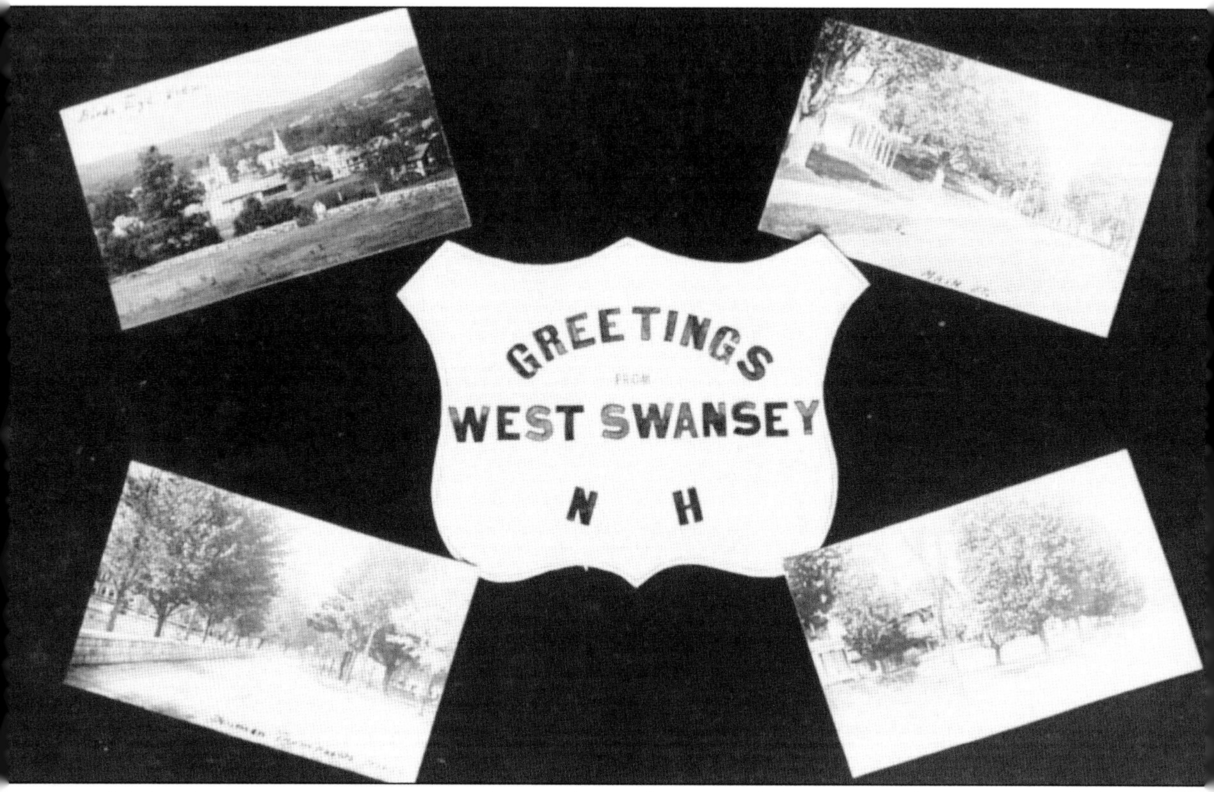

Multi-view postcards were extremely popular at the turn of the century. These views of Main Street, Denman Thompson's homestead, and the town from a distance give a whirlwind tour of West Swanzey.

One

SWANZEY

To separate Swanzey from Denman Thompson and *The Old Homestead* would be like separating Henry Ford from the automobile. The play was based on the people who lived in the town, and the townspeople became the play. Many even acted in it. It is a tribute to both that they grew from the same fiber.

Swanzey's past is full of colorful characters. Joyce Kilmer wrote *Trees* here; Langdon Moore, the gentleman robber, lived here and is buried in a chained-off grave site. Many of the rich and famous, like George M. Cohan and Paul Keith—who owned the Keith theaters and vaudeville circuit—visited here as guests of Denman Thompson.

Basically rural in feel, the area has always been peppered with factories, farms, small stores, and recreational areas. Today the roads are paved, the covered bridges fewer, the small businesses larger, and the population is greater. Antique shops are abundant, factories are fewer, and entrepreneurs abound. The fish and turtles are returning, as are the tourists who enjoy the colorful, picturesque beauty of the area. For those who enjoy historical archeology, the Swanzey Historical Society is a perfect source of information and guidance. There are many who yearn to return to what *The Old Homestead* represents.

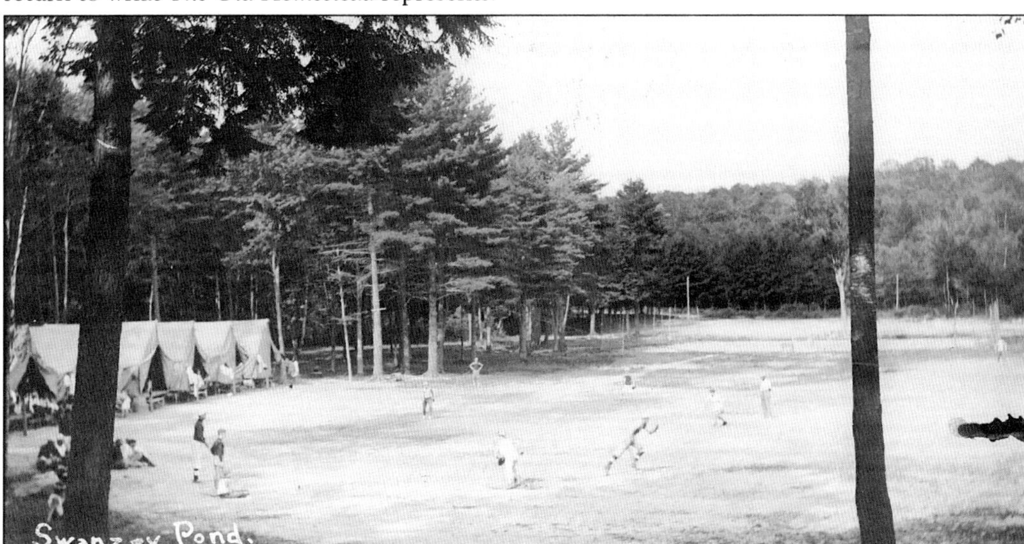

Baseball was as popular in 1912 as it is today, as this game played at Swanzey Pond on August 16 illustrates. Notice the tents on the side where the viewers are. The ballpark was a prime spot for picnics and day outings.

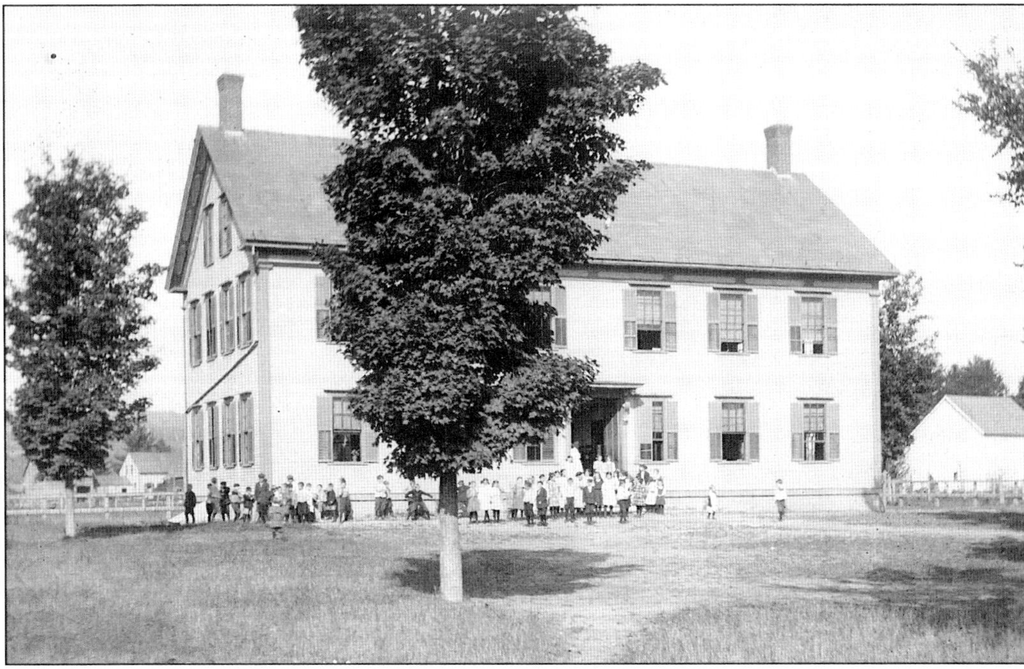

Children play outside during recess at the school in West Swanzey.

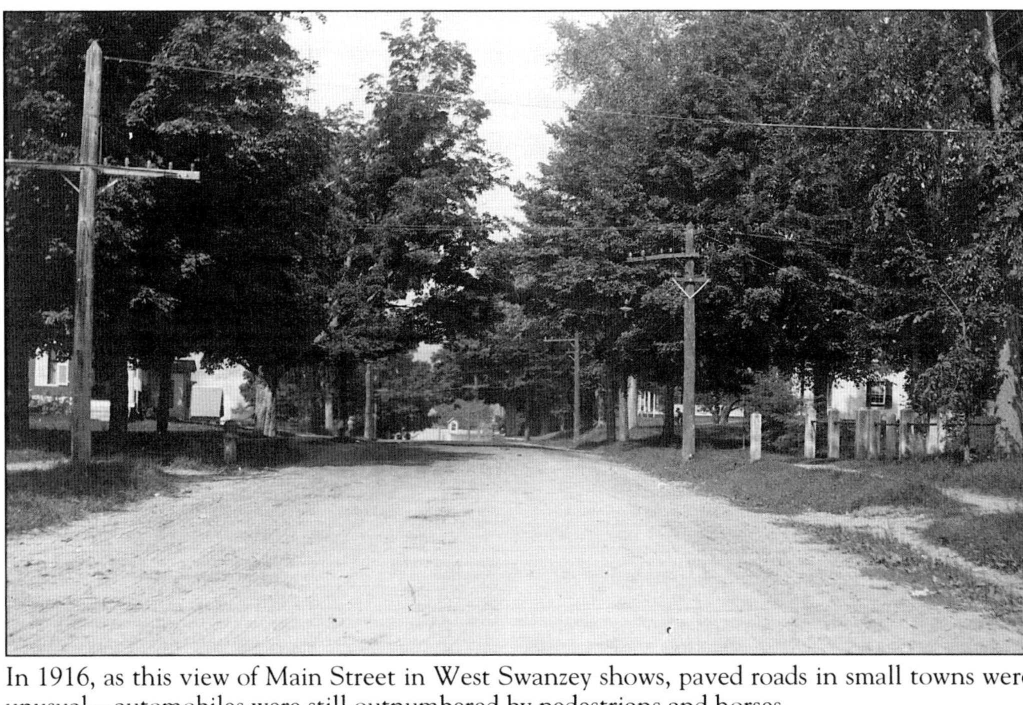

In 1916, as this view of Main Street in West Swanzey shows, paved roads in small towns were unusual—automobiles were still outnumbered by pedestrians and horses.

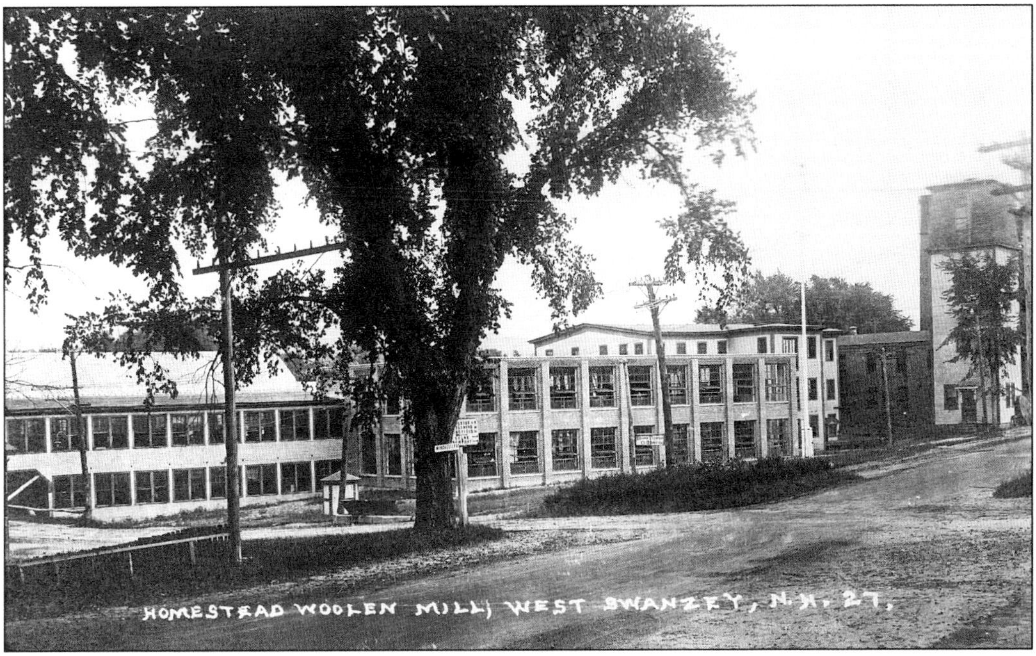

West Swanzey mills like the Homestead Woolen Mill were the mainstay of the labor force and major contributors to the economic well-being of the town.

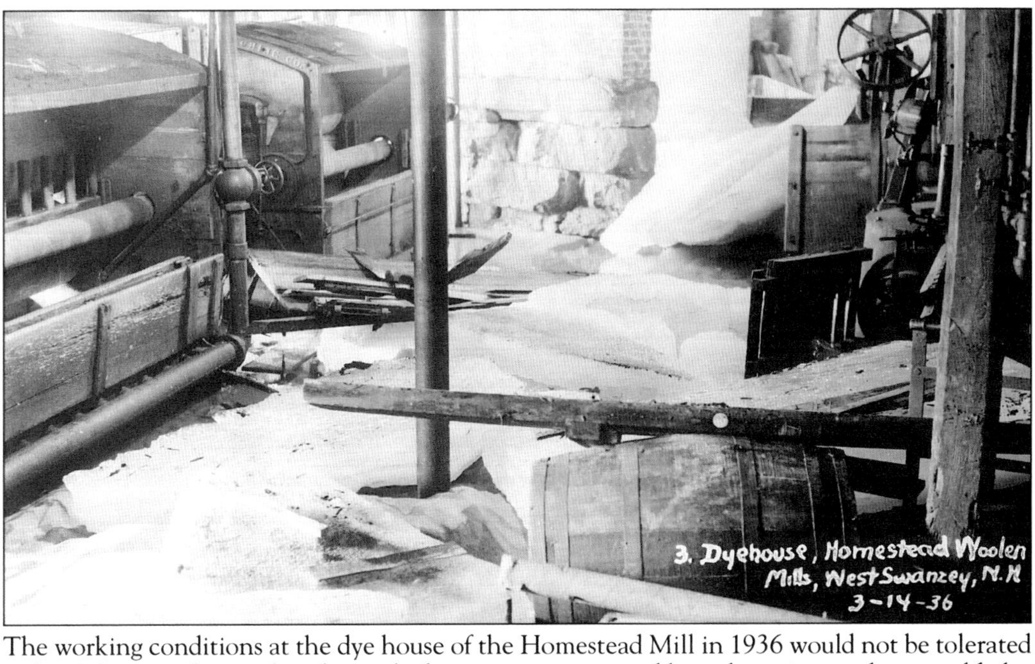

The working conditions at the dye house of the Homestead Mill in 1936 would not be tolerated today. Likewise, the careless disposal of toxic waste executed by unknowing workers would also be prohibited.

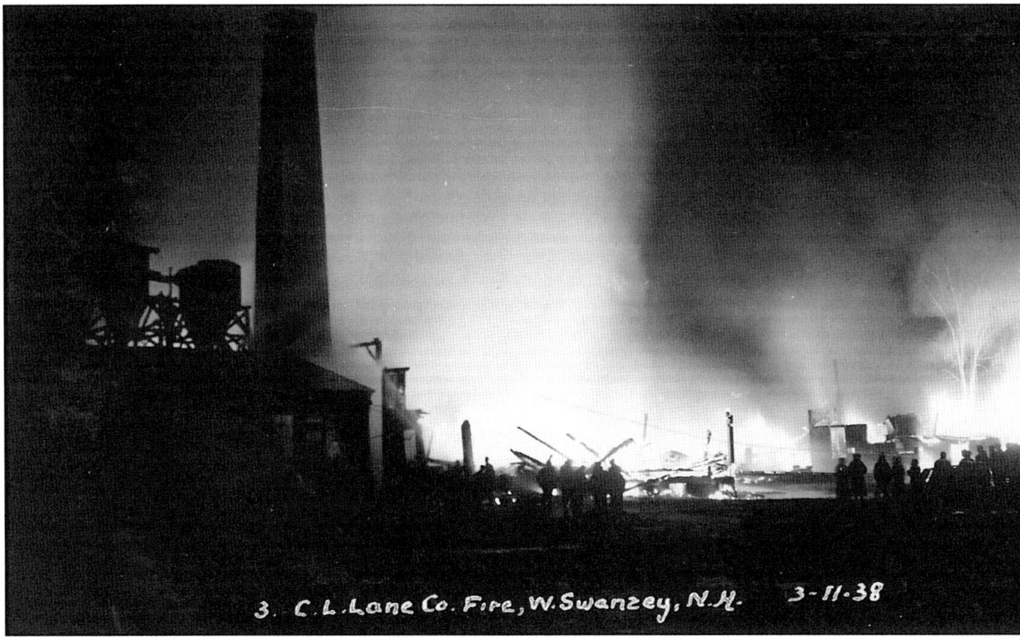

Fires have always been the bane of factories, which were often made of wood and housed flammable and sometimes toxic contents. This blaze took place at the C.L. Lane Company on March 11, 1938. The fires' effects on the lives of workers were often devastating.

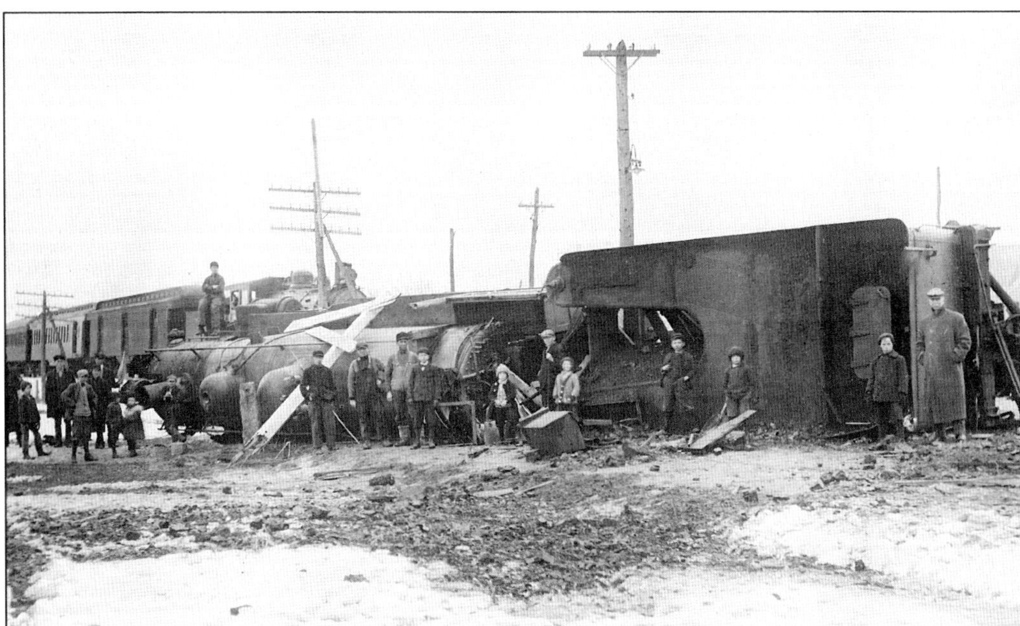

The train was the lifeline of many a small town, providing a major means of transportation for both passengers and products. The wreck shown here took place in West Swanzey.

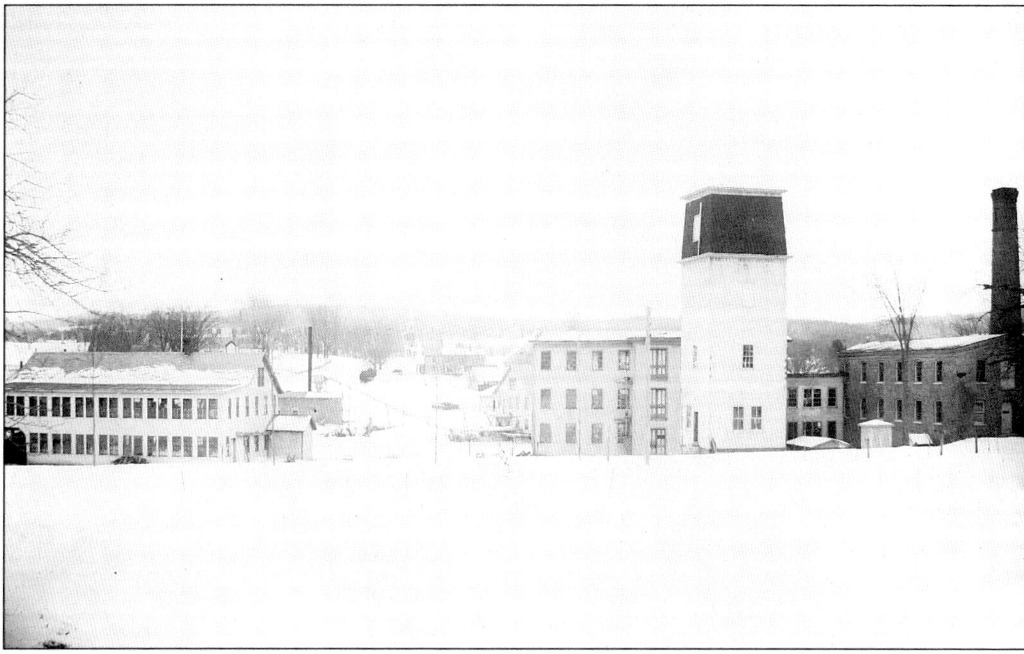

This view of West Swanzey looking east was taken in 1906.

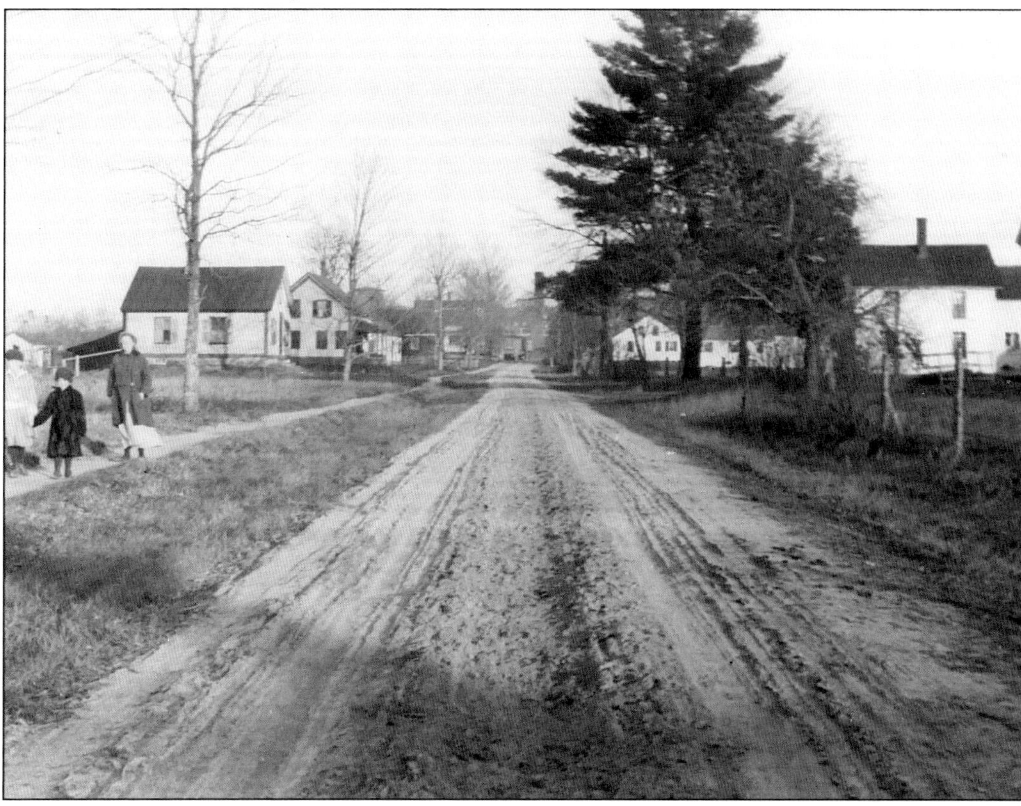

Unpaved roads, like West Street in West Swanzey, were common in the years approaching 1920, as the automobile was used only by the affluent.

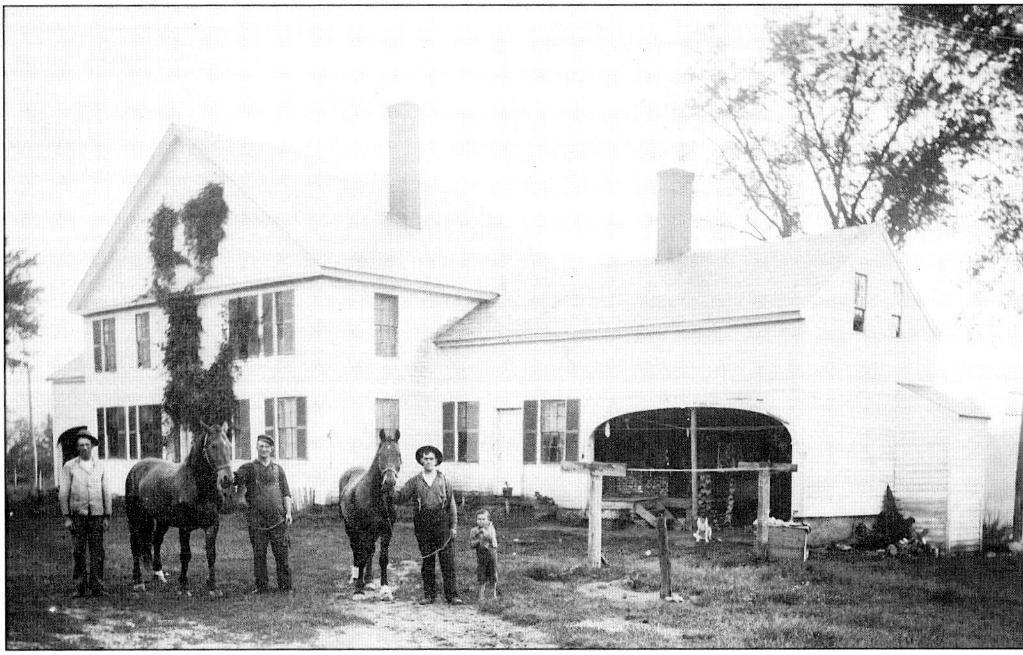

Posing outside a farmhouse on Lake Road in 1907 are, from left to right: Charles Holbrook, Bill Holbrook, John Conbay, and Gordon Conbay (John's son). The horse was still a major means of transportation at this time.

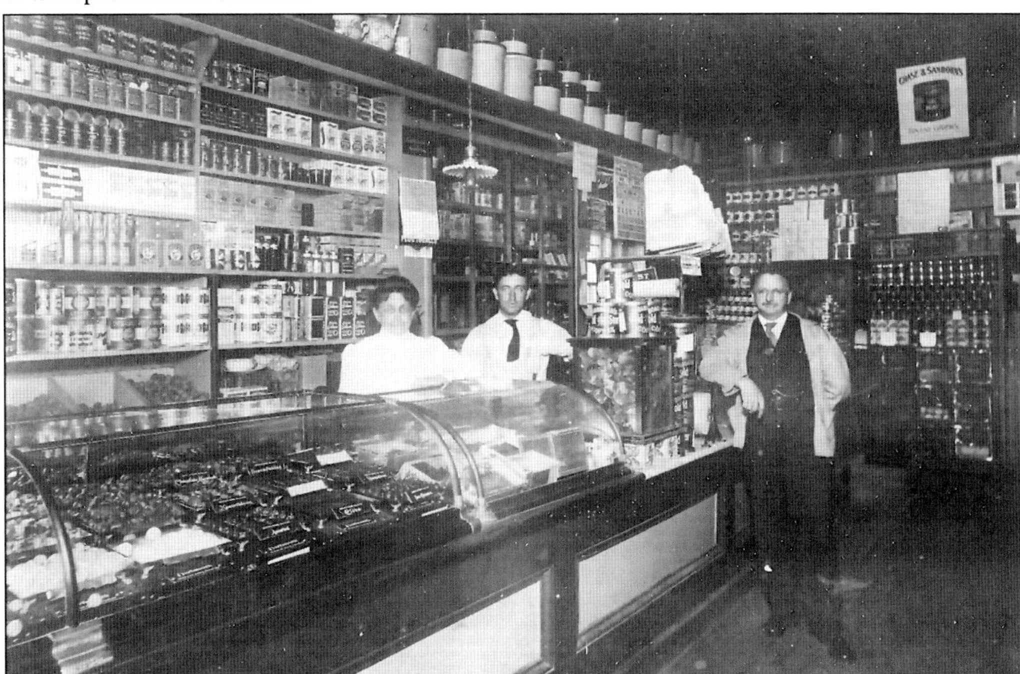

Mrs. Luella Howard was photographed behind the counter at J.O. Howard's store in 1910 with store clerk Carl Cross. Johnny Howard stands in front. These small grocery stores supplied everything that couldn't be grown or made at home. Notice the brand names like Chase & Sanborn and Arm & Hammer on the shelves.

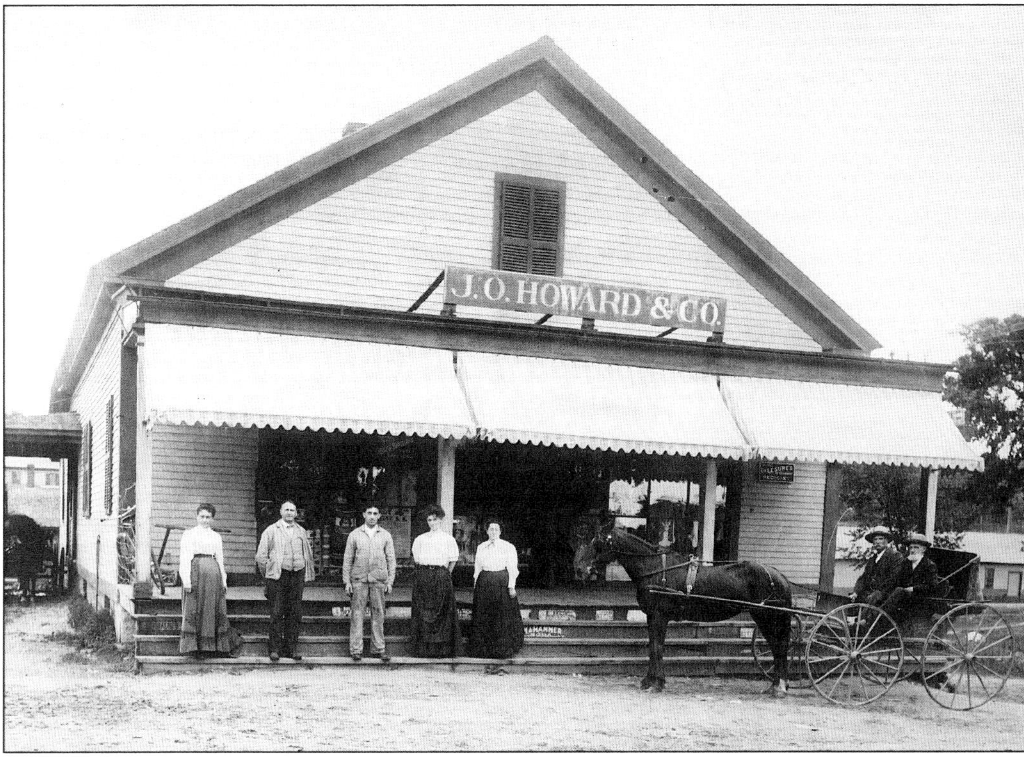

Mr. and Mrs. Howard stand with friends and customers in front of J.O.'s Howard store. Horse-drawn carriages were the means of transport for most people obtaining their weekly supply of foodstuffs.

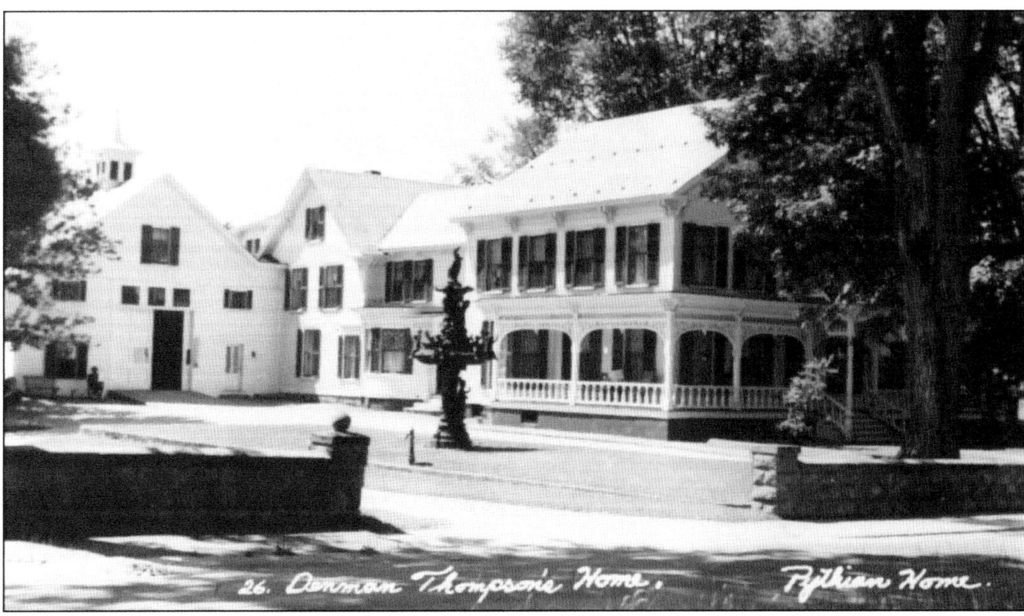

The Knights of Pythias fraternal order occupied the Denman Thompson homestead. The first meeting of the group took place on November 11, 1949, and the last was in December 1979. Lodge #73 was for the Knights, and #37 was for the Sisters.

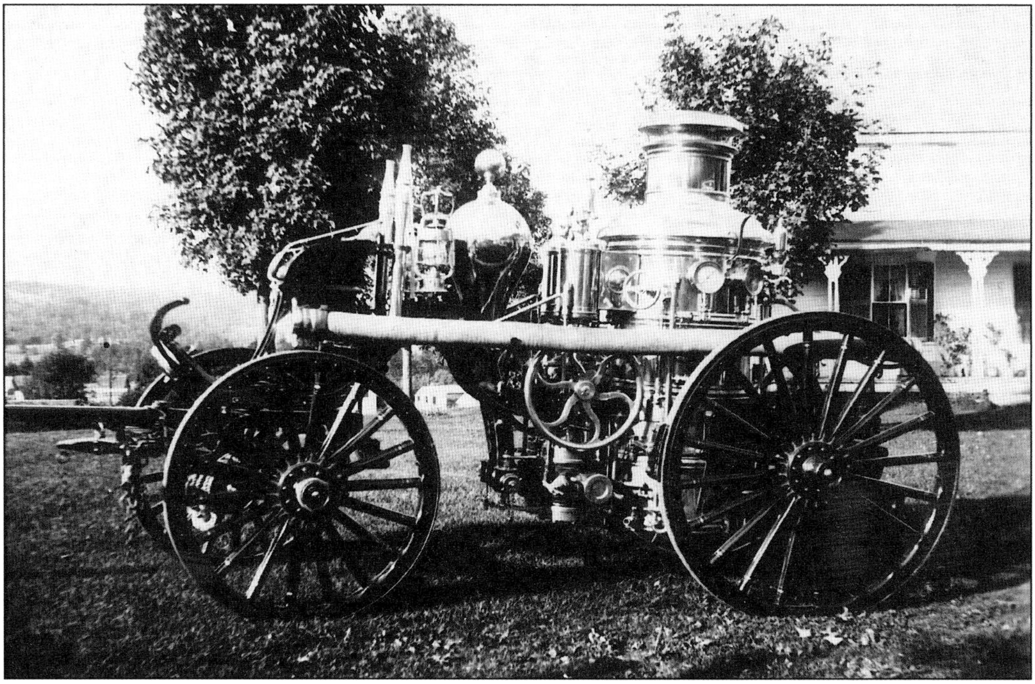

Fire pumps and wagons were generally manned by volunteers in 1901. These horse-drawn vehicles were often ornate and had a lot of brass trim. Unfortunately, because of the small amount of water they could pump and the time it took them to get to a fire, they were inadequate and often too late. The pumper has been fully restored and can be seen at the Swanzey Museum.

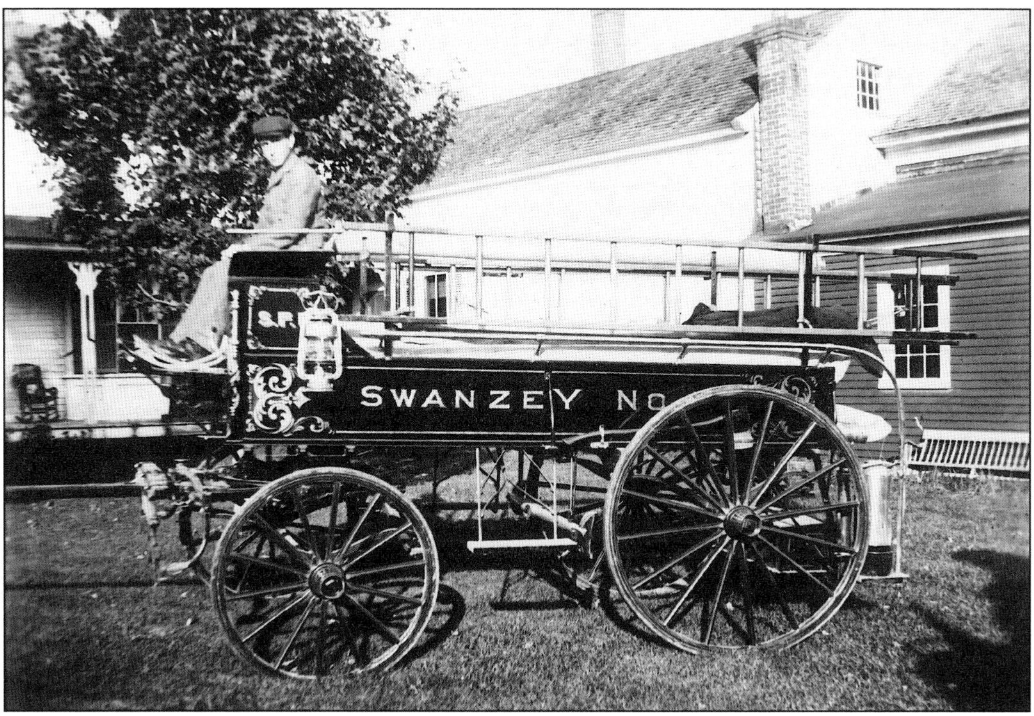

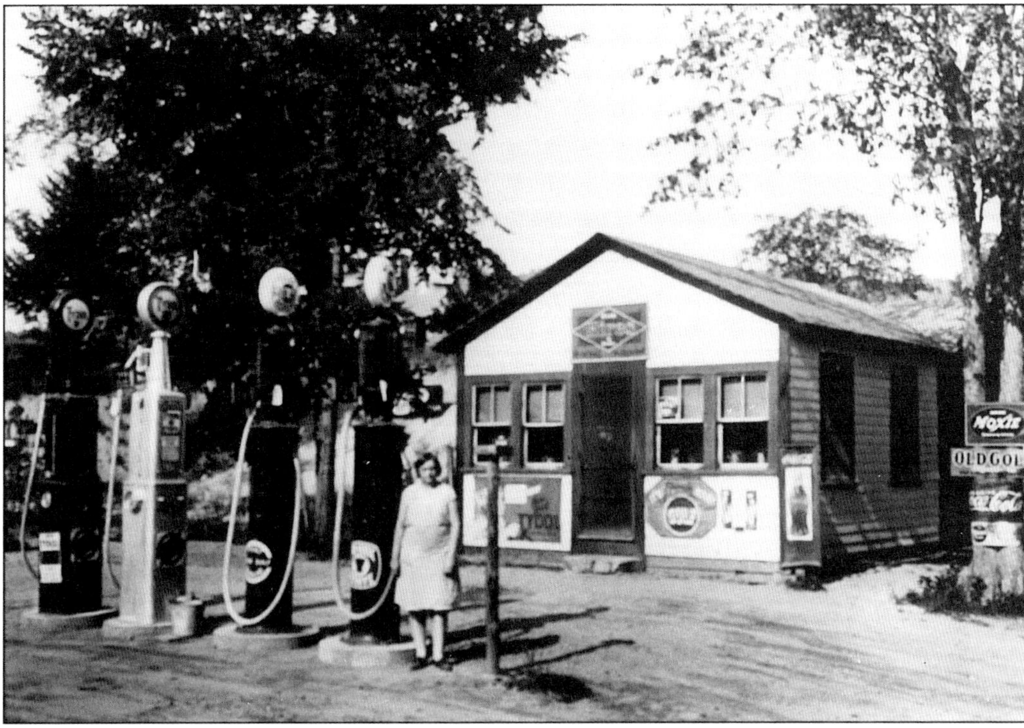

Mrs. Doris Nims stands near the pumps at Everett Nims' store and gas station on Keene Road (Route 10) in 1930. Note the glass globes on top of the pumps, and the tin and porcelain advertising signs for Moxie, Coke, and Old Gold.

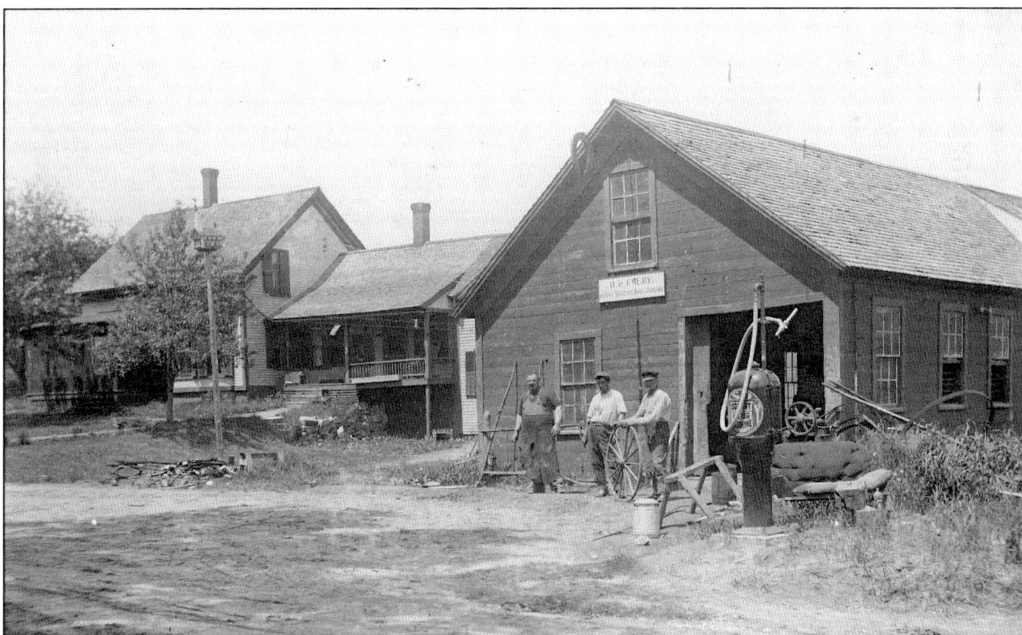

The blacksmith was an important part of the community, as he shod horses, fixed wheels, and repaired all types of necessary implements. Bert Emery's blacksmith shop is shown here in 1930.

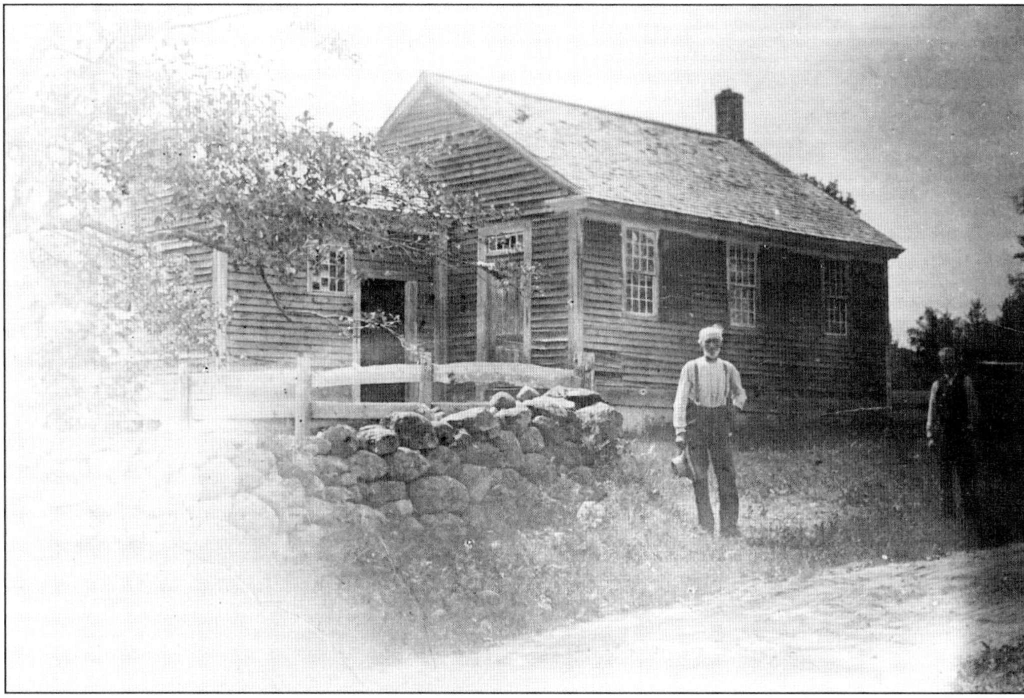

Webster Derby and Mr. Oakman are shown here in front of Schoolhouse #6 on Forrest Avenue. The schoolhouse was built in 1800, abandoned in 1886, and sold at auction for $26.

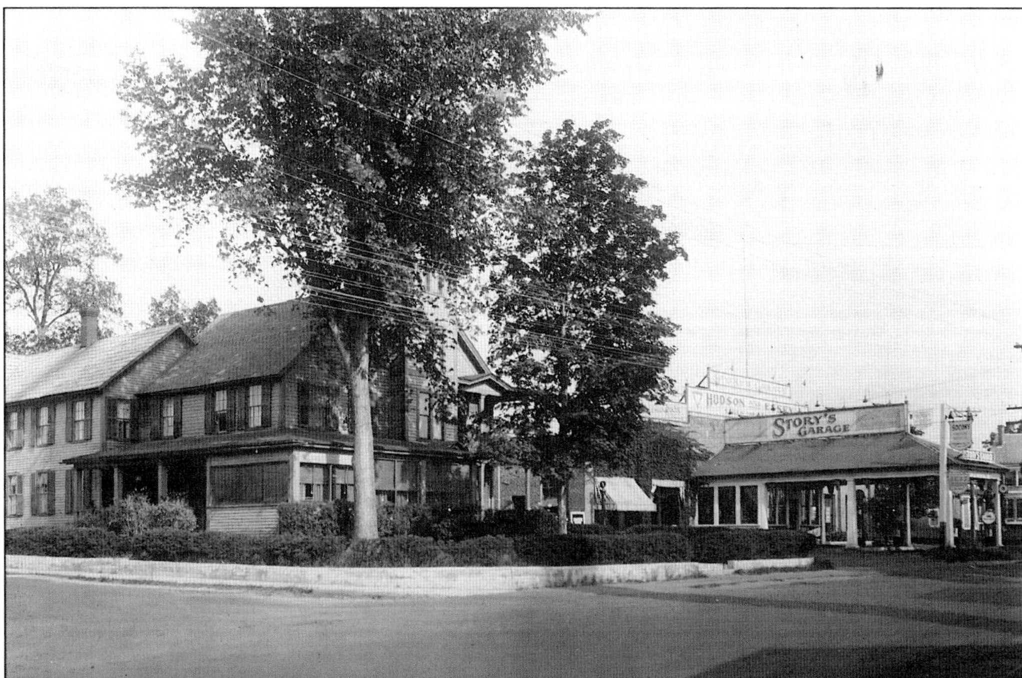

Mr. Story's house and garage appear on the corner of West and South Winchester Streets. At the time (the garage was built in 1925), it was very common for people to build their businesses beside their homes. Note the Socony sign hanging in front.

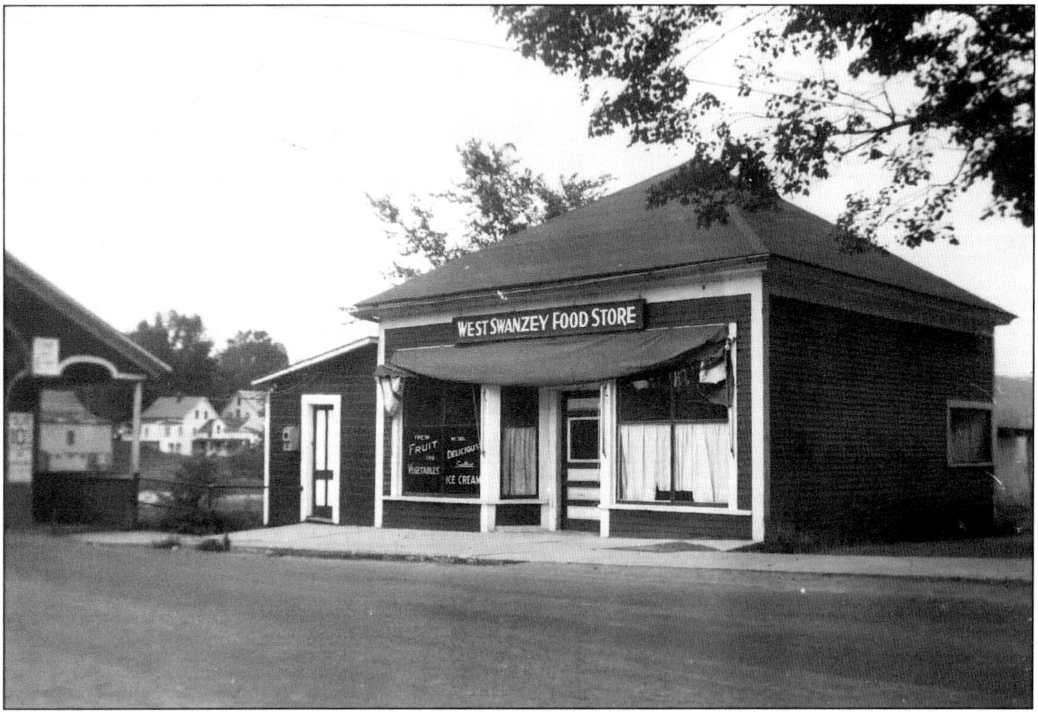

The West Swanzey Food Store was owned by a number of different people. Shown here in 1945, the building was originally built in 1917. In 1938 it was known as Gomarlo's. A "Delicious Sealtest Ice Cream" sign hangs in the window.

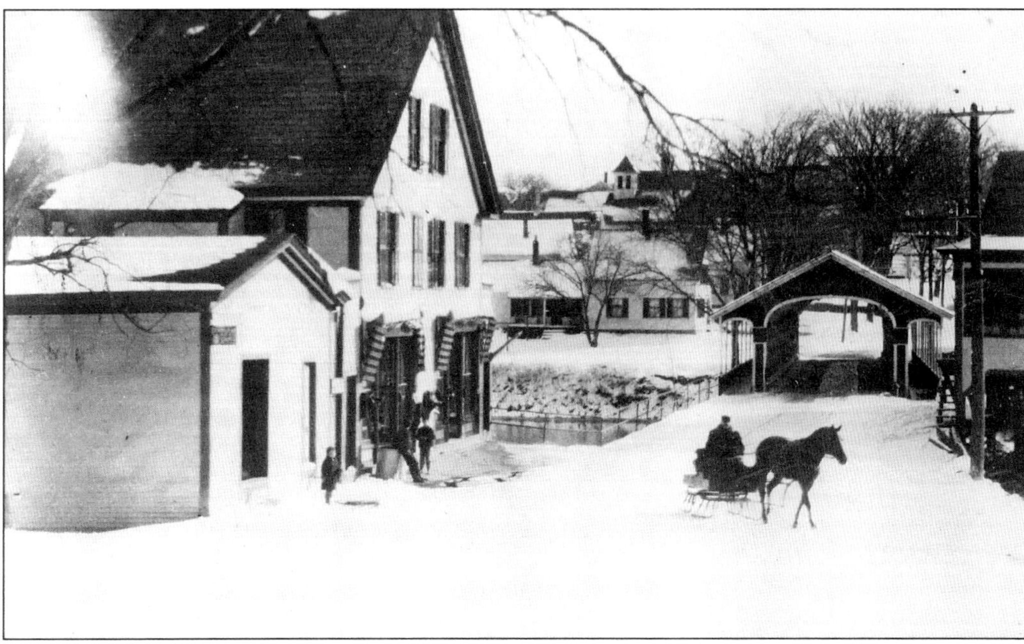

This 1914 picturesque winter scene of the Thompson Covered Bridge reveals both walkways and a horse and sleigh. The store was built in 1840; it was actually two stores connected by an enclosed passage.

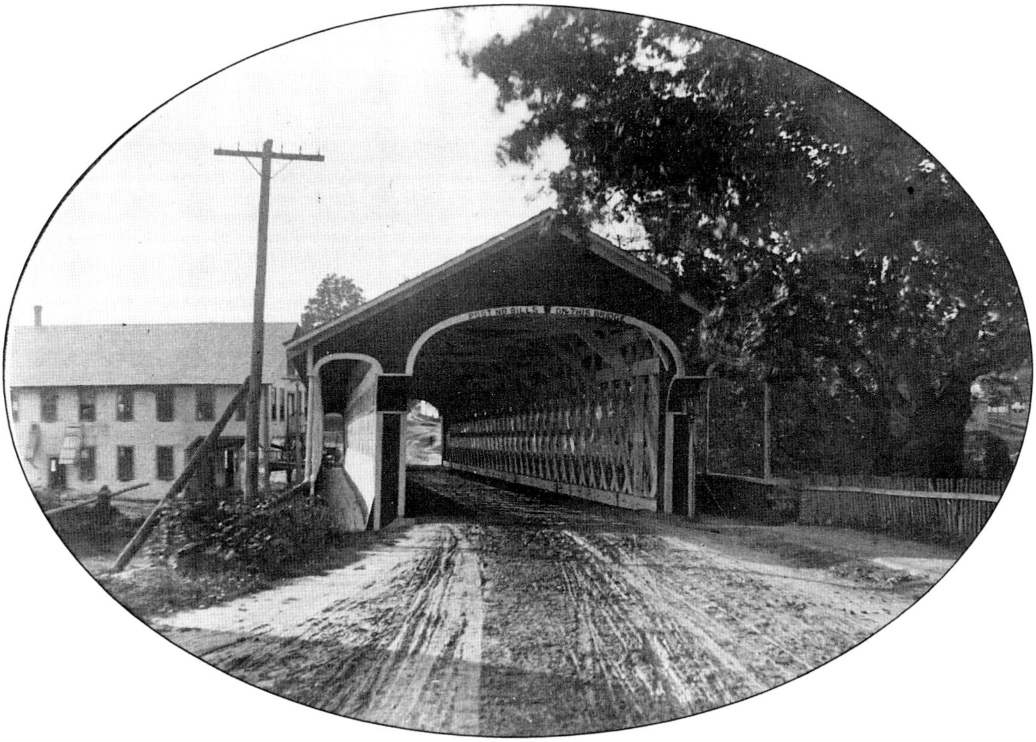

Note the sign on the bridge, which reads "Post No Bills On This Bridge." It was common for broadsides, advertisements, and posters to be plastered all over town whenever traveling salesmen or traveling groups like the circus came through.

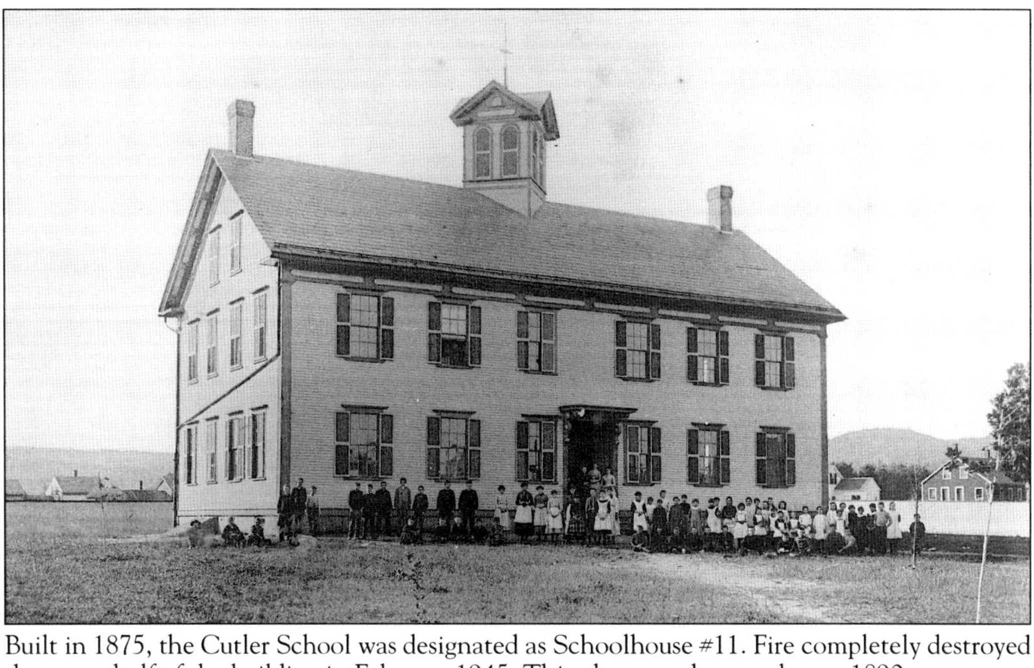

Built in 1875, the Cutler School was designated as Schoolhouse #11. Fire completely destroyed the upper half of the building in February 1945. This photograph was taken *c.* 1890.

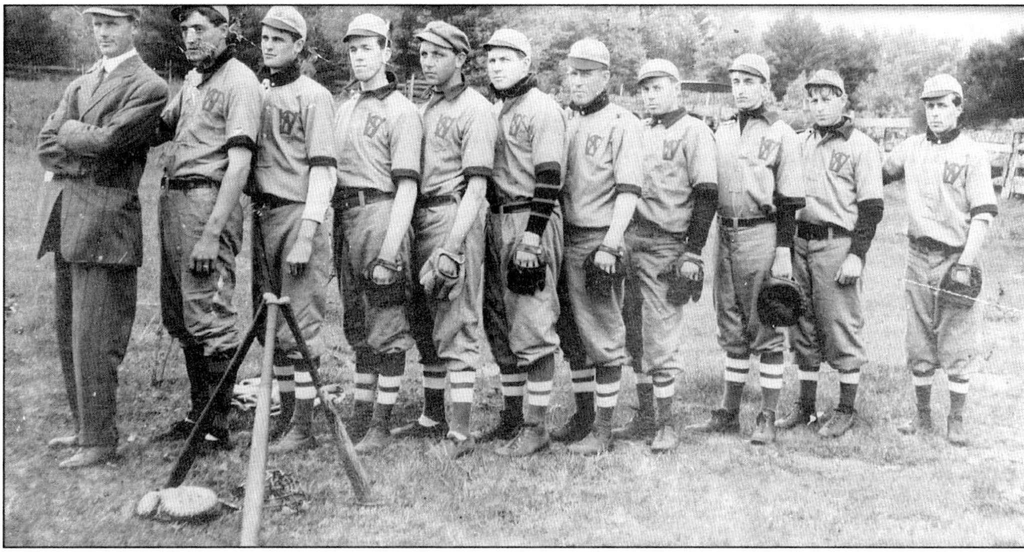

The West Swanzey baseball team is shown here with their old-fashioned baseball gloves. Baseball was an important means of socializing and recreation at the time.

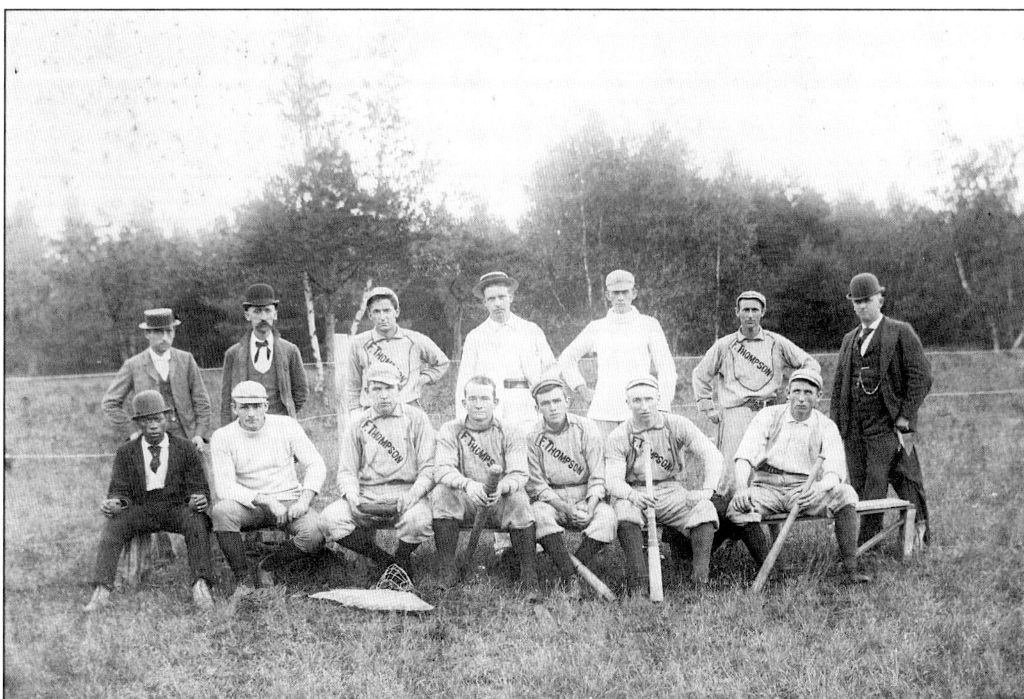

Franklin Thompson's baseball team has gathered around a supply of bats unlike the ones we use today. The black man in the derby was probably the coach, although his actual identity is unknown.

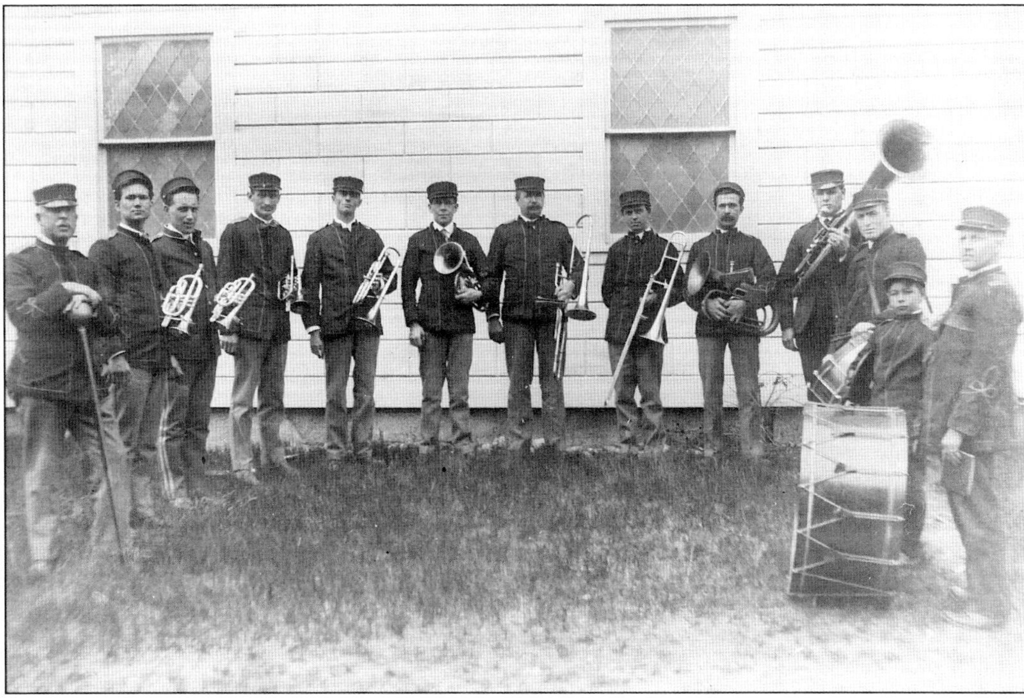

Bands were very important for all civic and social functions. This one assembled on May 20, 1907.

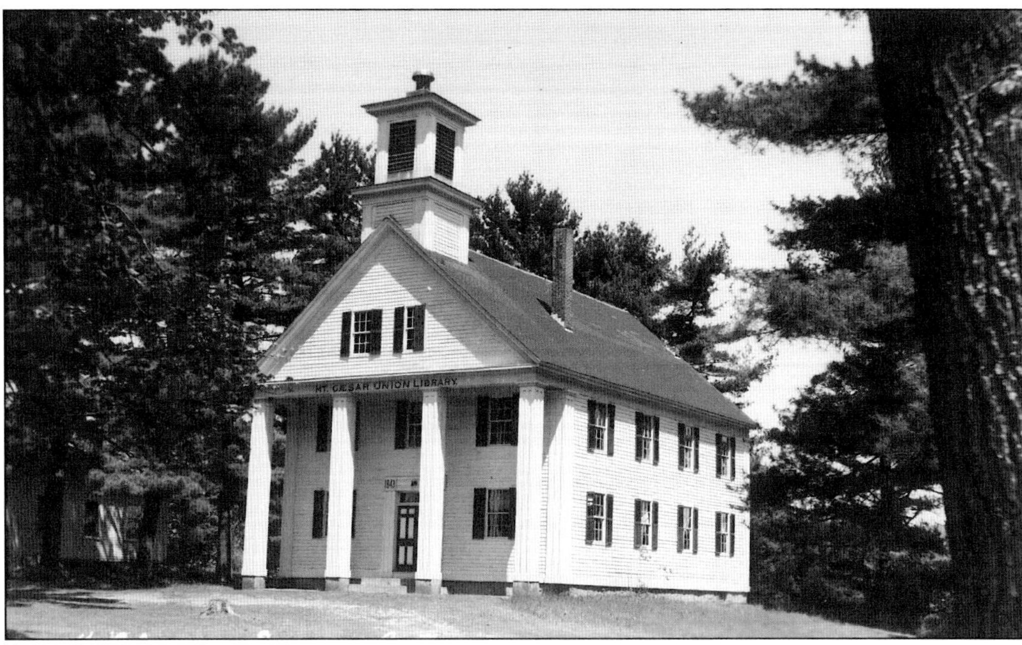

The library in Swanzey Center housed the town's intellectual core. Many small towns prided themselves on how well-stocked and well-used their libraries were. Today, however, times have changed, and many small-town libraries are open for a just few short hours a week.

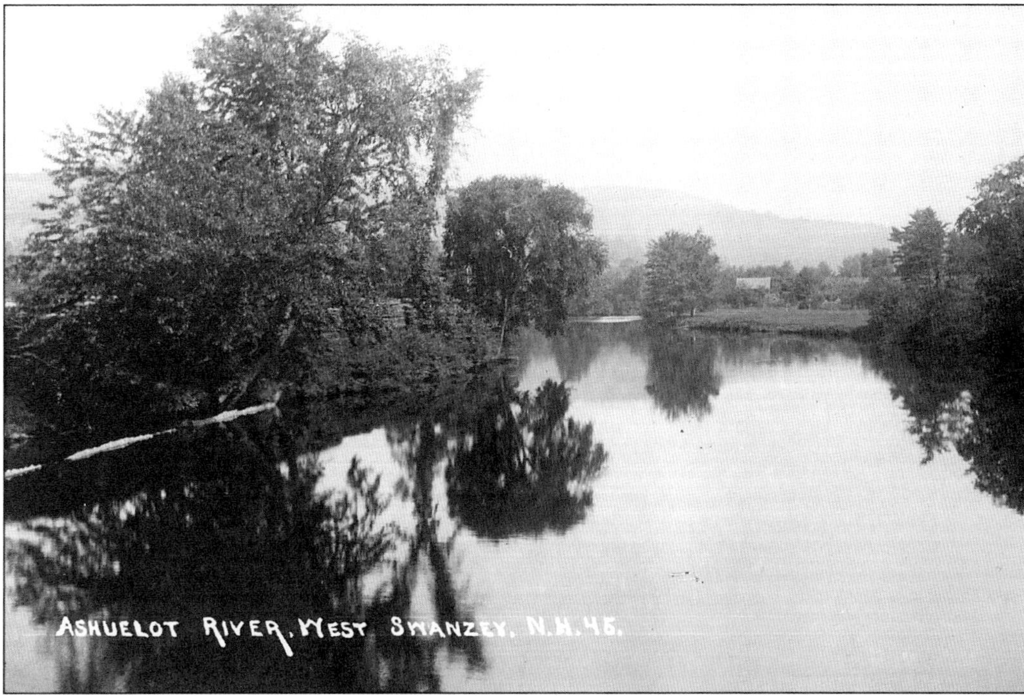

This 1934 view of the Ashuelot River in West Swanzey shows the waterway before it became polluted. Over the years, the river has slowly been detoxified and the fish are now returning.

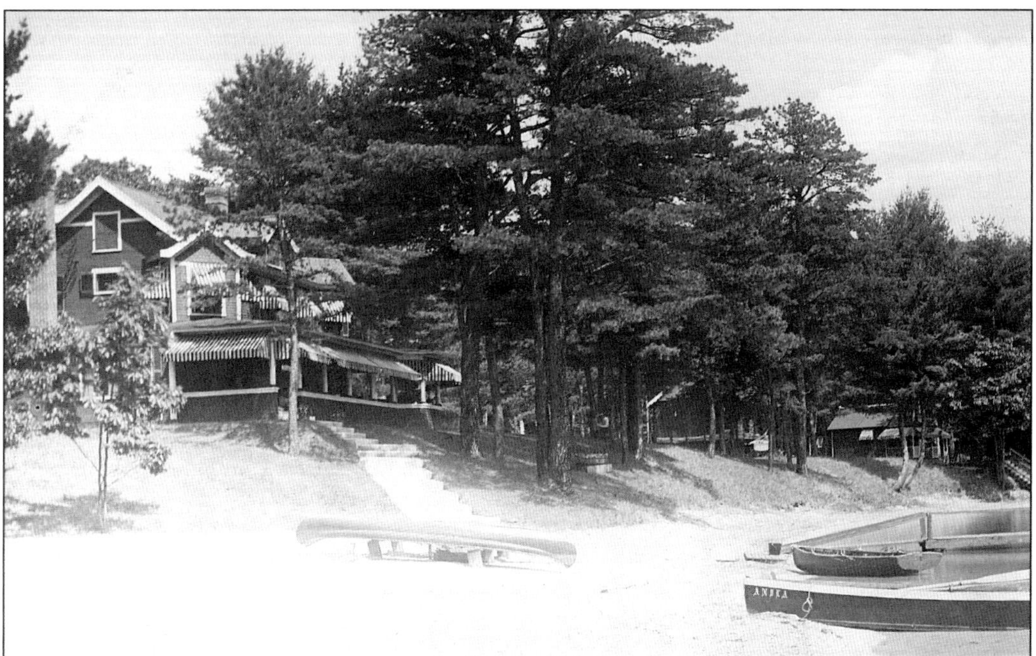

This 1909 photograph of Mrs. Kilpatrick's cottage at Swanzey Pond shows that it has long been fashionable and pleasant to have a summer home on the lake. These summer homes had to have enough room to accommodate guests.

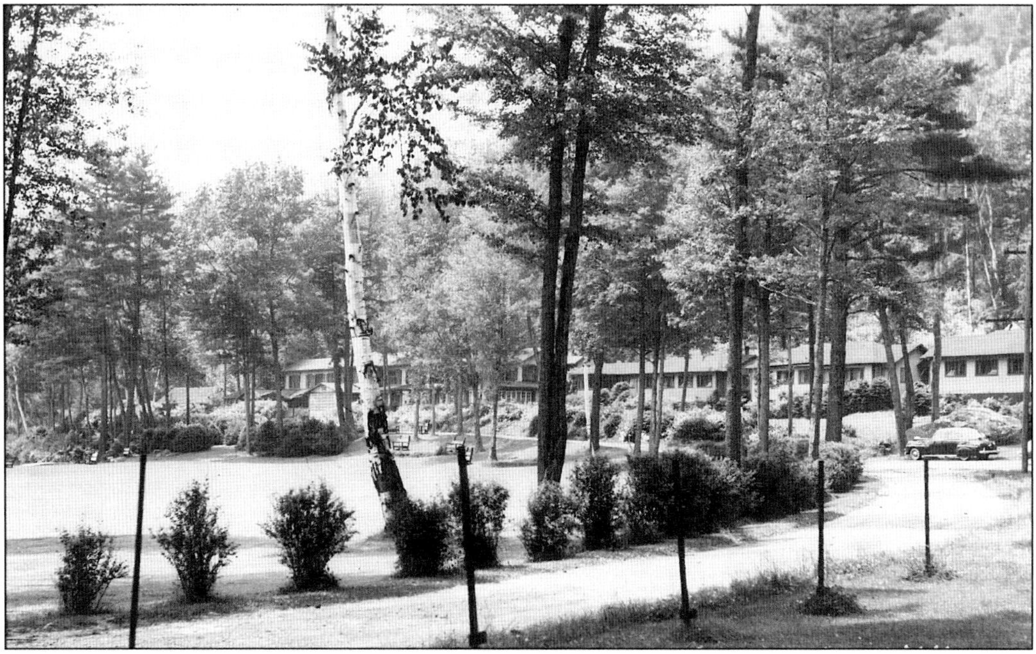

Camp Wawona on Swanzey Lake is shown here in 1943. Camps with cabins that people can rent weekly or seasonally have always been popular in this area.

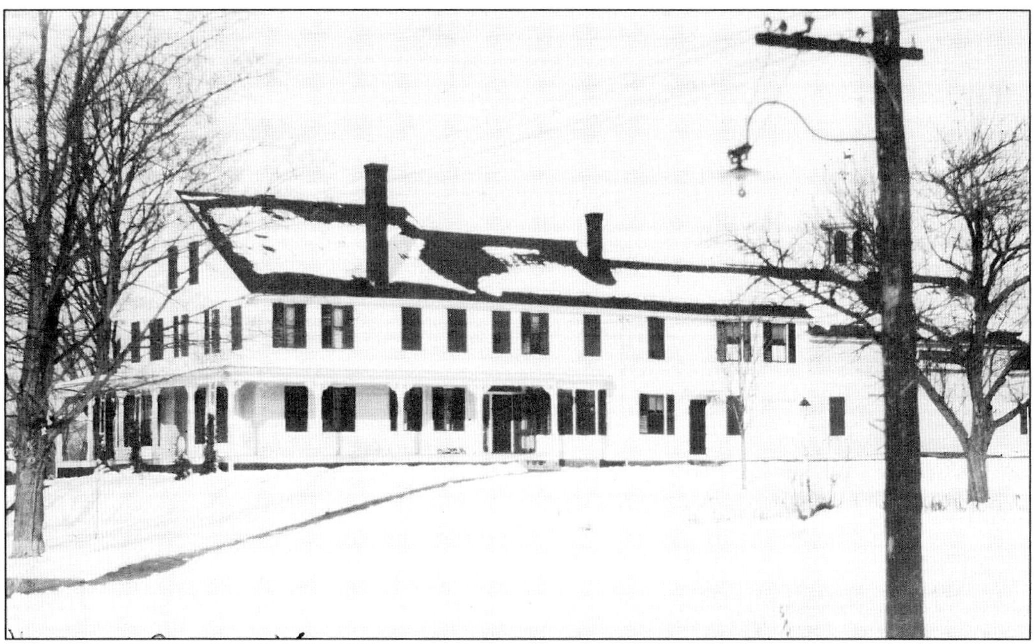

Large family homesteads, like the home of George Whitcomb, were heated by wood and often had both summer and winter kitchens.

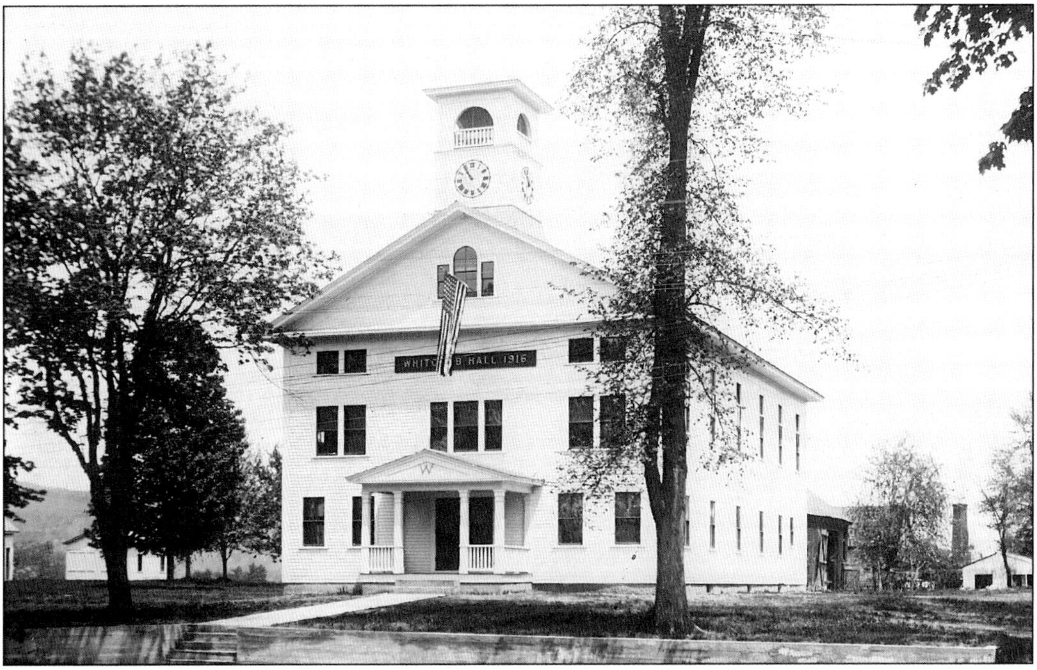

Whitcomb Hall was given as a gift to the town by George Whitcomb.

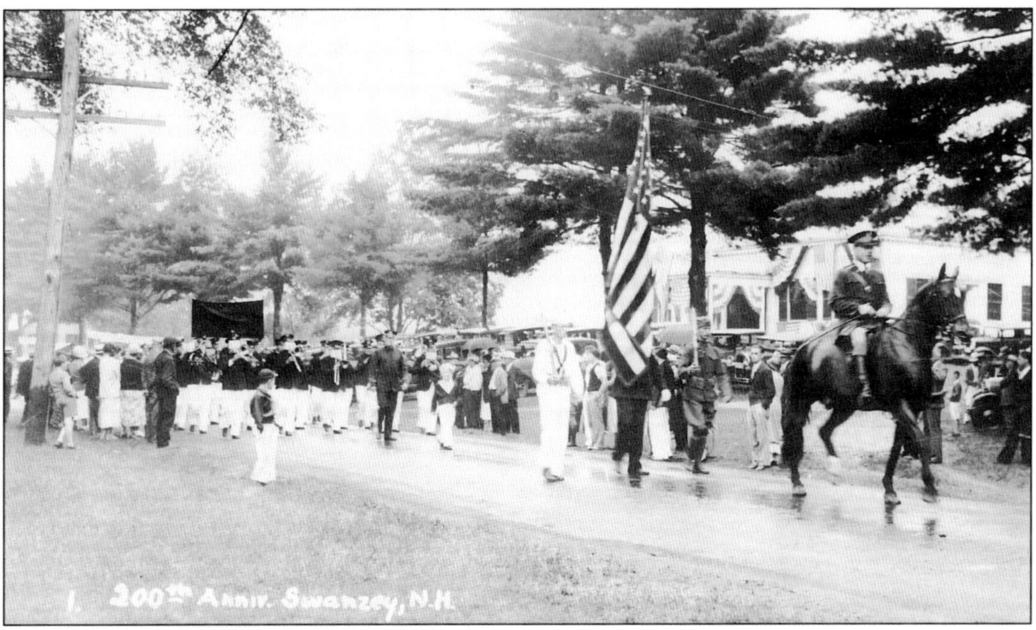

The 200th anniversary of Swanzey in 1933 was a major event featuring parades and floats. Veterans, social, and civic organizations from Swanzey and adjoining towns participated in the celebrations. This image shows the visiting band from Keene.

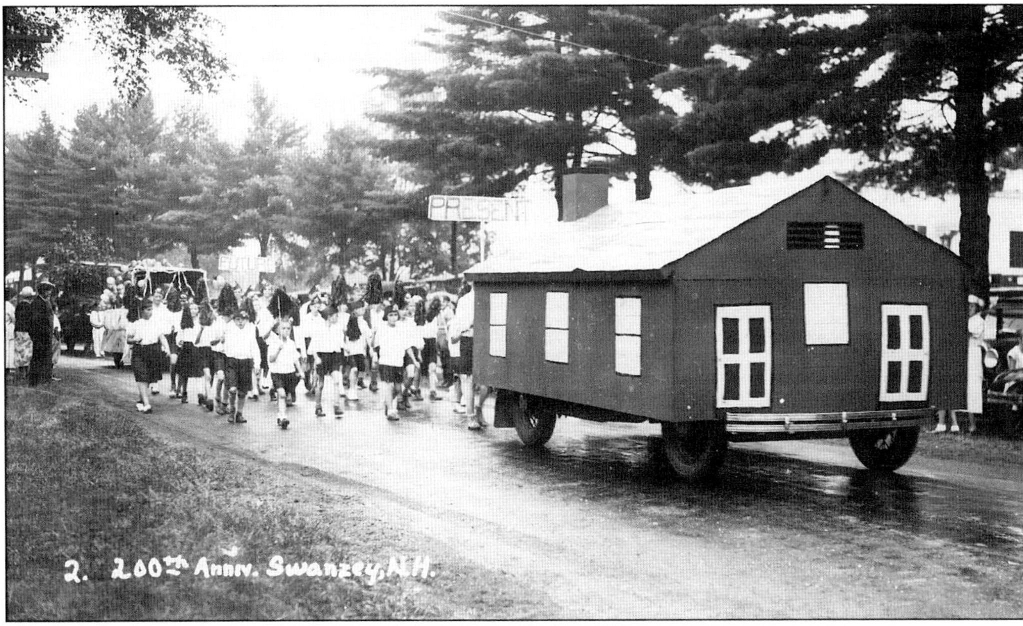

A schoolhouse float on wheels is followed by local children.

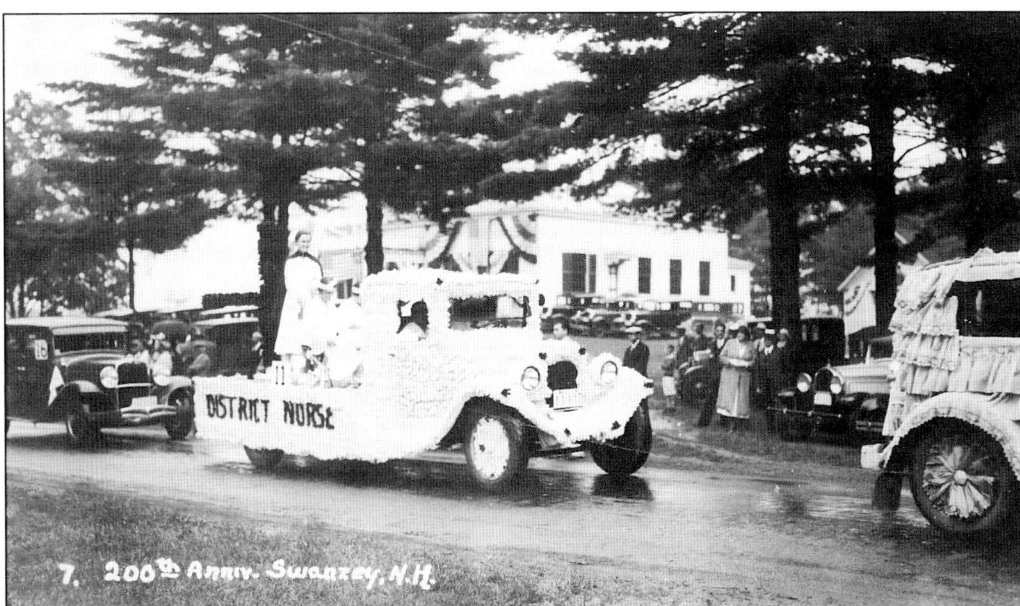

The flowered truck of the district nurse was float #11 in the parade. Note the flag and decorations on the building in the background.

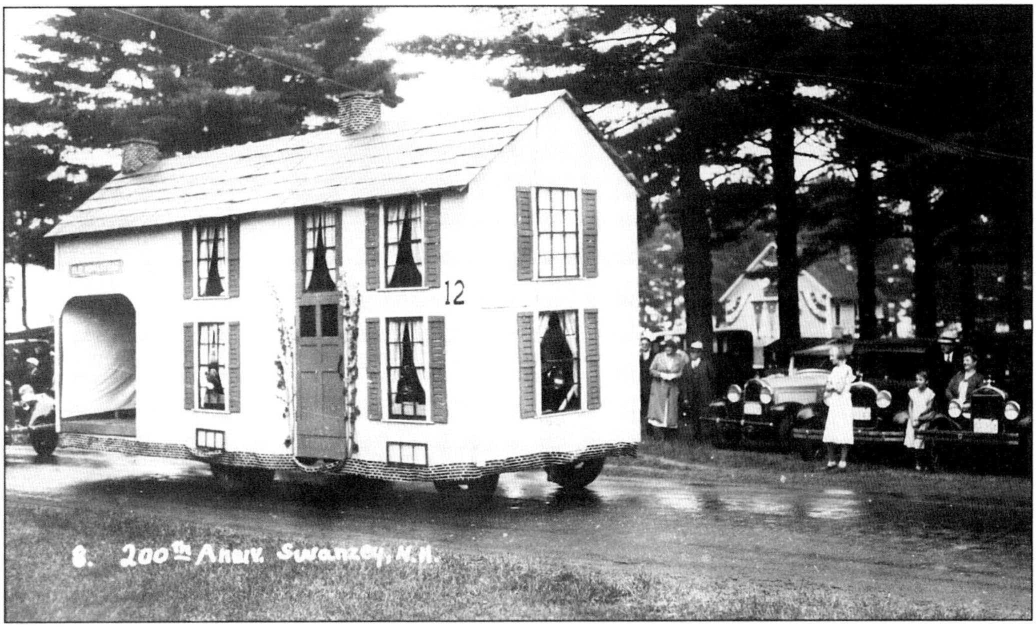

Float #12 won third prize in the parade. The building after which it was modeled can be seen in the background past the trees.

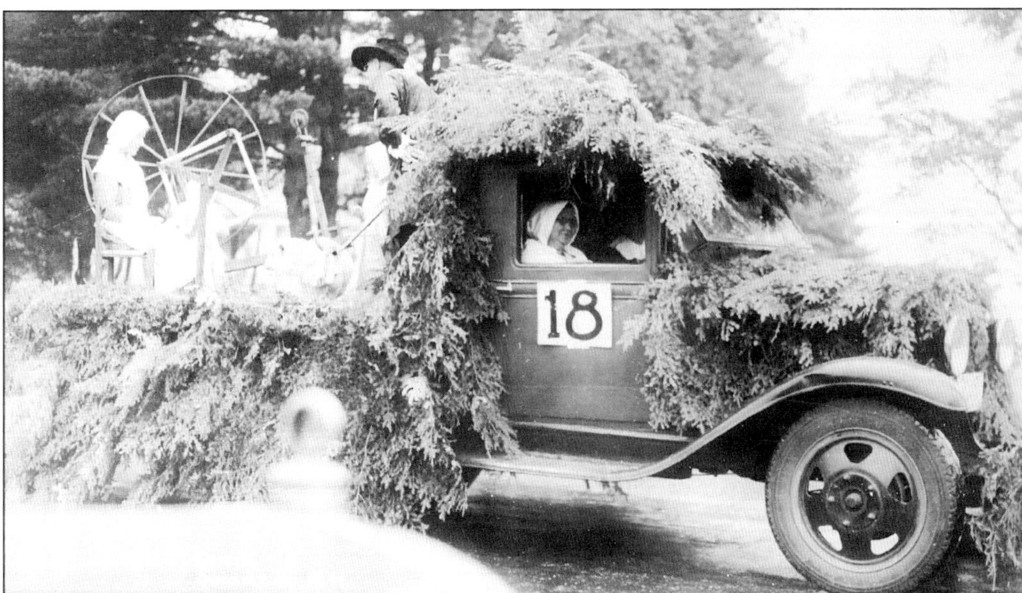

Float #18 was a historical rendition of pilgrims John and Priscilla Alden. Both spinning and flax wheels are shown, as well as the sheep from which the wool would come.

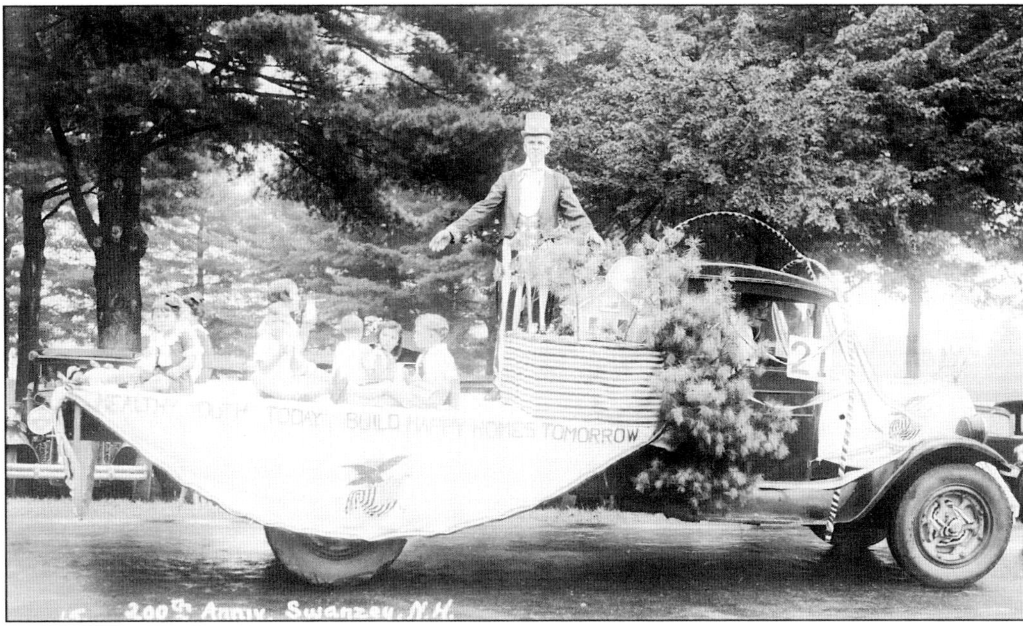

Float #21, entitled "Healthy Youth Today Build Happy Homes Tomorrow," involved the participation of 4H Club children and Leland Bogue as Uncle Sam.

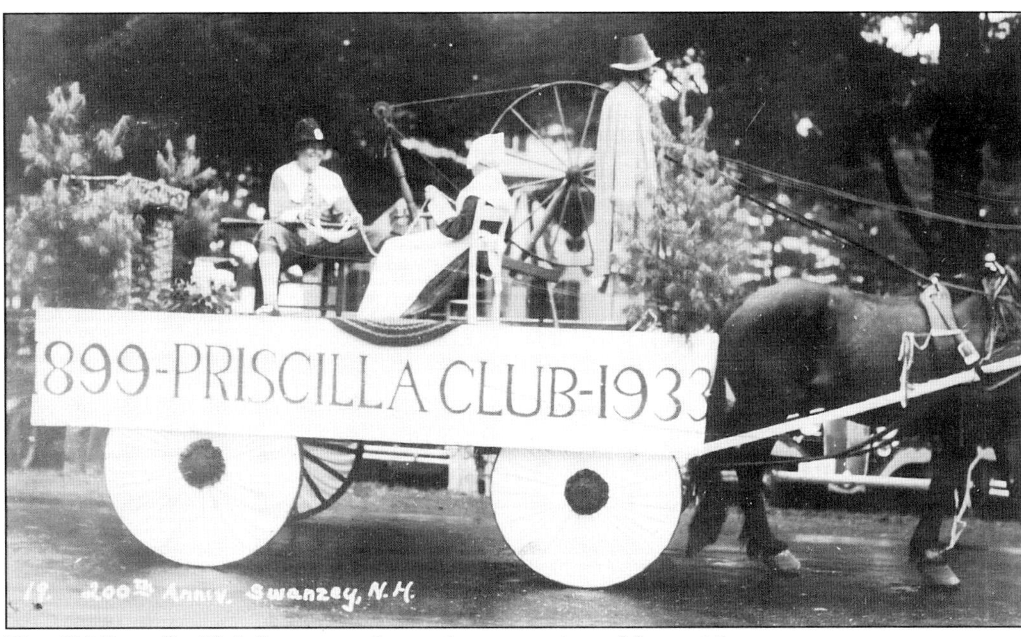

The 899 Priscilla Club float was a horse-drawn version of float #18.

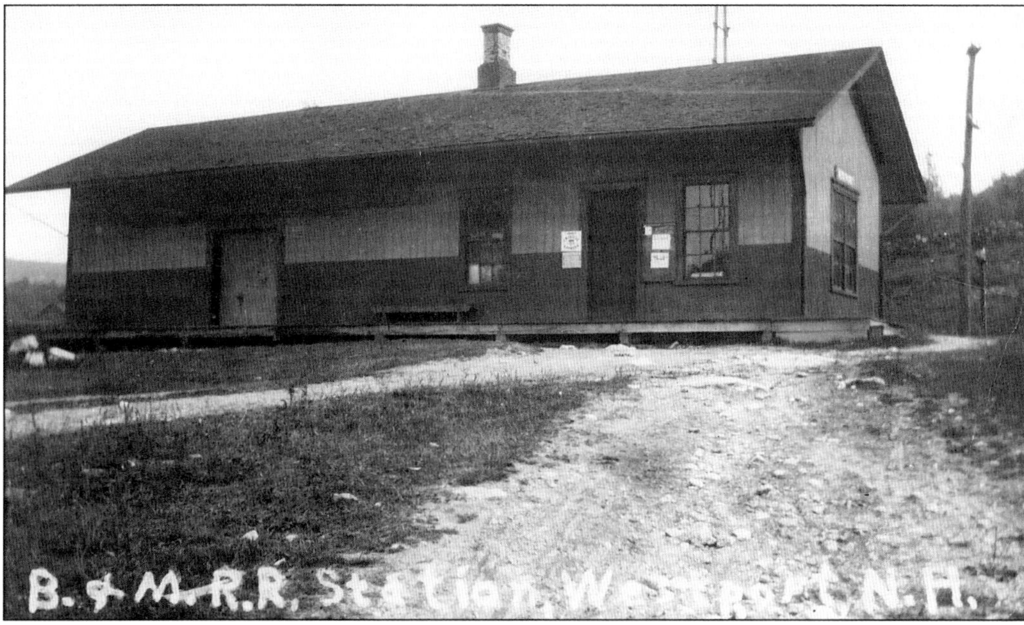

The railroad was the lifeblood of many a town, as it not only brought passengers but also transported commodities to and from local businesses. The station in Westport is shown here.

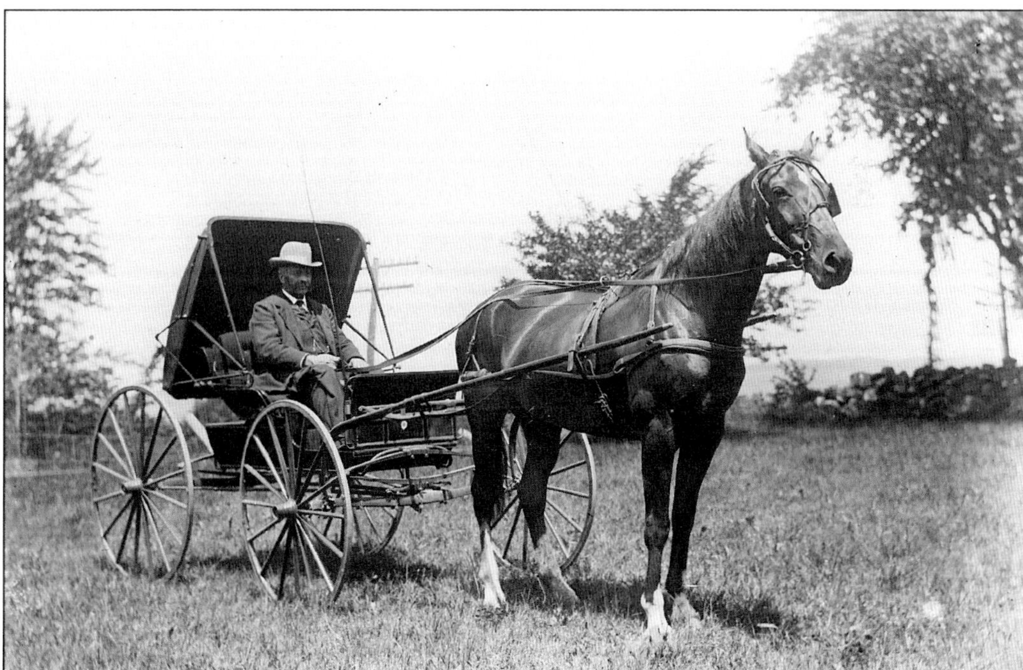

Horse-drawn carriages were only practical during clement weather. The driver is Dr. George Cutler.

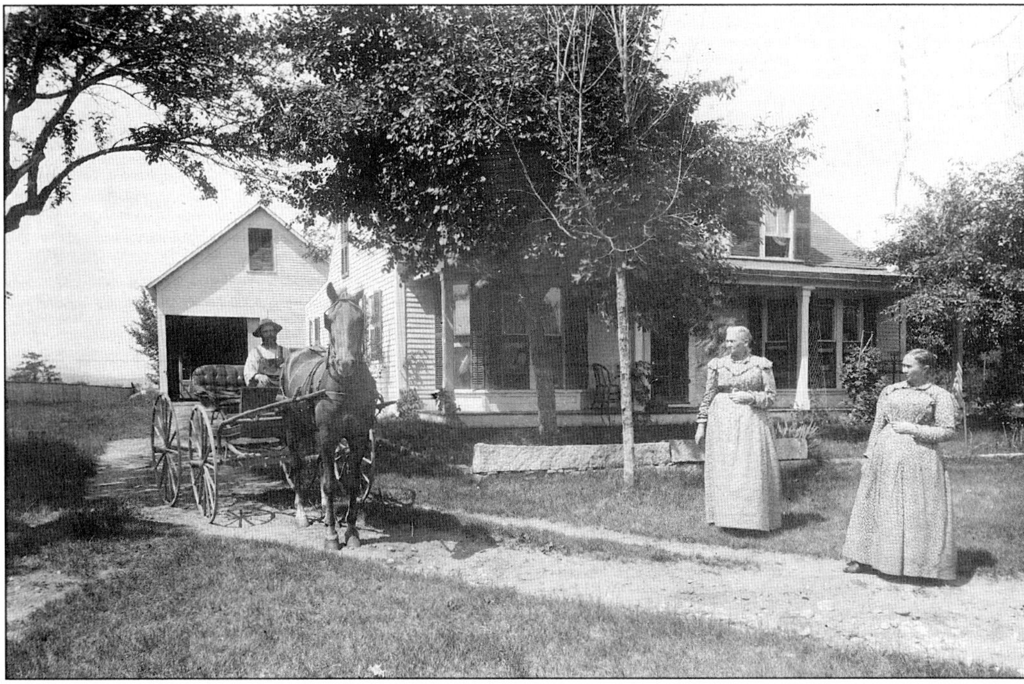

This horse-drawn team with Johnny Horse was driven by Andrew Haskell *c.* 1900. Near the tree is Ellen Alexander, and near the road is Nan Ward.

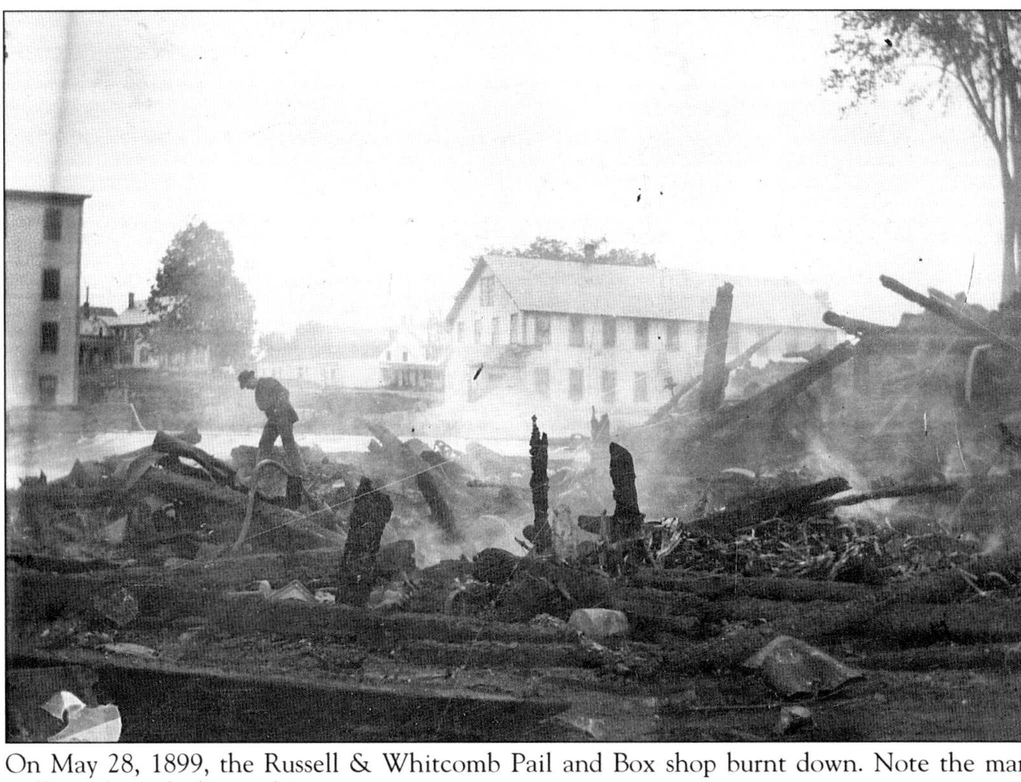

On May 28, 1899, the Russell & Whitcomb Pail and Box shop burnt down. Note the man walking through the smoking ruins.

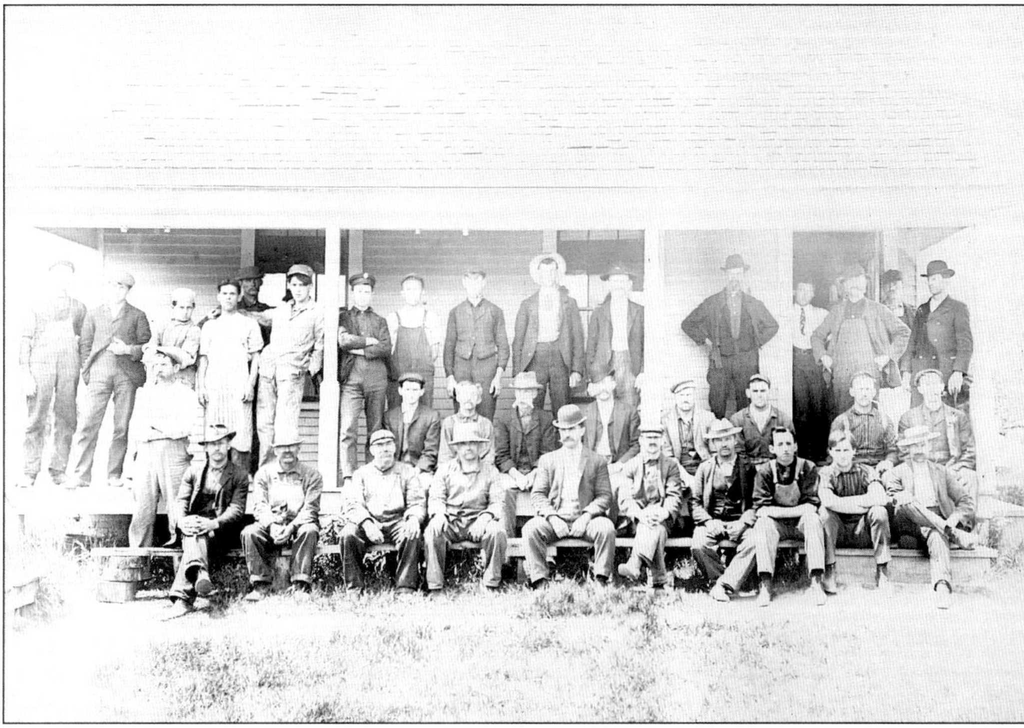

This photograph, probably taken shortly before the fire, shows the Whitcomb Pail and Box shop and the men who worked there.

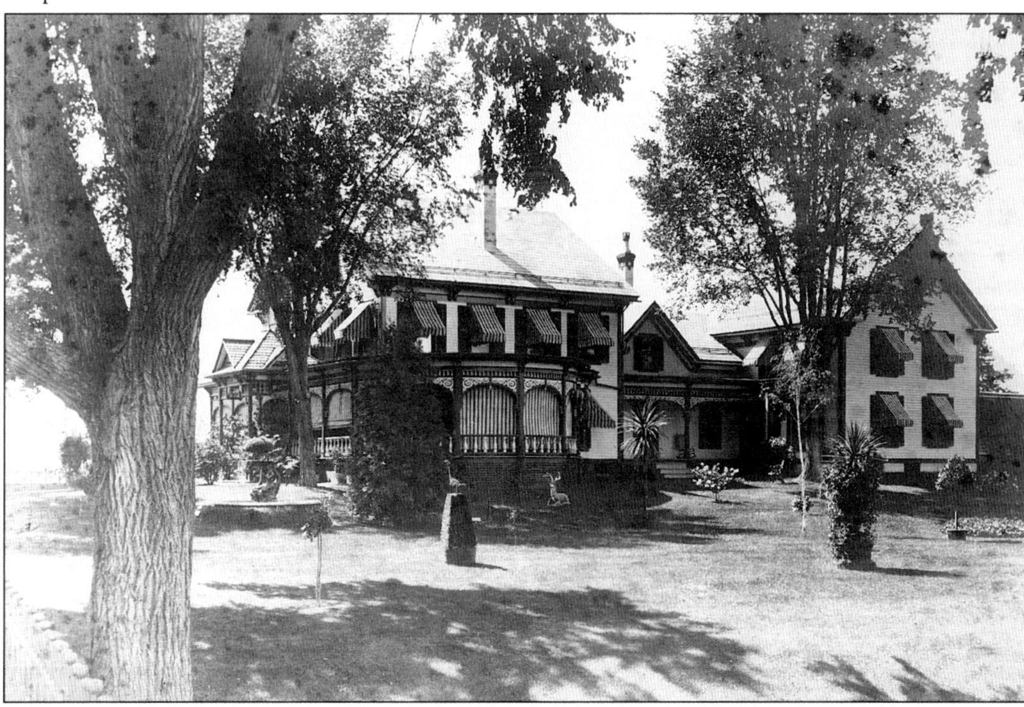

The Old Homestead epitomizes the southwest corner of New Hampshire and has become a symbol representing the character and fiber of area residents.

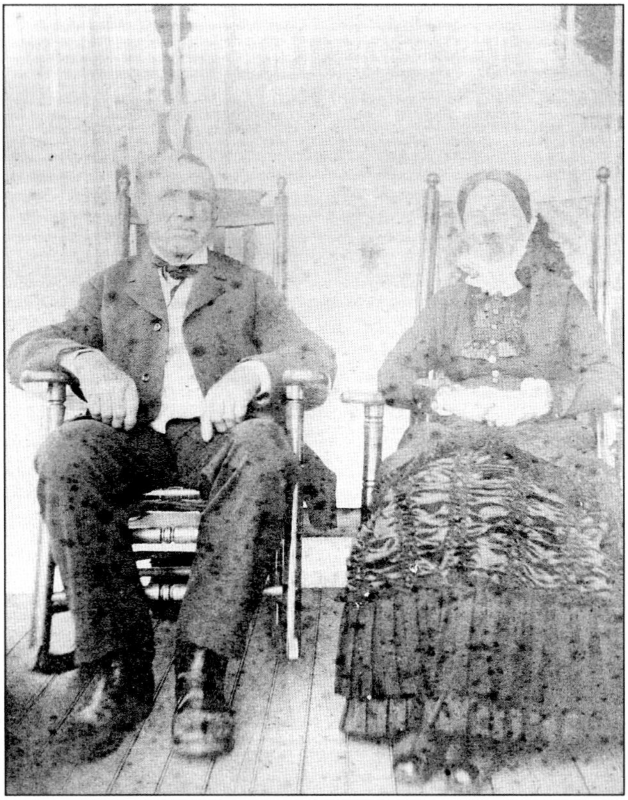

This image from Mr. and Mrs. Rufus Thompson's golden wedding anniversary is half of a stereoview card made on August 15, 1881. Mr. And Mrs. Thompson were the parents of Denman Thompson.

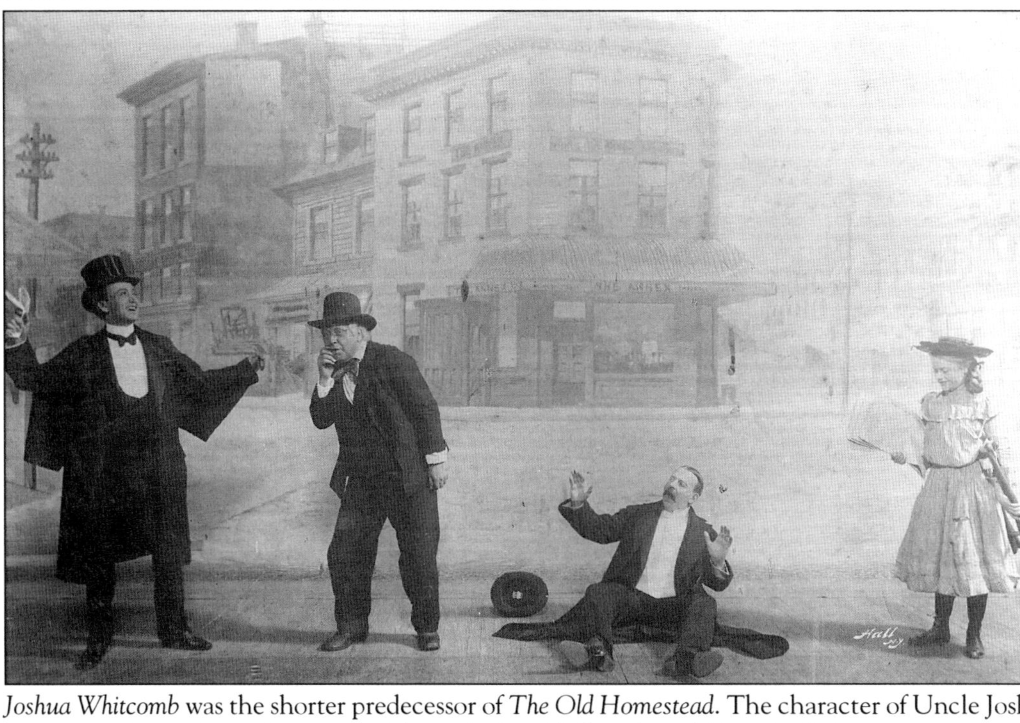

Joshua Whitcomb was the shorter predecessor of *The Old Homestead*. The character of Uncle Josh was an amalgam of two Swanzey residents, Joshua Holbrook and Captain Otis.

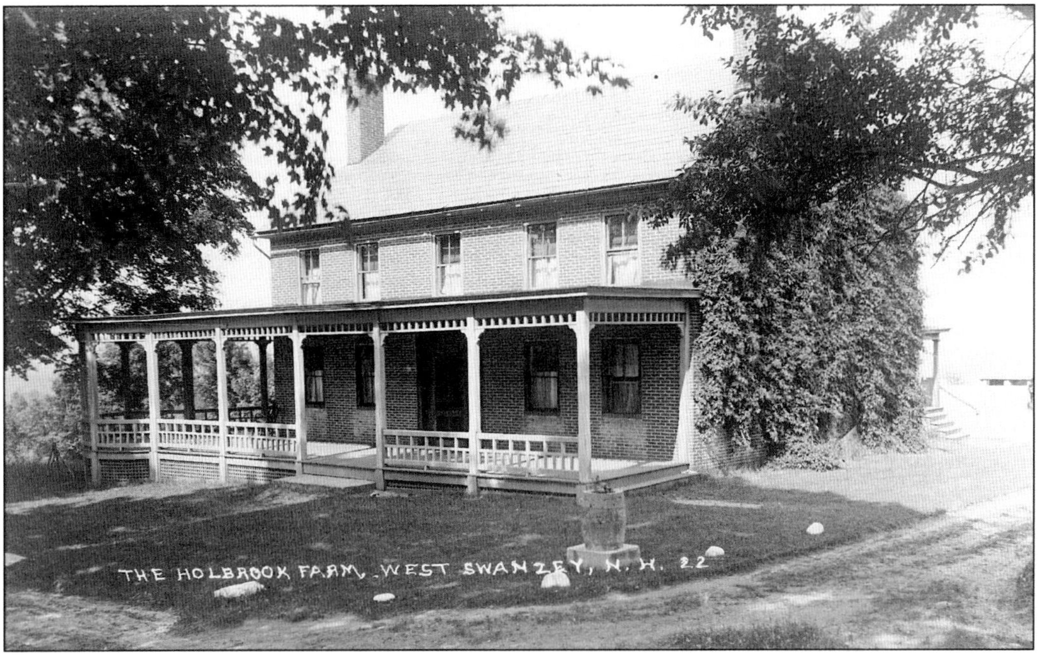

The Holbrook farm is typical of the type of homestead that is found in this area. The long porches that wrap around much of the house were the sites of a good deal of evening socializing and some summer kitchen chores, like cleaning string beans.

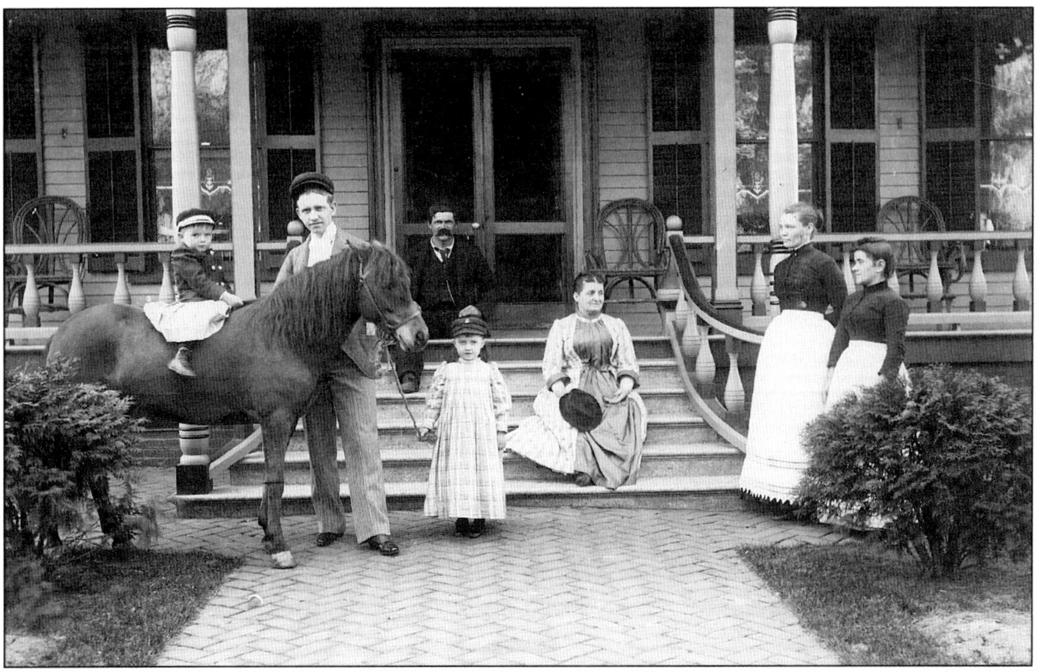

Mrs. Denman Thompson sits on the stairs of the Thompson home while two maids look on. The little boy on the horse is dressed in the style of clothing that was typically imposed on male children at the turn of the century.

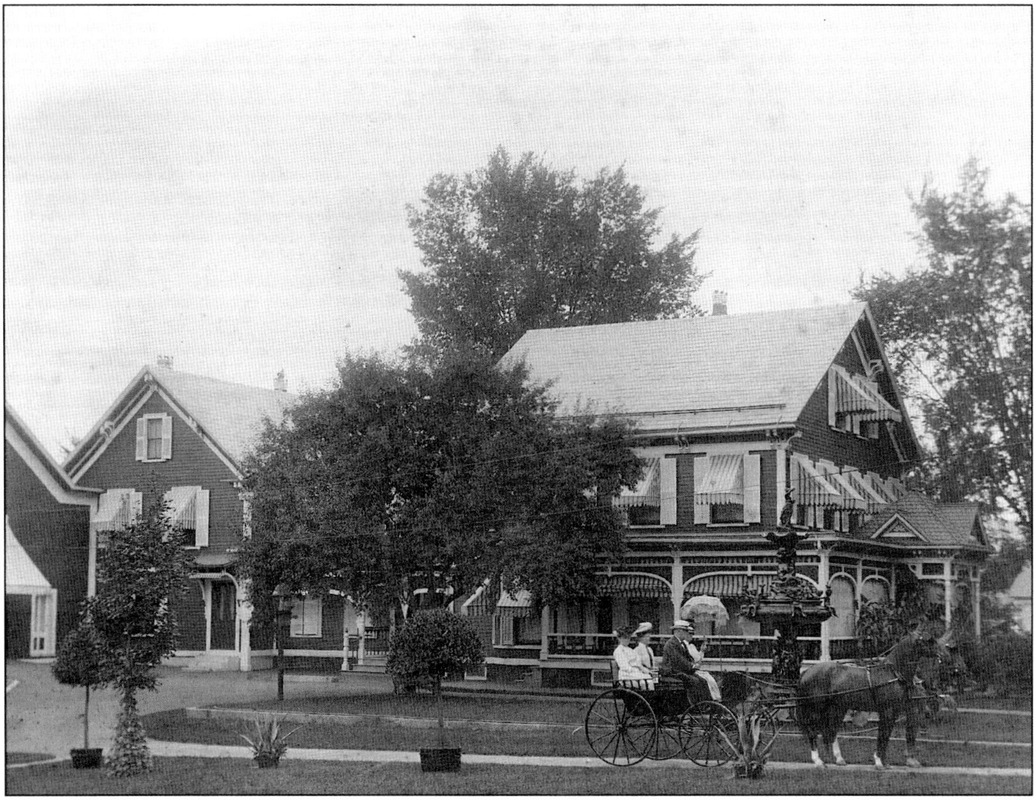

Denman Thompson and his family are shown here in a two-horse-drawn carriage. Mrs. Thompson is sporting a fancy parasol.

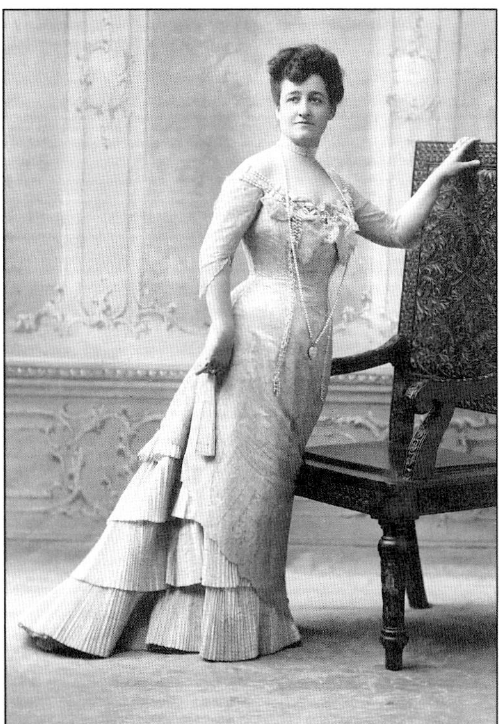

Denman Thompson's daughter, Annie Kilpatrick, appeared with her father in the play.

Annie took the part of Rickety Ann in Thompson's play.

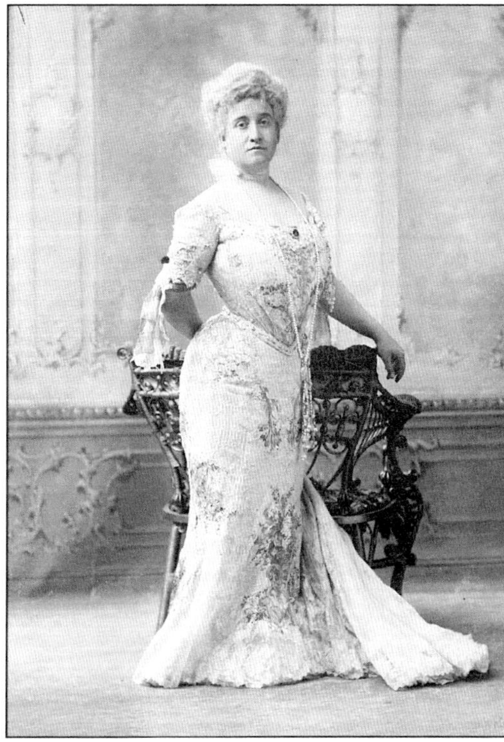

Horses were groomed and trained for sport and show as well as for drawing carriages and plowing fields. Note the windmill that was on the property.

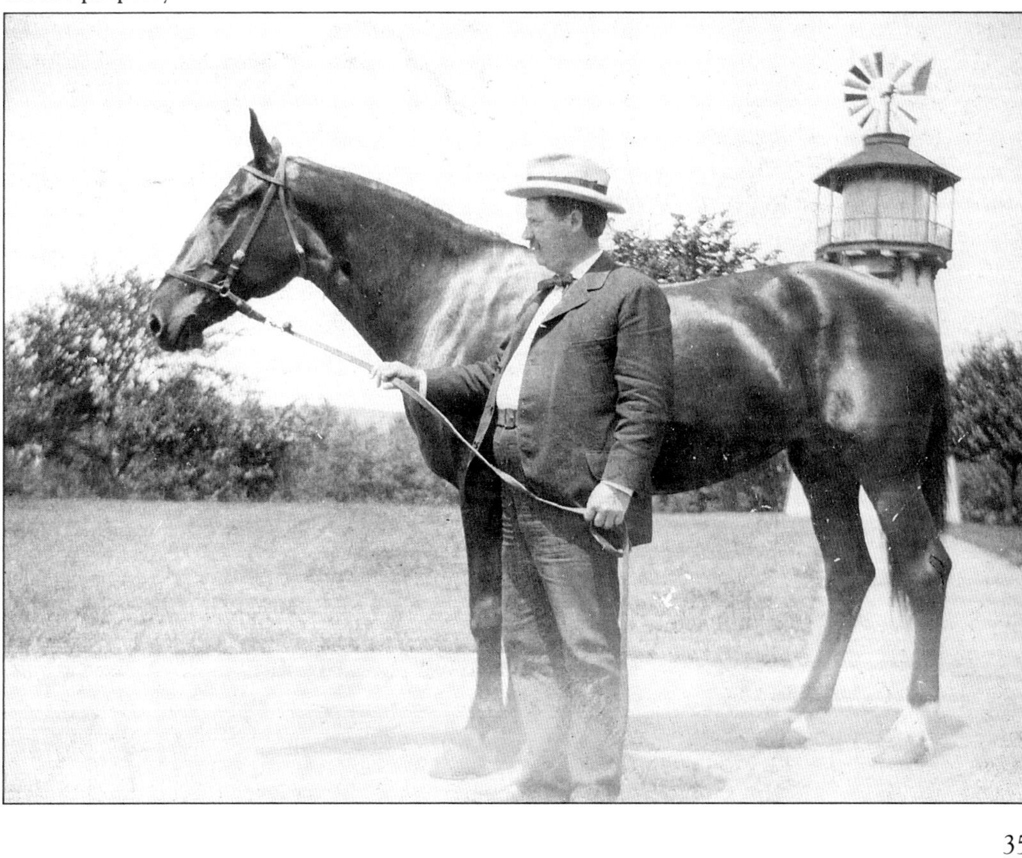

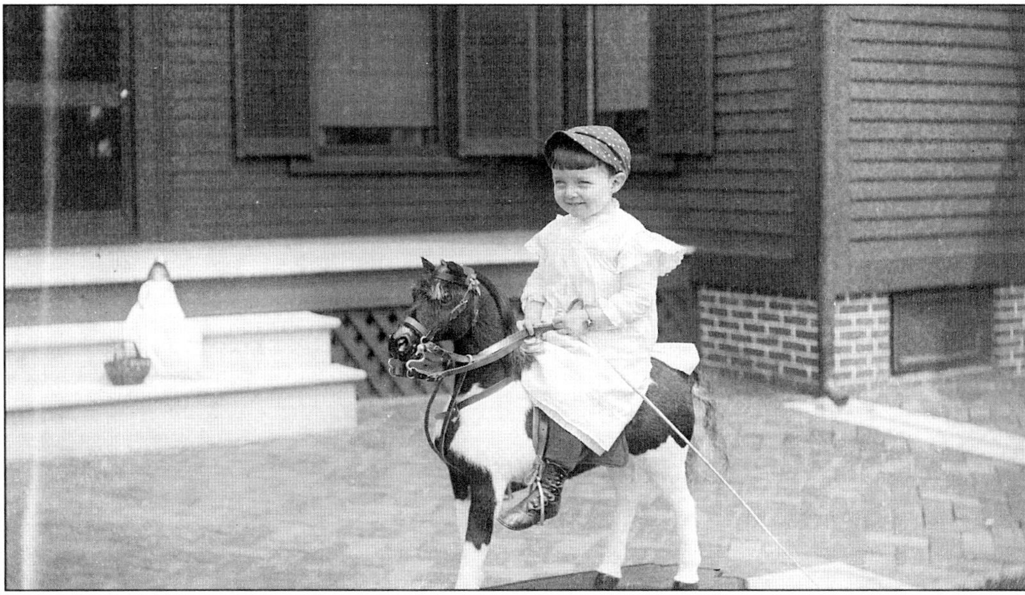

Not all horses were spirited high-steppers. Thompson enjoyed spoiling the children in his life with fanciful gifts.

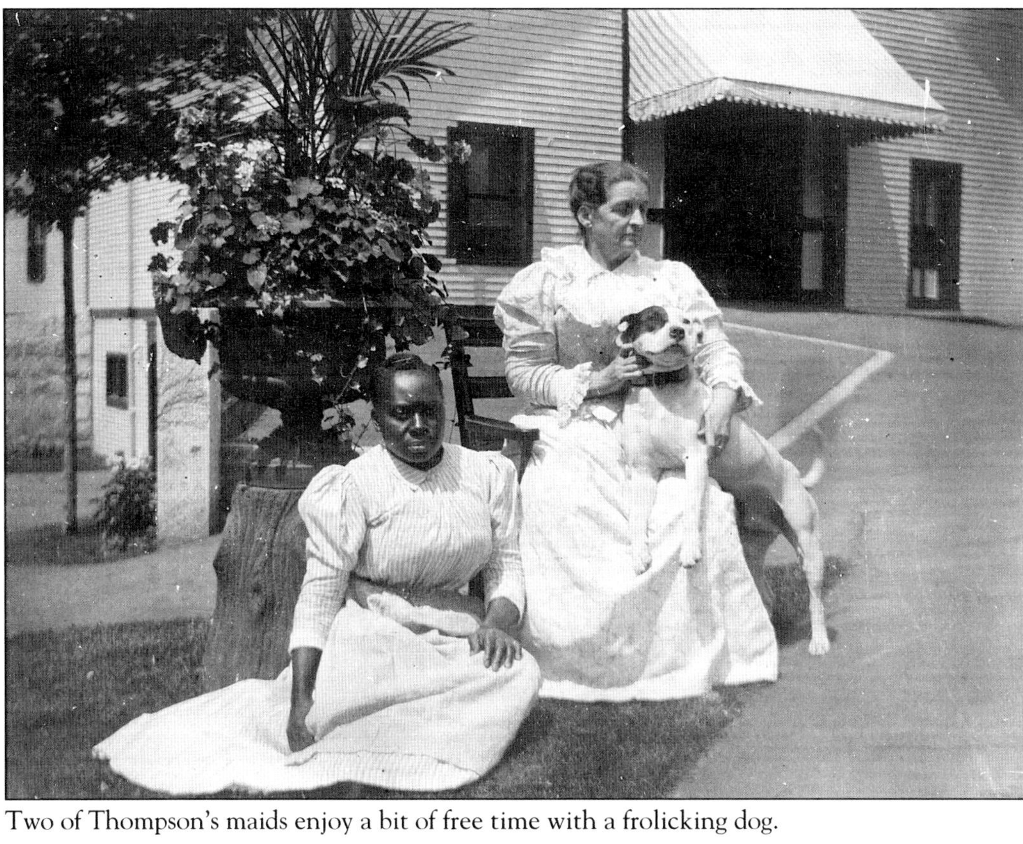

Two of Thompson's maids enjoy a bit of free time with a frolicking dog.

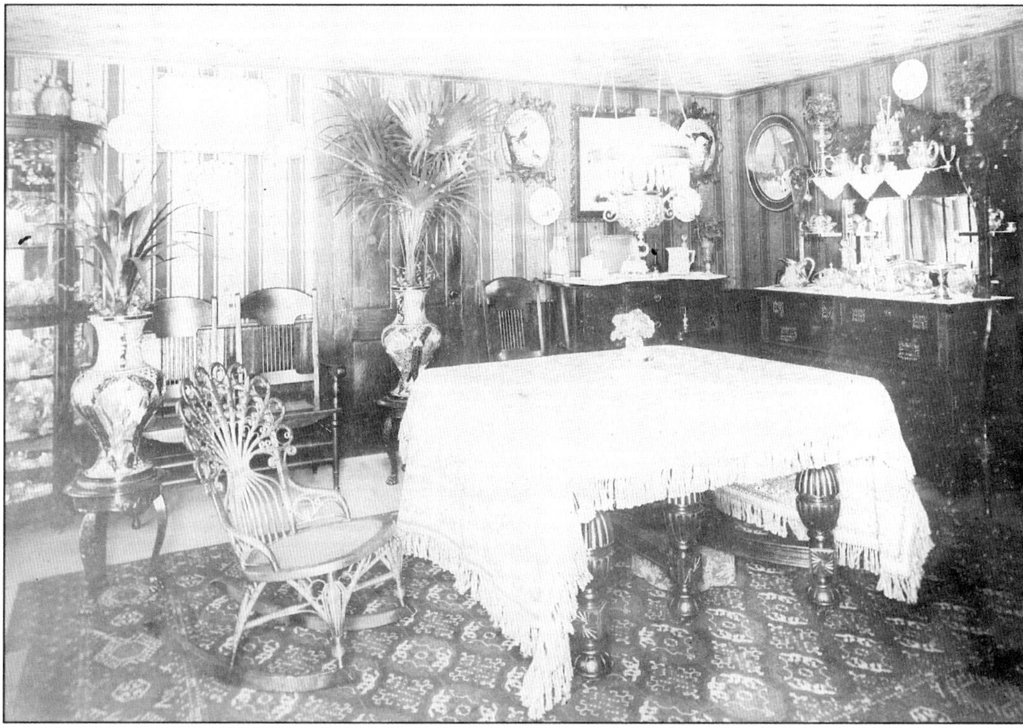

The ornate wicker and mahogany furniture, porcelain, and decorative ornamentation of the interior of the Thompson homestead reveals that the family was extremely affluent.

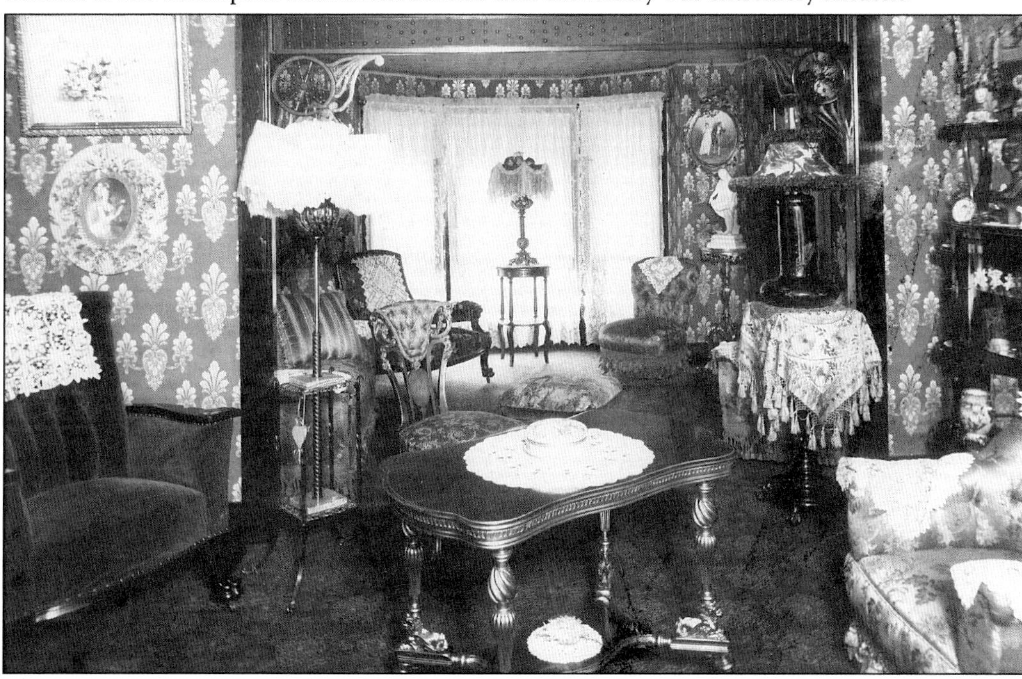

The sitting room was not only a place to entertain friends but also a place to read the newspaper or sit by the sunny window while doing needlework. Notice the heavily carved furniture and strategically placed fancy lamps.

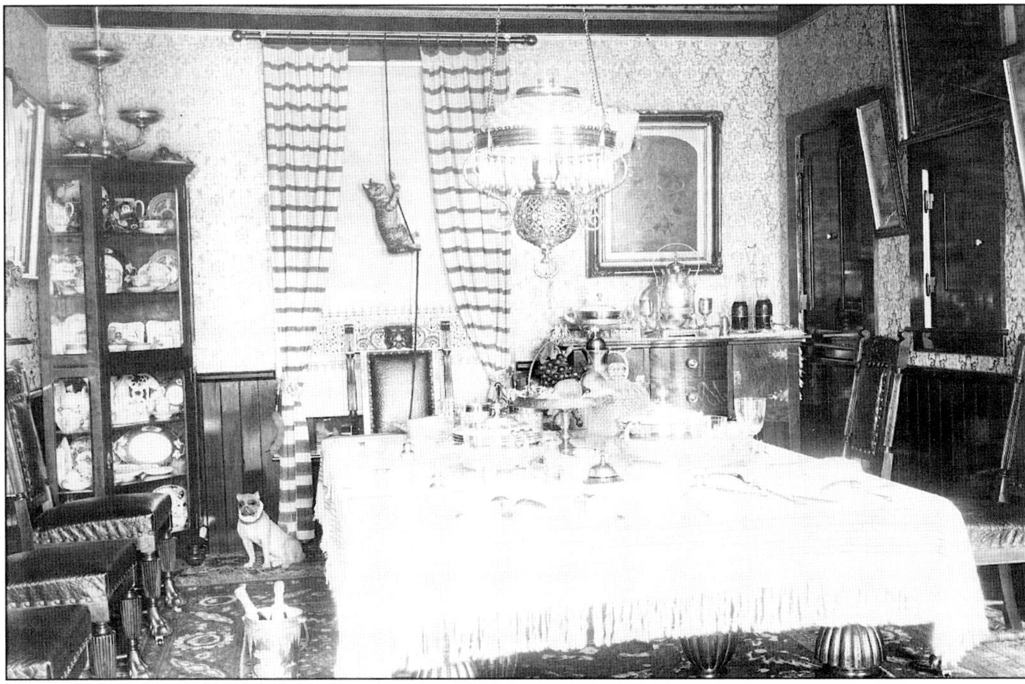

Very few people could afford the ornate china, sterling, and plate glass that is strewn with magnificent abundance about this room. The champagne bucket on the floor gives one the feeling that this picture was taken just before a party or the arrival of a guest like Chauncey Olcutt or the Jersey Lily.

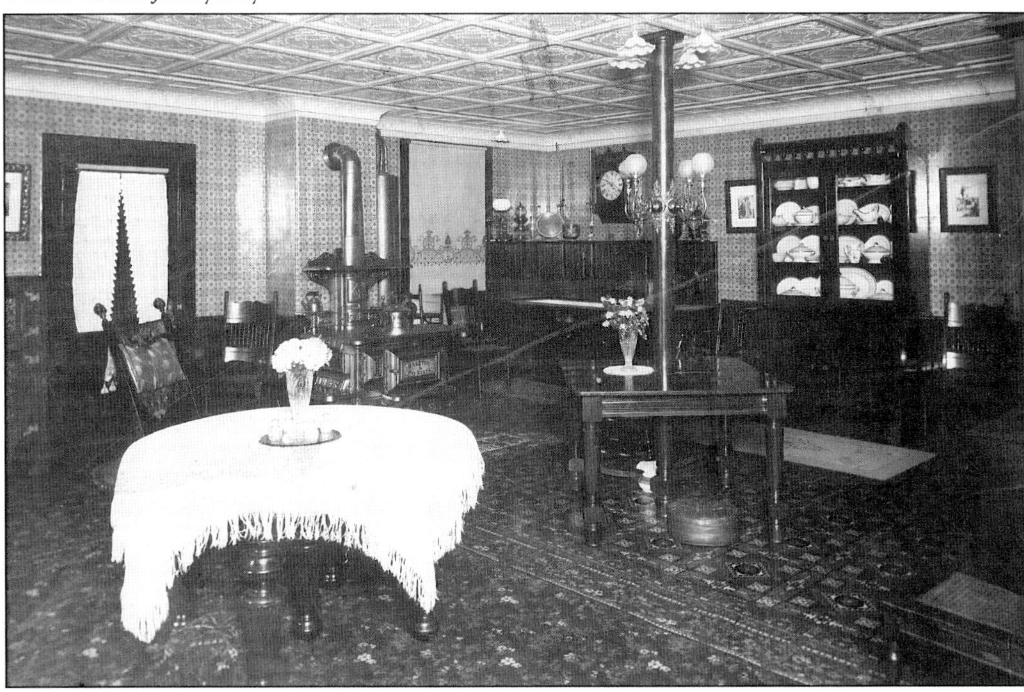

Carpeted kitchens were not the norm. The cast-iron wood-burning kitchen stove, however, was the heart of every home, whether the residents were rich or poor.

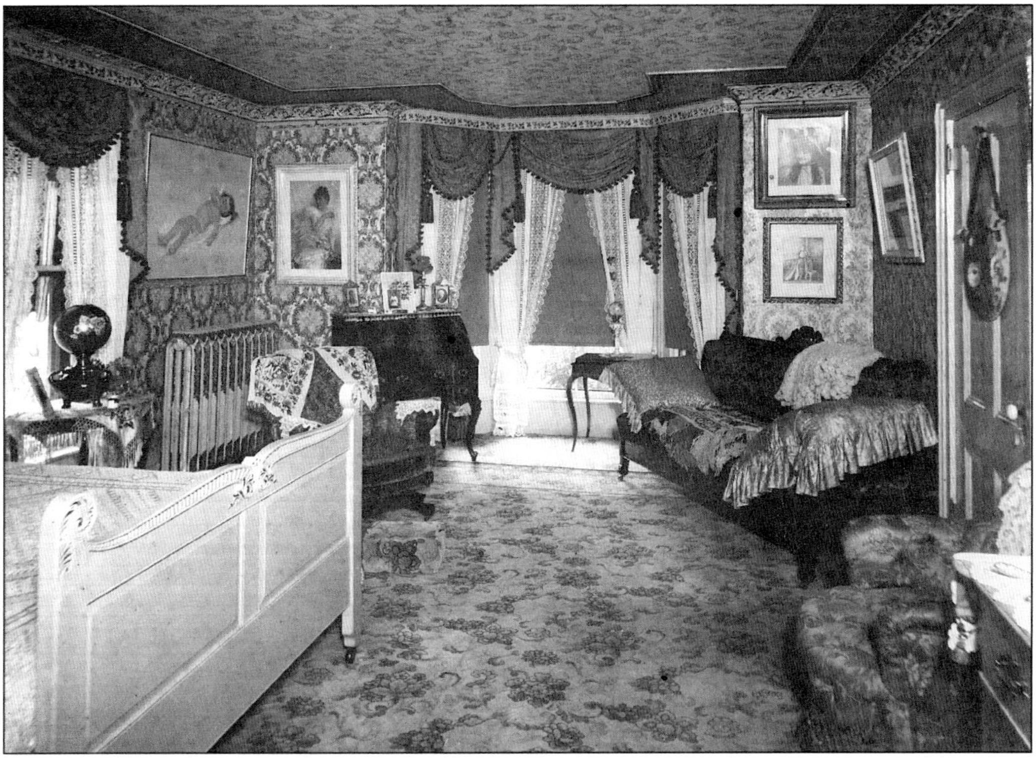

Bedrooms were not just for sleeping in but for writing one's letters and taking one's afternoon rest. Notice the photographs on the wall, some of which represent family members.

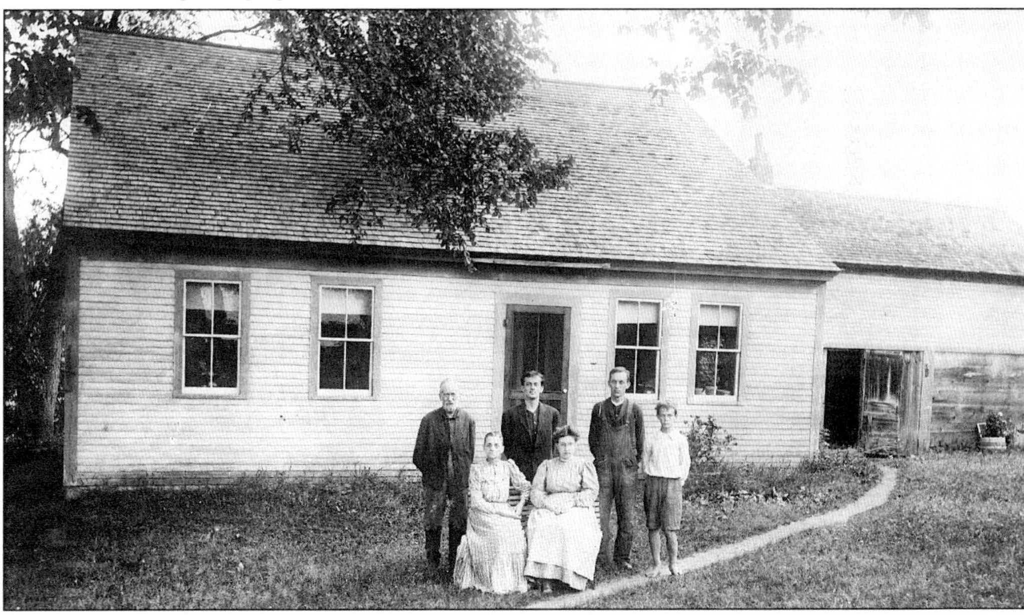

This is the Carlton farm in East Swanzey. Harvey Carlton lived comfortably and could afford a maid, but there is no evidence of the posh lifestyle that Denman Thompson's family enjoyed. Notice that Carlton's grandson is barefoot; both the clothing and the homestead are plain and wholesome.

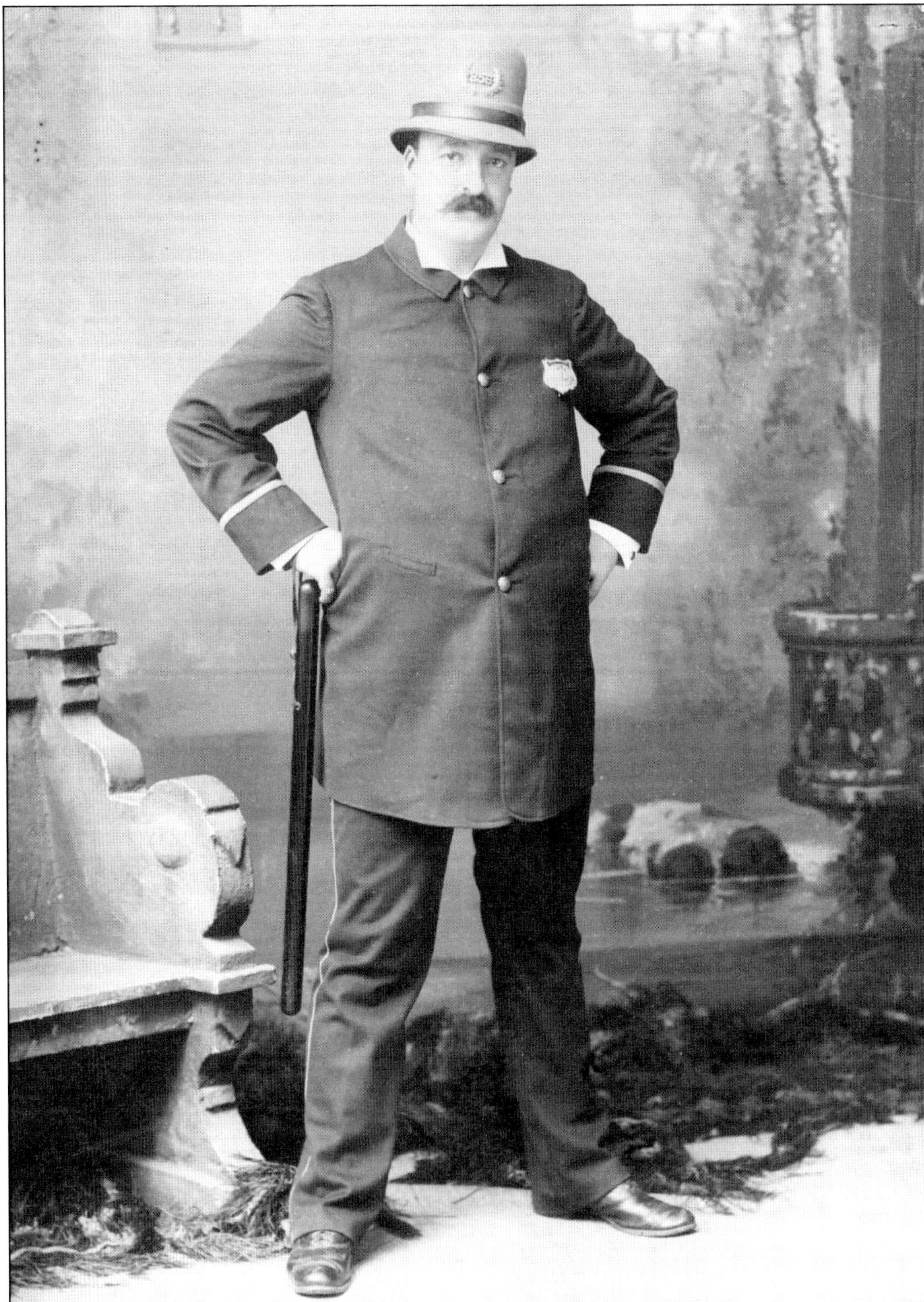

Mr. Tom Law is shown here dressed to play "One of the Finest" in Denman Thompson's original *The Old Homestead*. This image has been taken from a large cabinet photograph that was probably used in the theater lobbies.

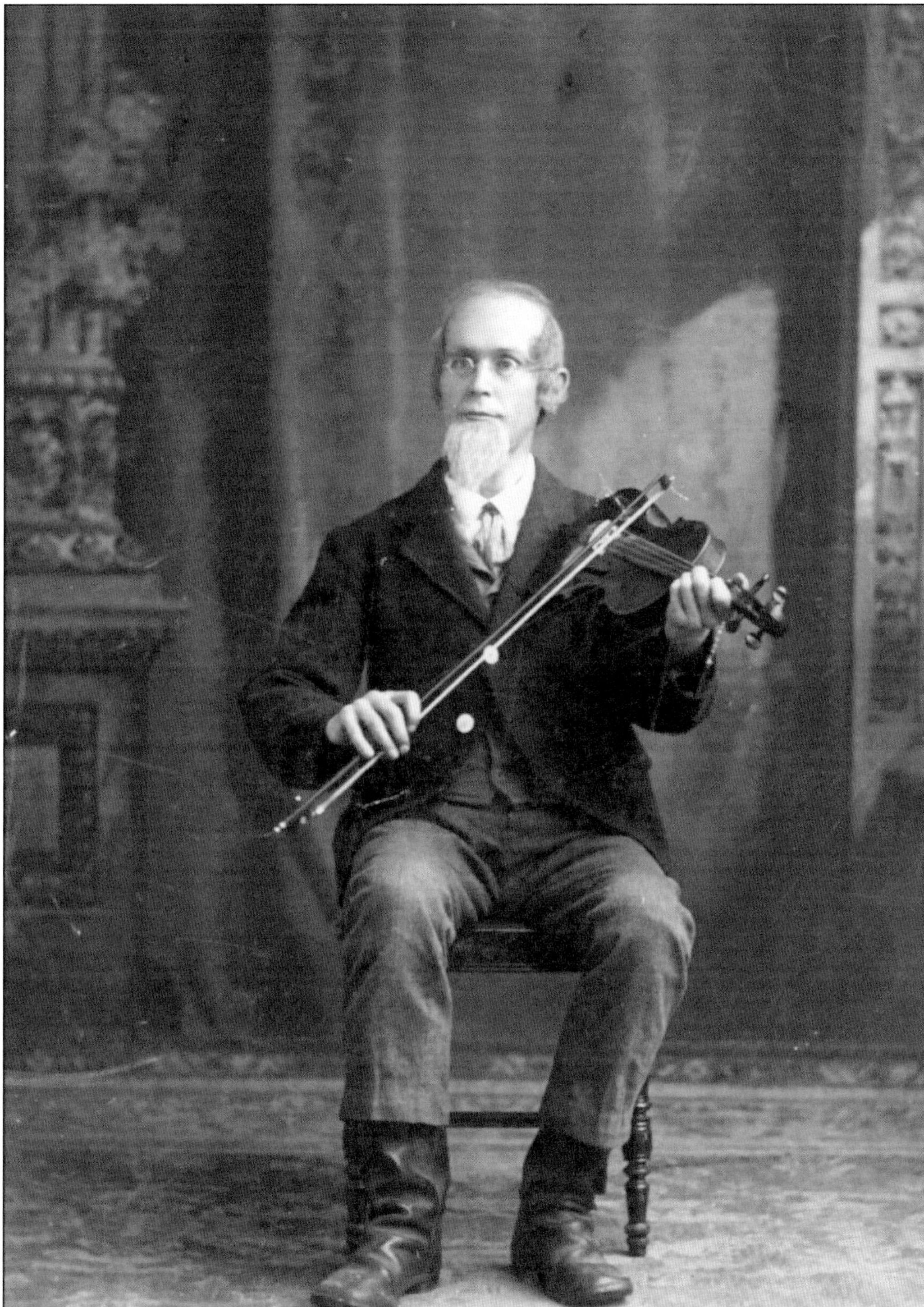

The fiddler was an important addition to any function, as he made the music that people danced to. This actor was in one of the many performances of Thompson's play.

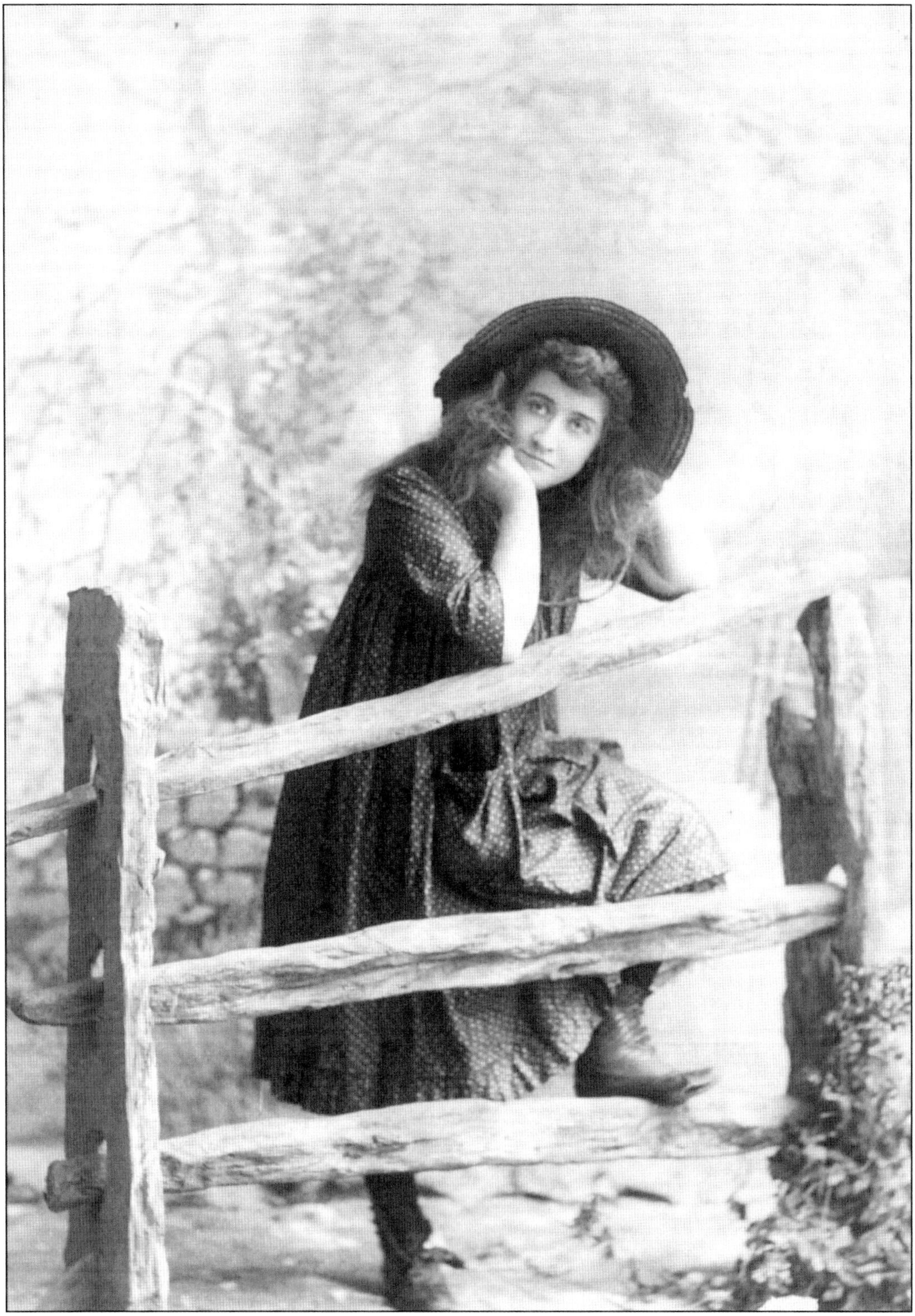

Thompson's daughter Annie is shown here dressed for a scene from *The Old Homestead*. She played the part of Rickety Ann.

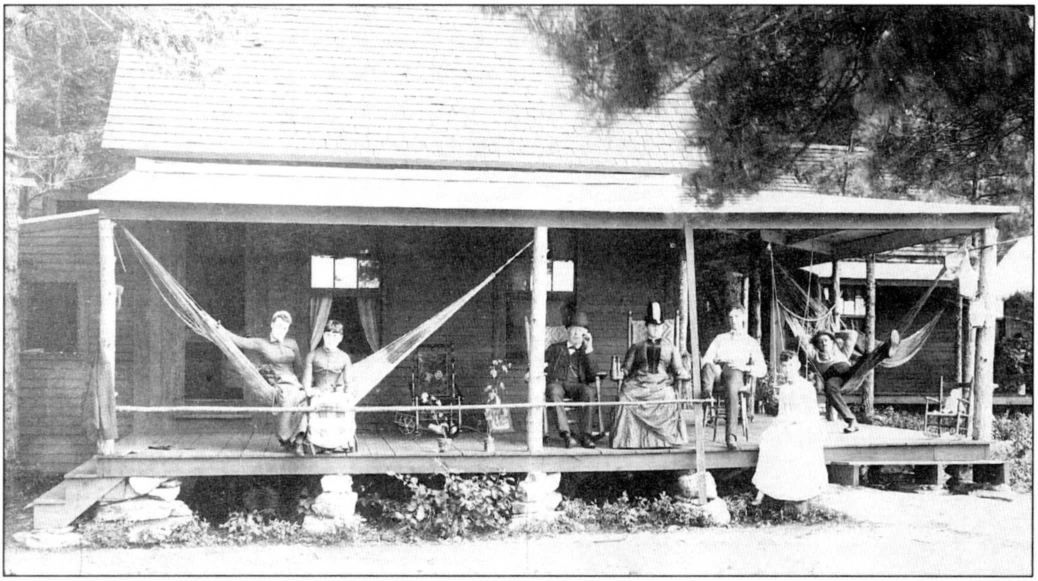

Although the modern trend is for families to have a summer home in New Hampshire and a winter home in Florida, summer homes in the early twentieth century were not necessarily a long distance away from the family's permanent residence. Rather, the summer cottage was often located at a relatively nearby lake or recreational area. The summer cottage of the Thompson family was on the lake. The family is shown here on the porch enjoying a relaxing afternoon. They are all dressed "properly," with none of them wearing bathing suits or even casual clothing.

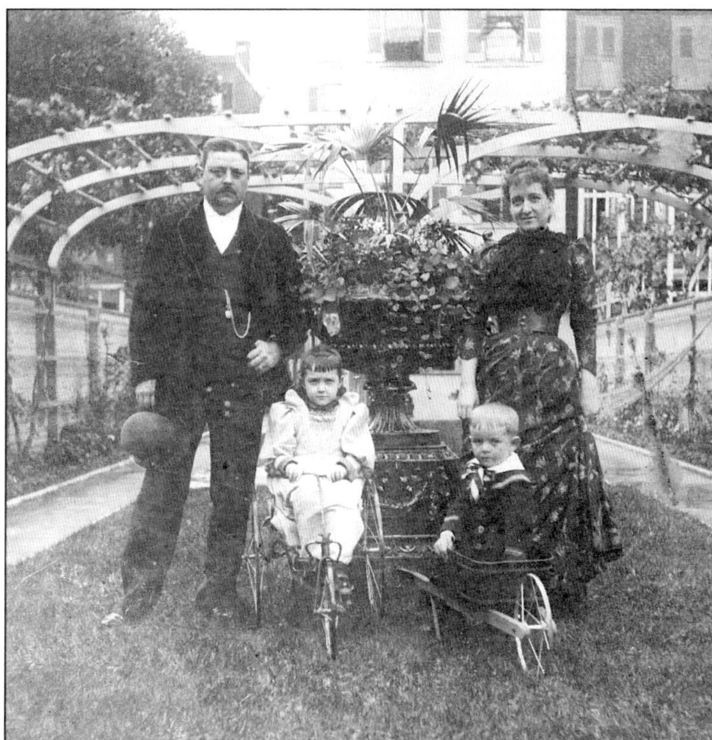

Thompson's daughter and son-in-law represented the MacFarland family.

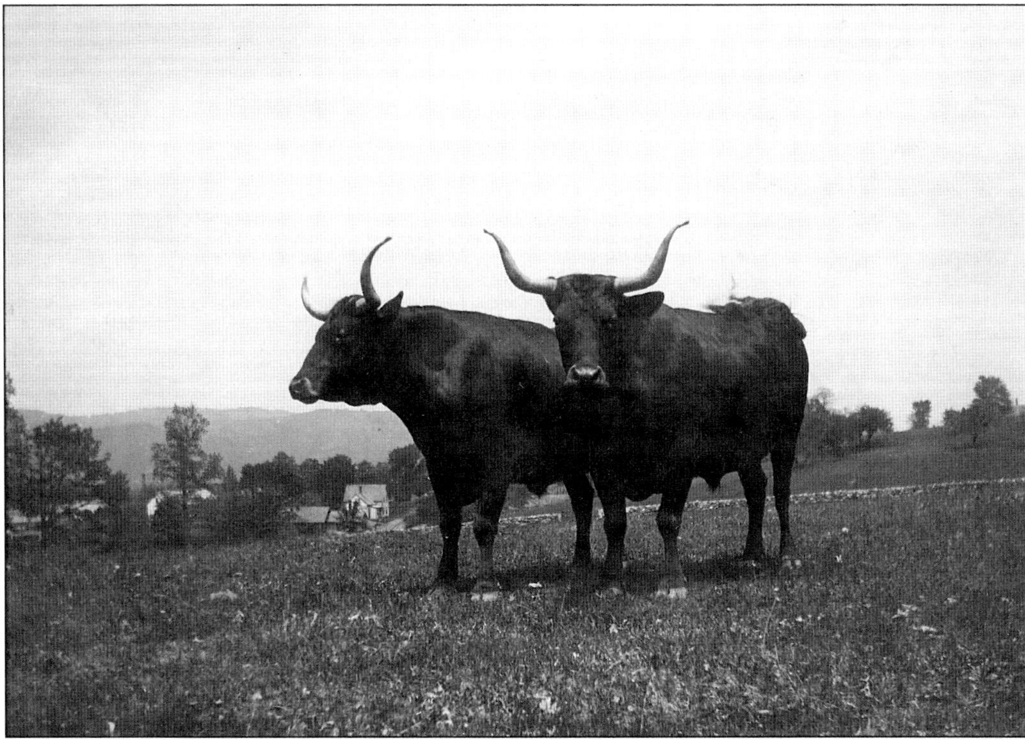

Denman Thompson's oxen appeared in the play and were quite pampered.

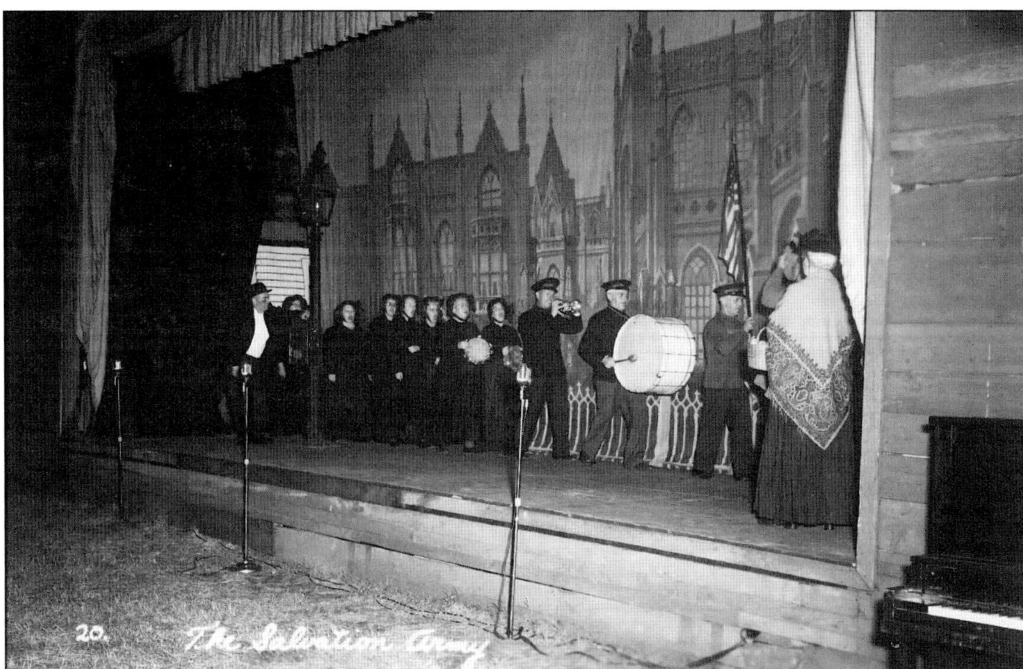

This scene from *The Old Homestead* shows the Salvation Army.

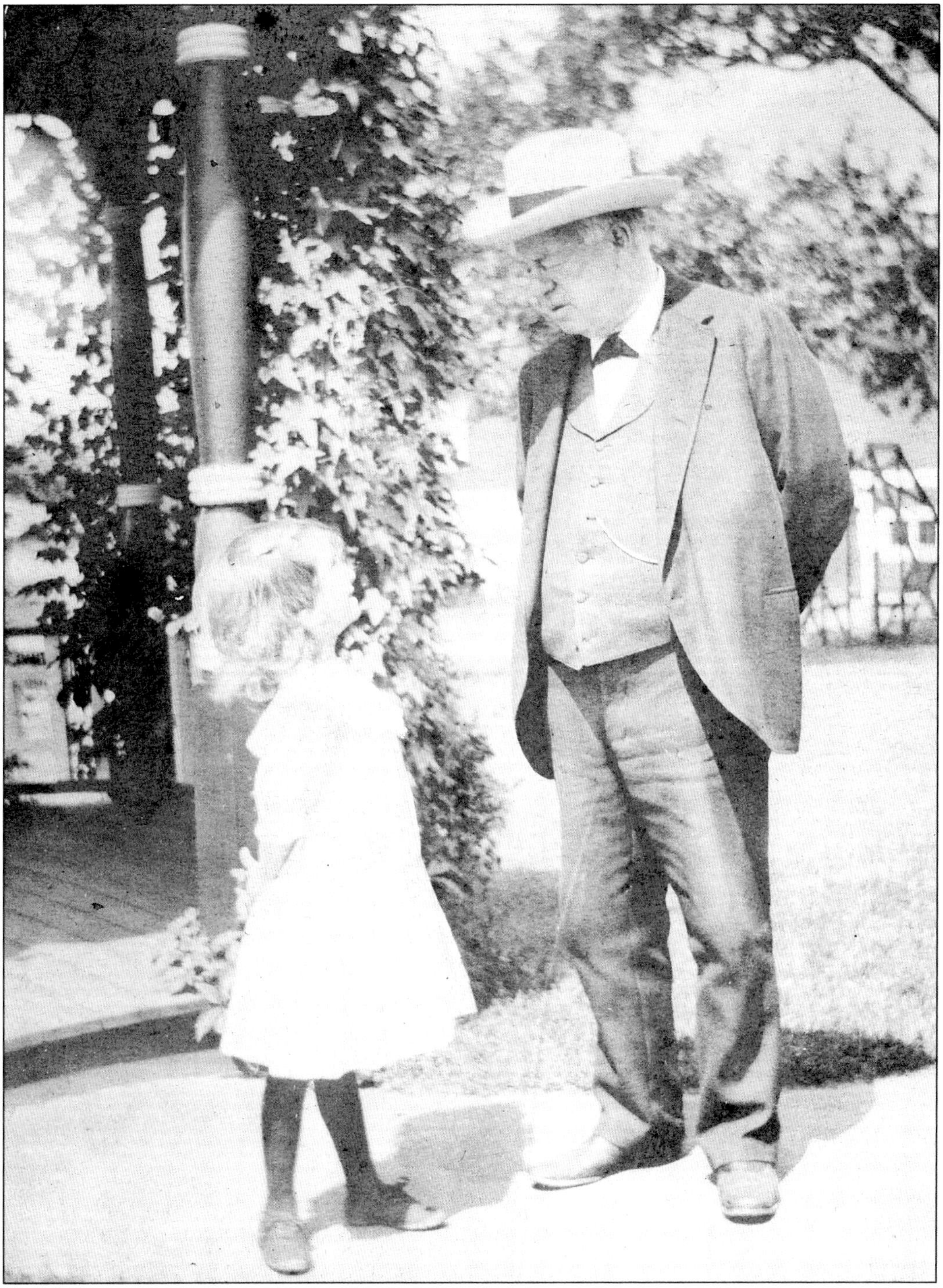

Denman Thompson appears here with his granddaughter.

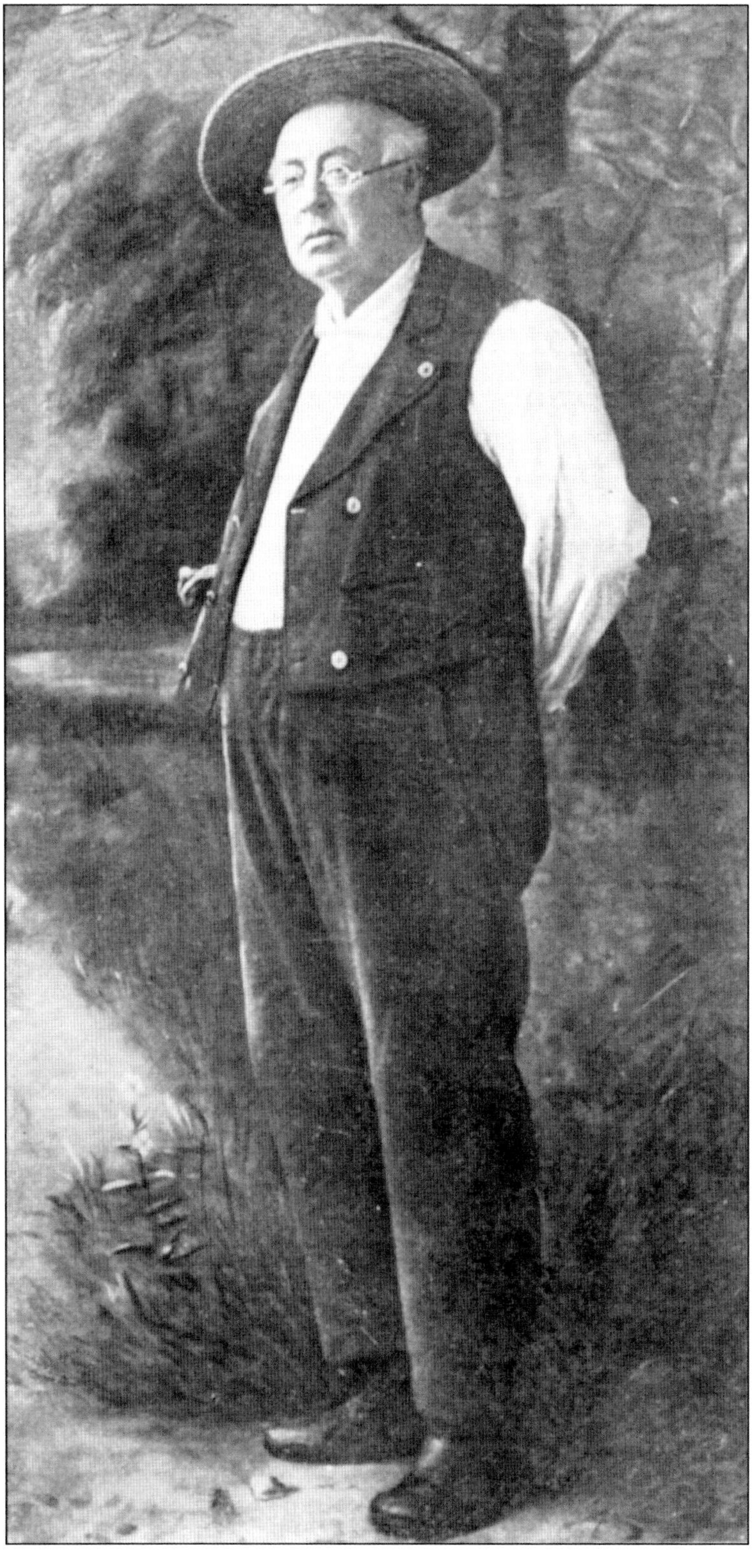

Denman Thompson is shown here playing the part of Uncle Josh. The reverse of this picture postcard offers an advertisement for Denman Thompson 10¢ cigars that reads: "They are as good as the play!" Thompson was a shrewd businessman and made a considerable fortune from sources other than the actual play.

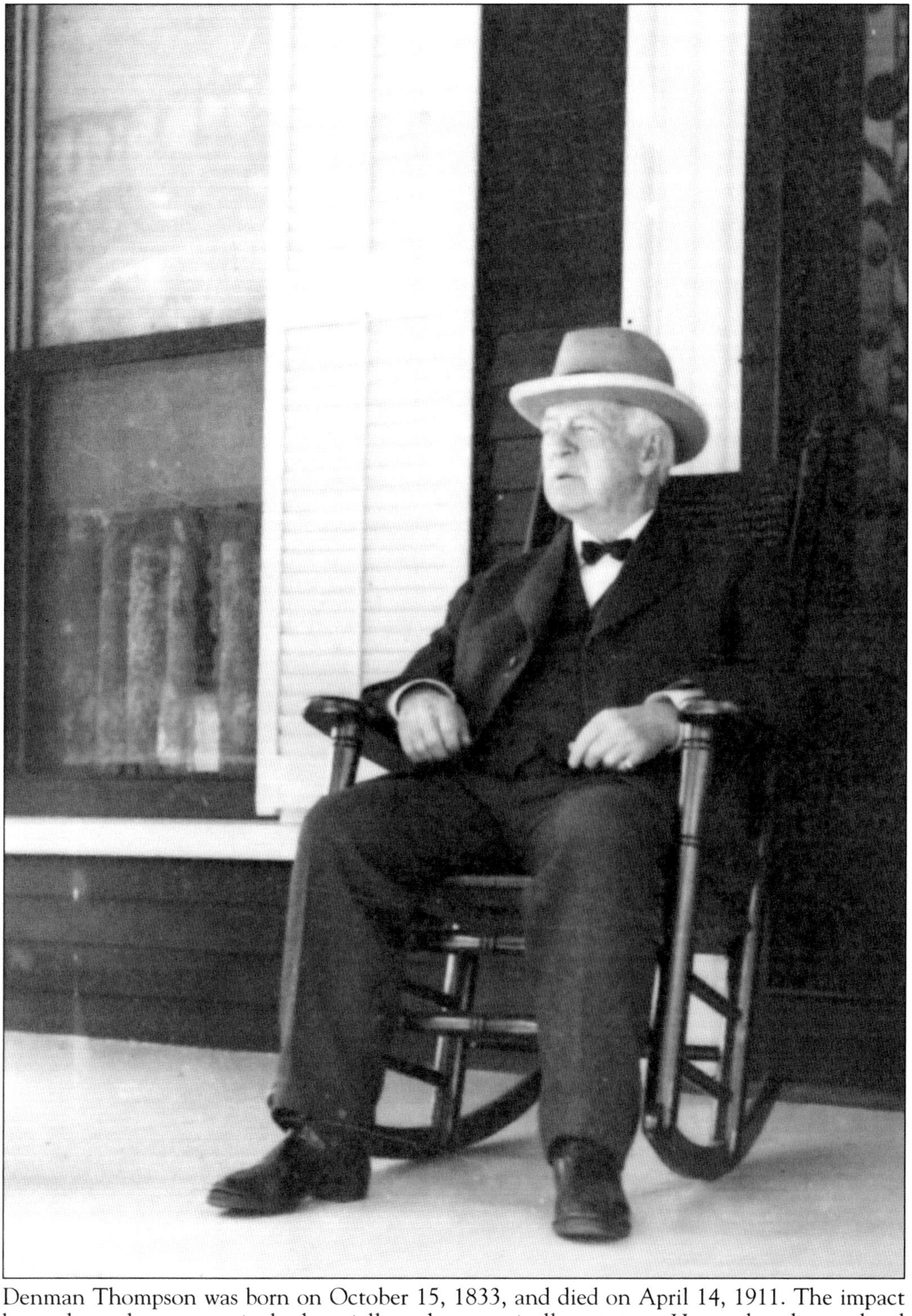

Denman Thompson was born on October 15, 1833, and died on April 14, 1911. The impact he made on the community both socially and economically was great. He employed many local people as staff, chauffeurs, actors, etc.

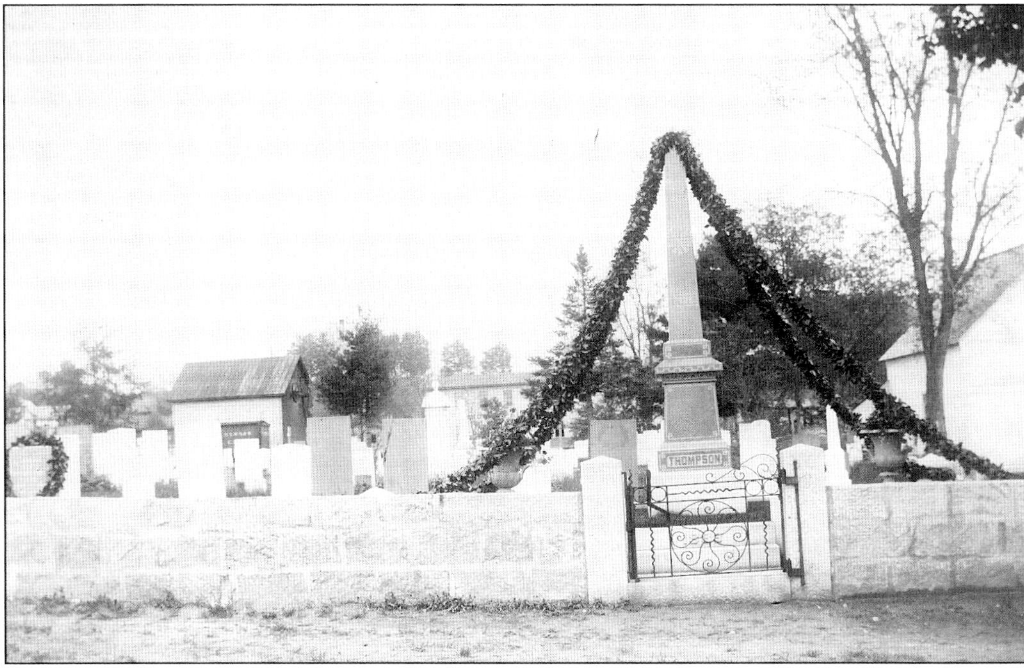

The town graveyard holds Denman Thompson's grave; gentleman robber Langdon Moore was not allowed to be buried here. The burial ground began in 1798 but records were not kept until 1940.

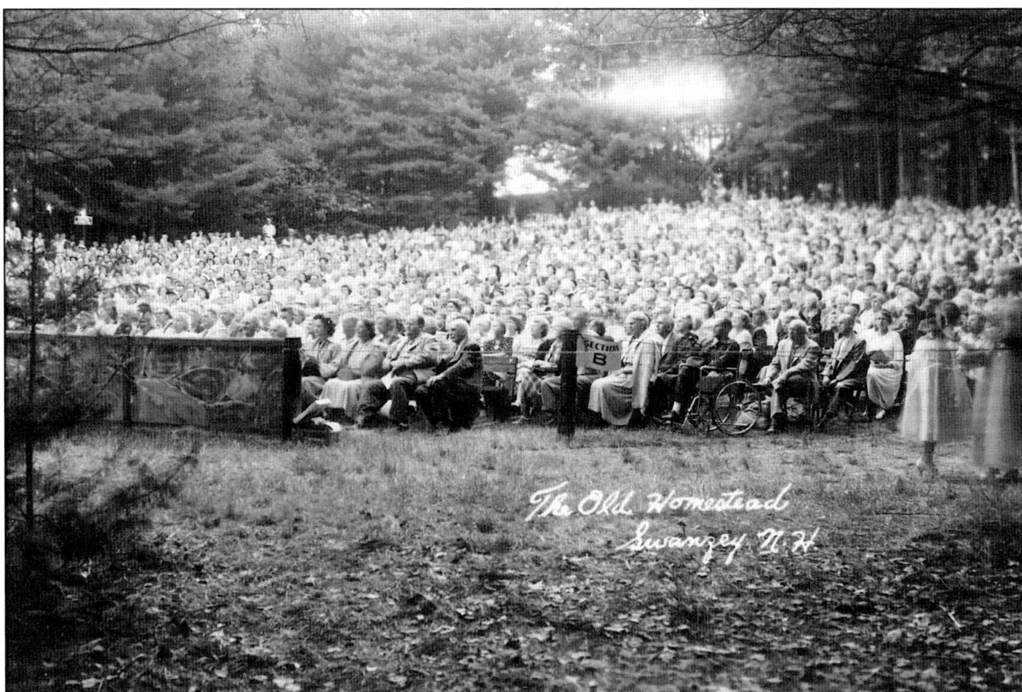

Swanzey residents and guests watch one of the yearly revivals of *The Old Homestead* at the Potash Bowl. Usually *Trees*, which was set to music, is sung at the same performance.

Two

Ashuelot

Ashuelot, or Ashuelot Village, is often referred to as West Winchester. The area is actually part of Winchester, although it is basically self-sufficient. The village has unsuccessfully tried to separate itself from Winchester a number of times over the course of its history. It is similar to its larger neighbors in the types of industries, homes, and lifestyles it has seen over the years, but it has always been less populated. The town was once known for its working ore mine. Much of Ashuelot's present-day life is wrapped up with that of the neighboring towns.

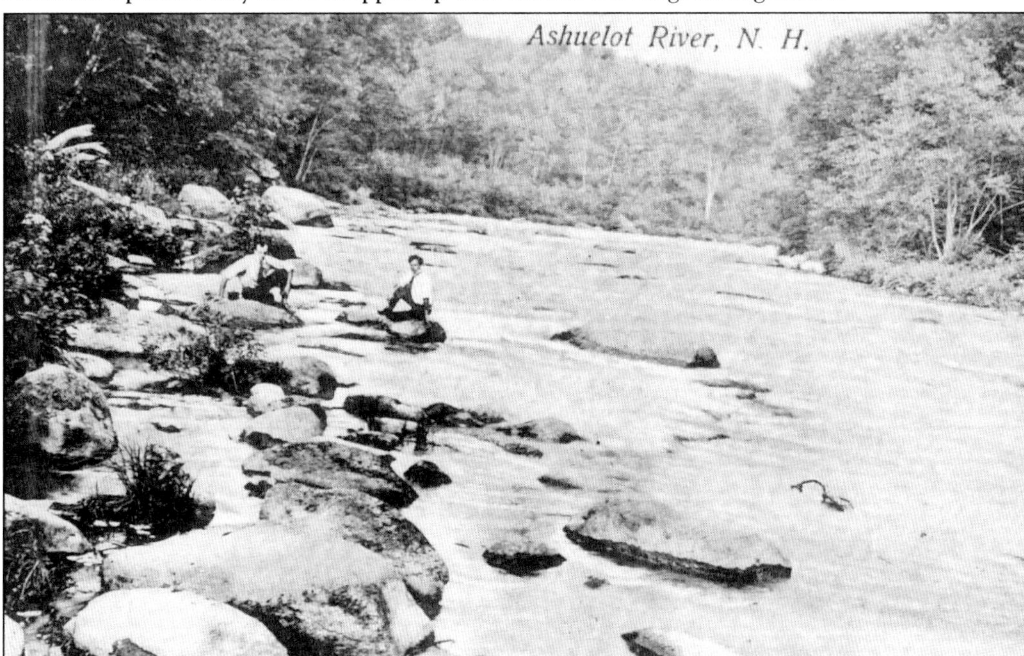

The Ashuelot River was used as a means of transportation by Native Americans even before European settlers came. It was once full of fish and wildlife, but with the advent of factories, mills, and industry, it became very polluted. The river is only now beginning to return to its naturally pure state.

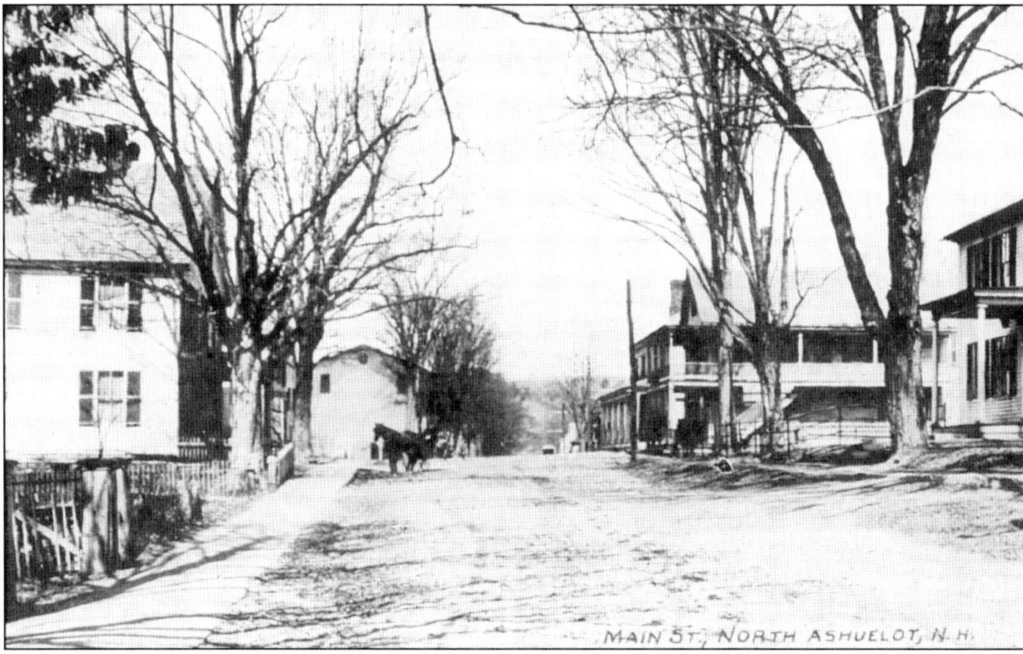

Main Street in Ashuelot was still not paved in 1921. Main streets before 1950 were integral parts of most communities, as they were often the sites of the most important and earliest buildings. Main streets were also often where much of the community social life took place.

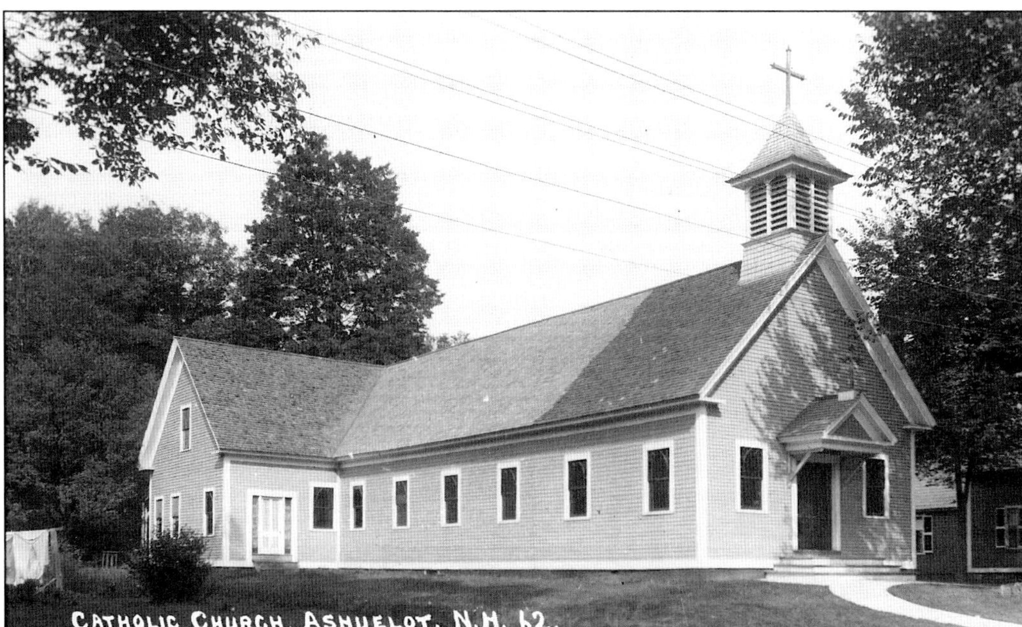

The Catholic church, unlike many Catholic churches of its time, was Spartan in its architecture and simple beauty.

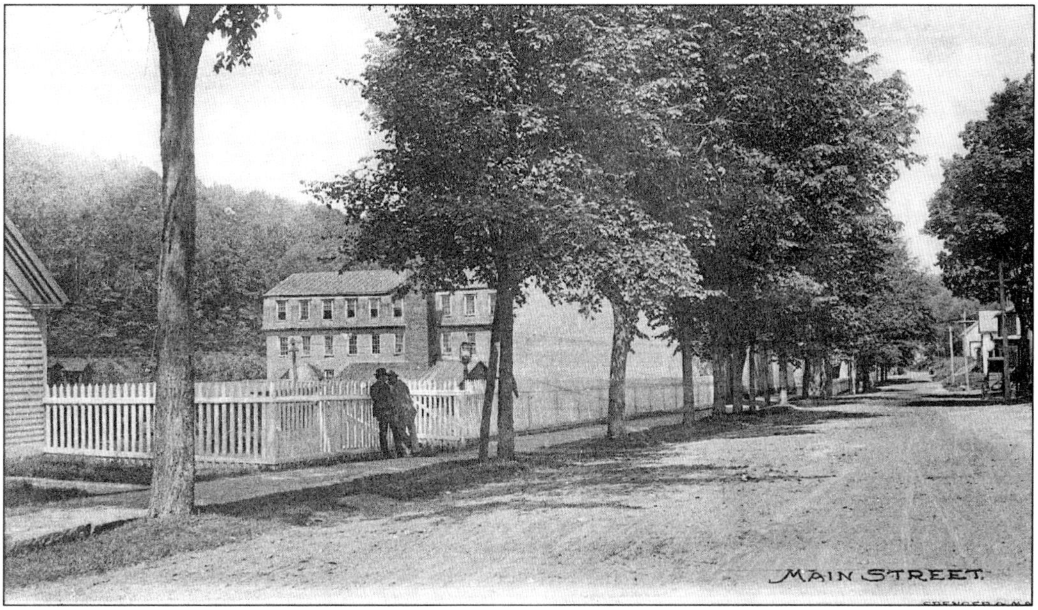

The Sheriden Woolen Mill was one of many woolen mills in this area that utilized the water power of the Ashuelot River. Mr. Sheriden owned the mill from 1901 to 1916. His home was known as the Norton house and is currently being restored by the Winchester Historical Society for use as a museum.

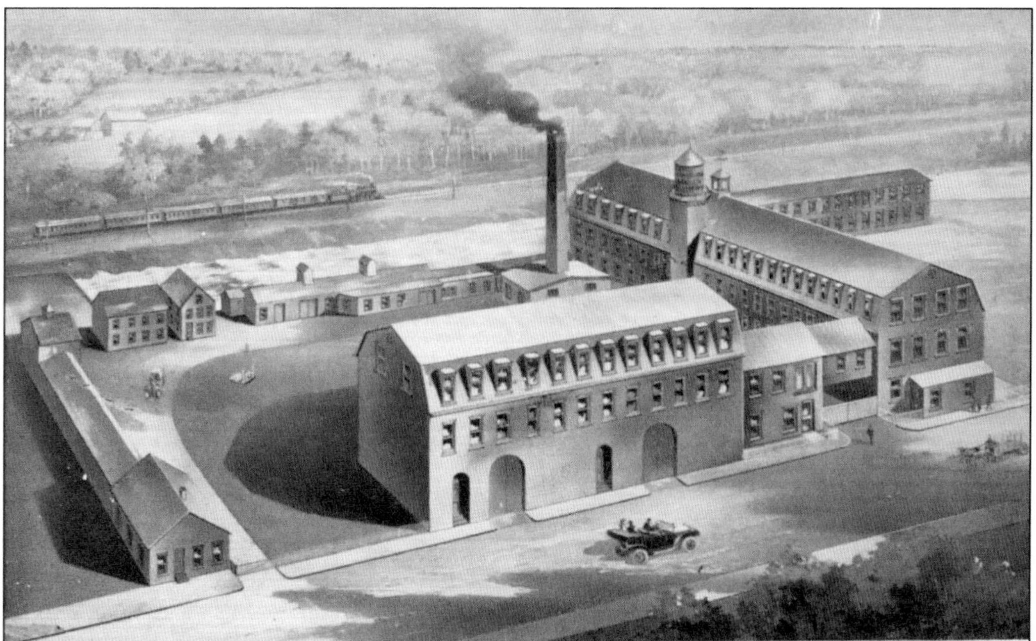

A train passes in the background of this view of the Hampshire Woolen Company, while motorized vehicles can be seen on the street in front. This is an idealized view of the mill. Note the black smoke being emitted from the smoke stack.

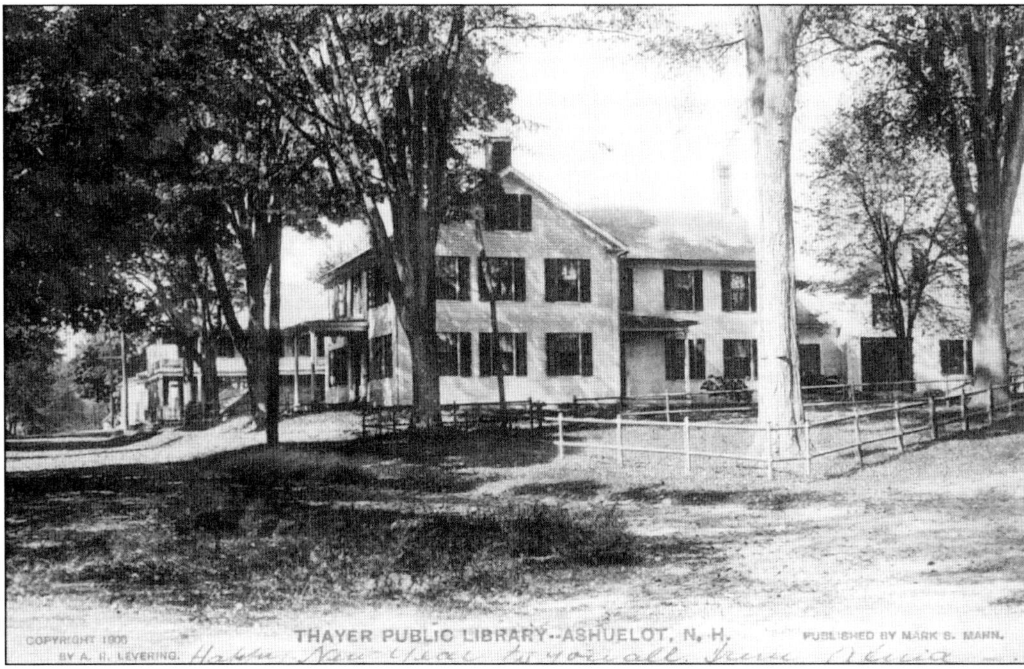

The Thayers, like other philanthropic families, funded public buildings and community projects, including the Thayer Public Library.

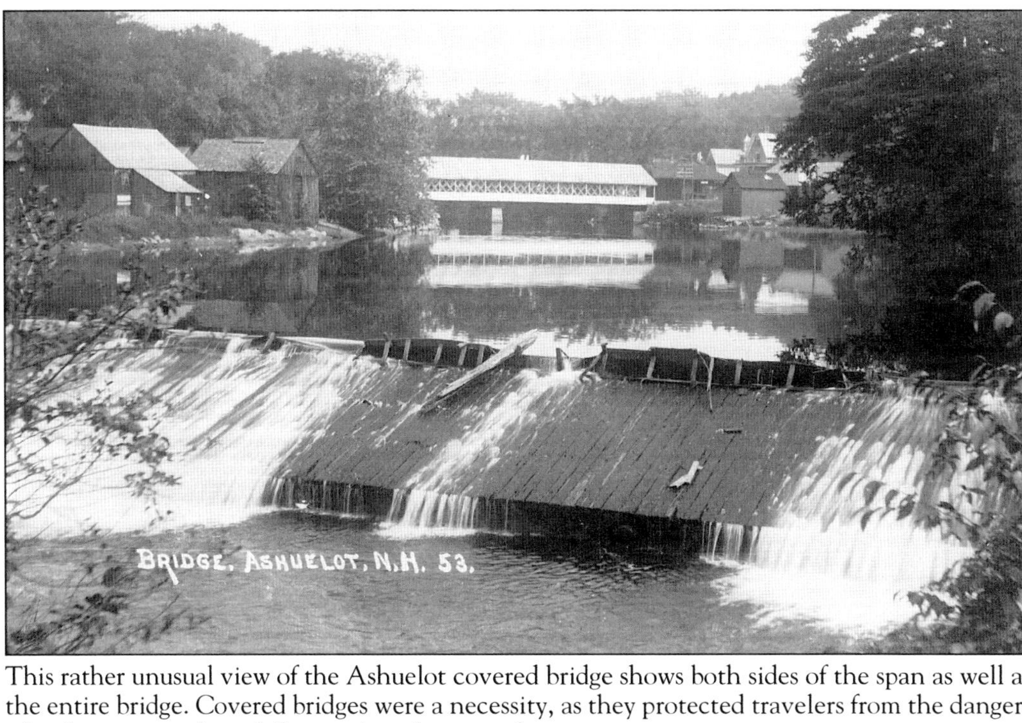

This rather unusual view of the Ashuelot covered bridge shows both sides of the span as well as the entire bridge. Covered bridges were a necessity, as they protected travelers from the dangers of inclement weather while crossing often treacherous waters.

Three

WINCHESTER

In many ways Winchester's social history is similar to that of other southwest New Hampshire towns. The town was the site of a silver mine belonging to the Connecticut Valley Mining Company, and Shipman's Tavern was a stopover for many a vaudeville performer and summer traveler bound for the large hotels in the White Mountains. Over the years, Winchester has lost its early industries and suffered tremendously from fires, the 1936 flood, and the 1938 hurricane.

The trains no longer stop here but Forrest Lake is still a mecca for bathers, boaters, and lazy-day fishermen. Until 1883, Forrest Lake was known as Humphrey's Pond. Many of the original homestead families have moved from the area since the demise of most industry, and only slowly have people from urban areas moved in to revitalize the area and enjoy the slower pace of life it offers. With the arrival of new small businesses, however, the downtown area is once again filling in. It is hoped that with time the few remaining abandoned buildings will be removed, and smarter, more ecologically sound buildings will take their place.

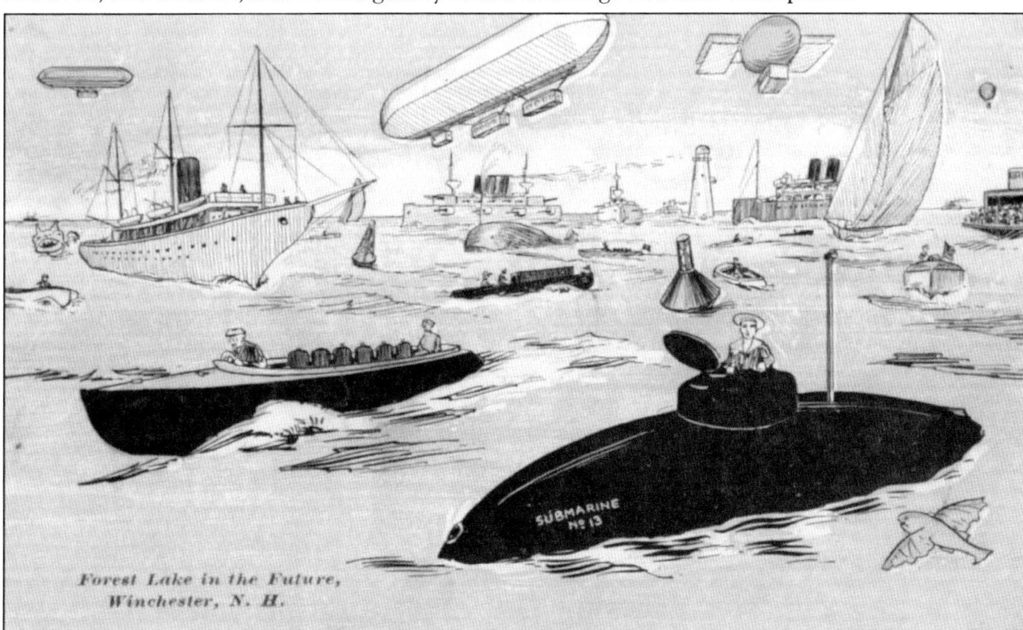

Forrest Lake has still not attained the space-age glory envisioned for it in this picture!

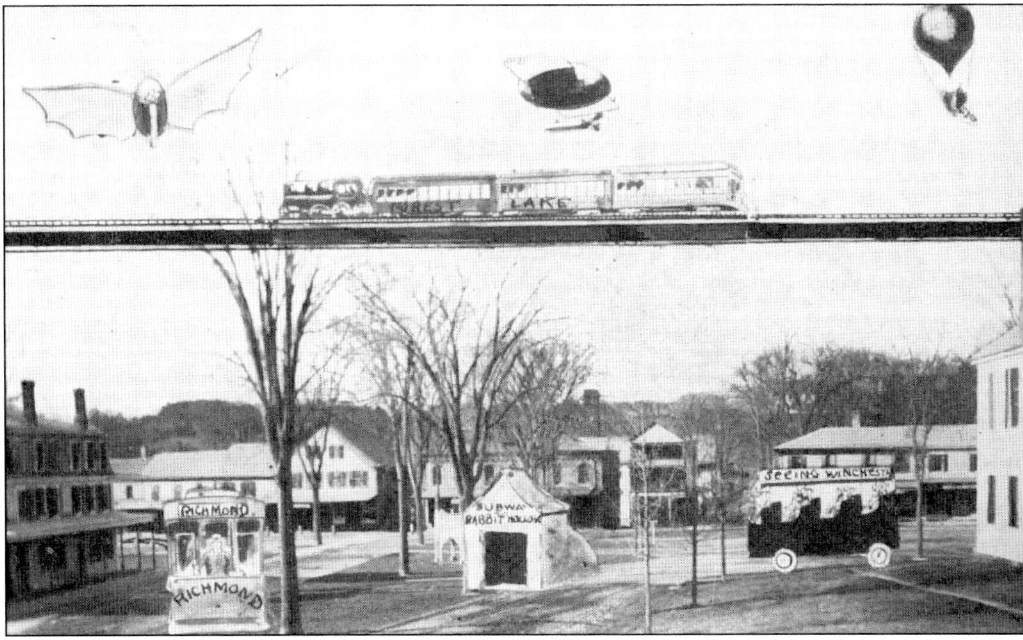

This "in the future" postcard is one of many that were made statewide to demonstrate the sense of humor of New Hampshire residents! The subway, skytrain, sight-seeing buses, dirigibles, and buses to Richmond are all still "in the future;" the occasional hot air balloon is sighted, however.

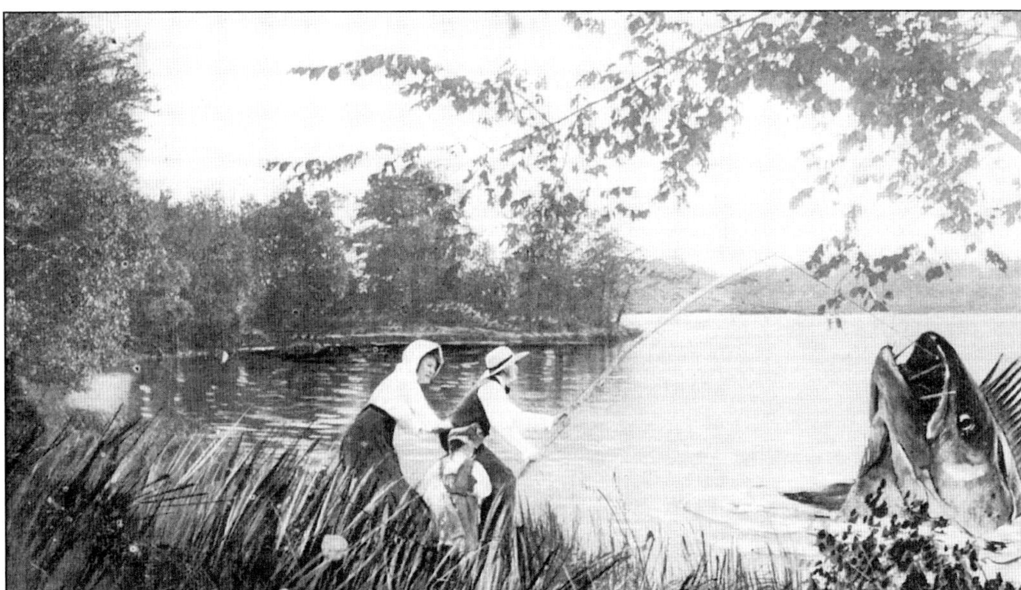

No historical evidence exists that fish of this size were ever pulled, or attempted to be pulled, from Forrest Lake. Perhaps it is just a fisherman's wish, or tale.

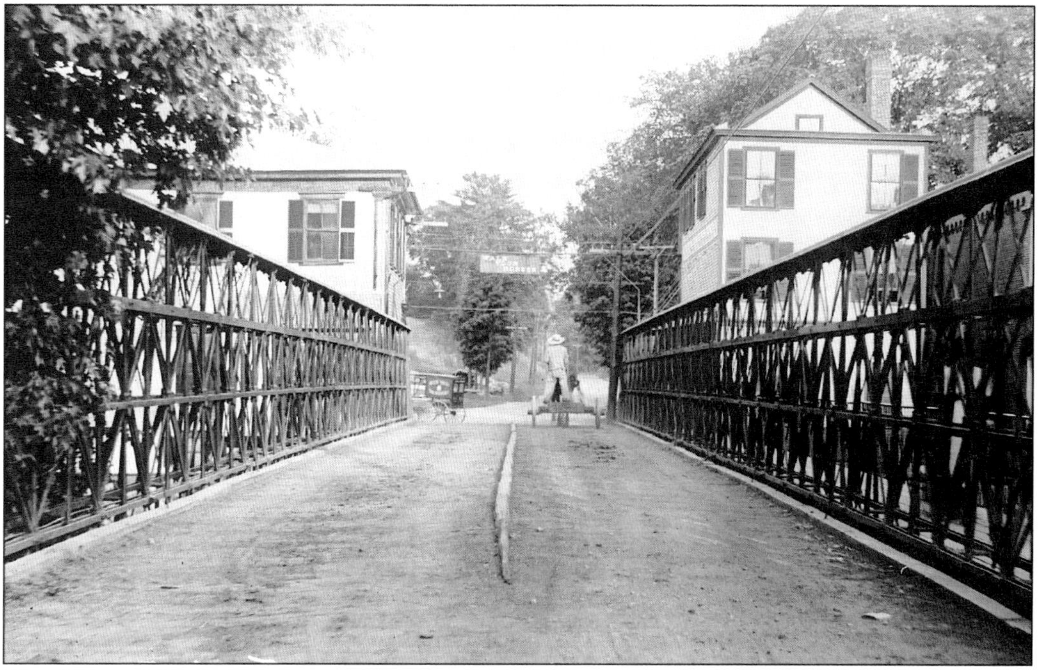

The driver of the farm wagon stands as he crosses the unpaved bridge across the Ashuelot River in 1912.

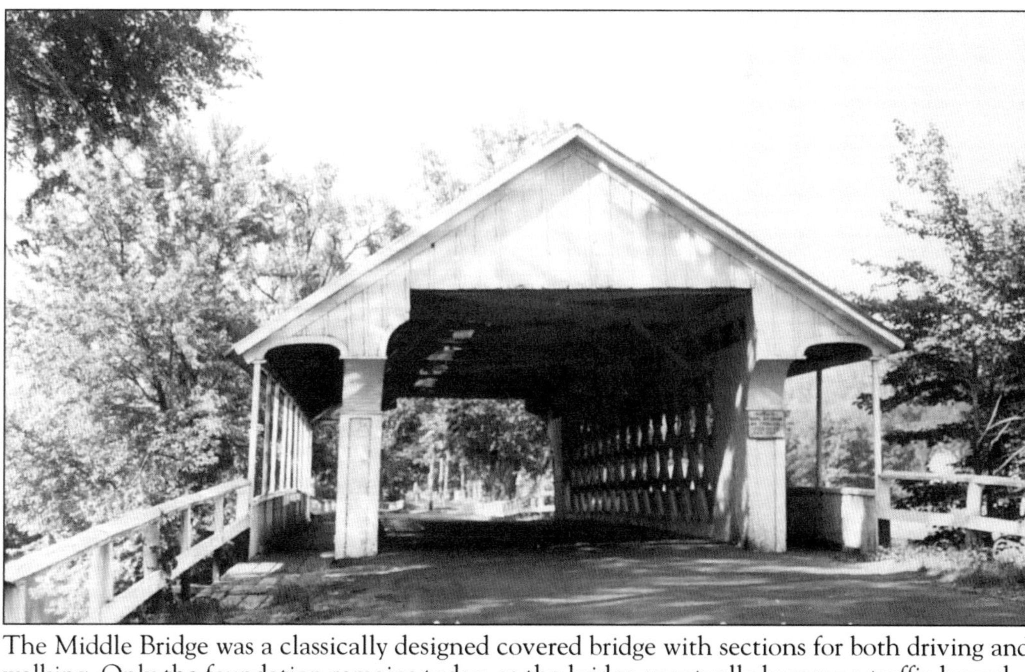

The Middle Bridge was a classically designed covered bridge with sections for both driving and walking. Only the foundation remains today, as the bridge eventually became a traffic hazard.

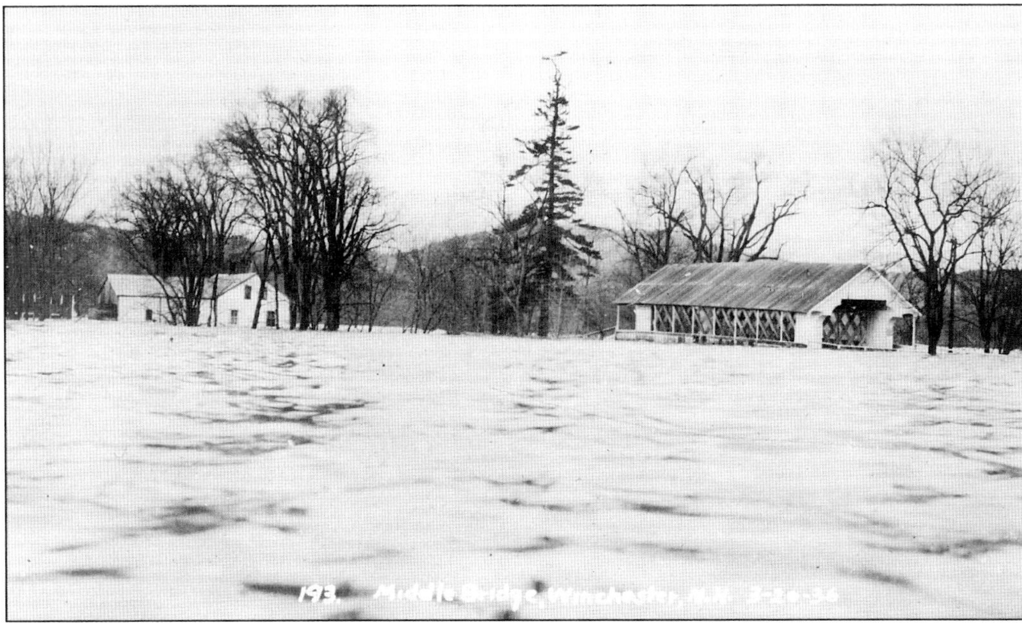

This shows the Middle Bridge during the flood of 1936. The bridge, as well as the home in the distance, is partially under water. This flood led to the building of dams as safety guards on the Ashuelot River.

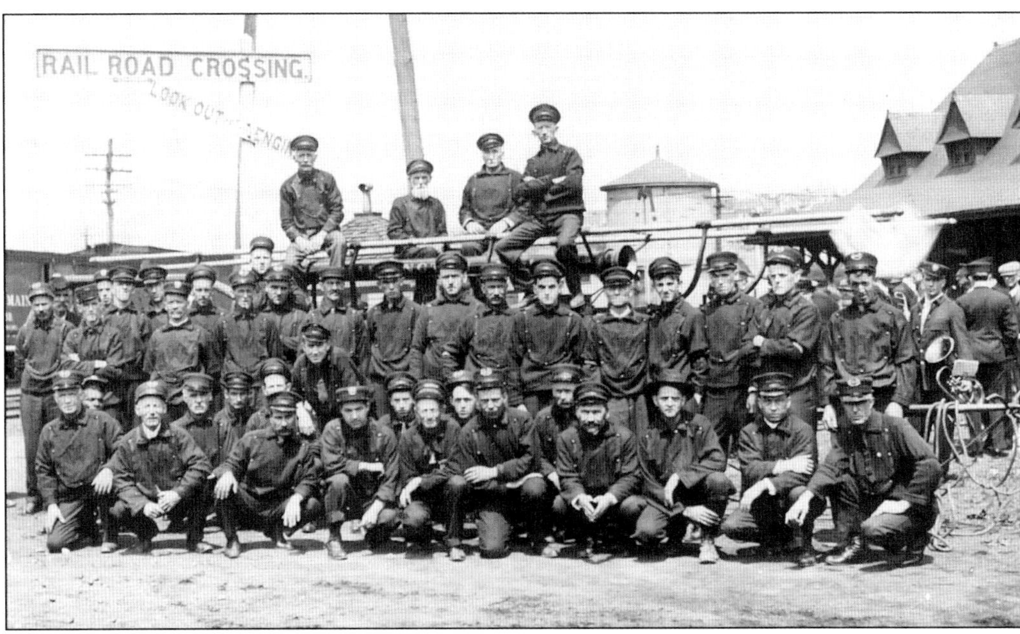

The Winchester Fire Department poses with their Arlington pump engine in 1912 at the railroad crossing. This engine was sold at auction in 1968 for $4,000. Today, it is once again housed in the town fire station.

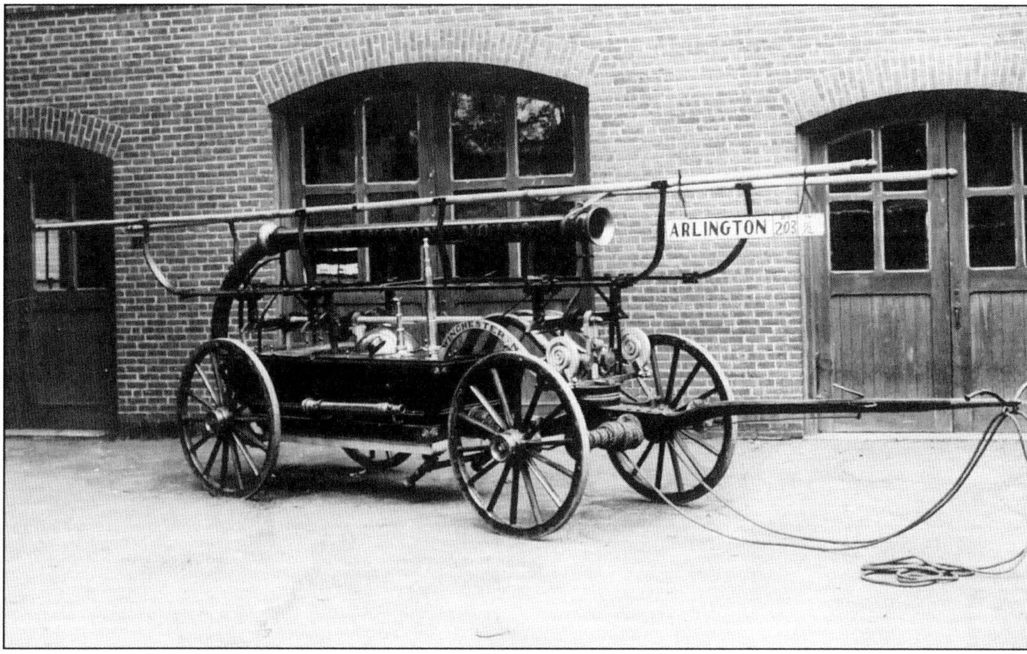

This close-up view shows the well-maintained Arlington, the pride of all parades in town. It carried 203 feet of half-inch fire hose.

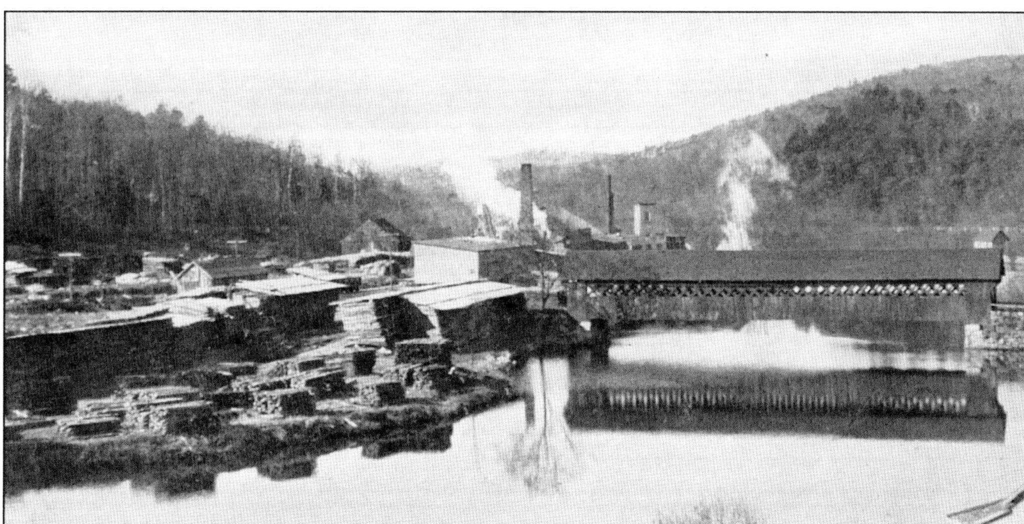

Lumber stacked at the side of the river is shown here near the box factory and bridge at Lower Ashuelot.

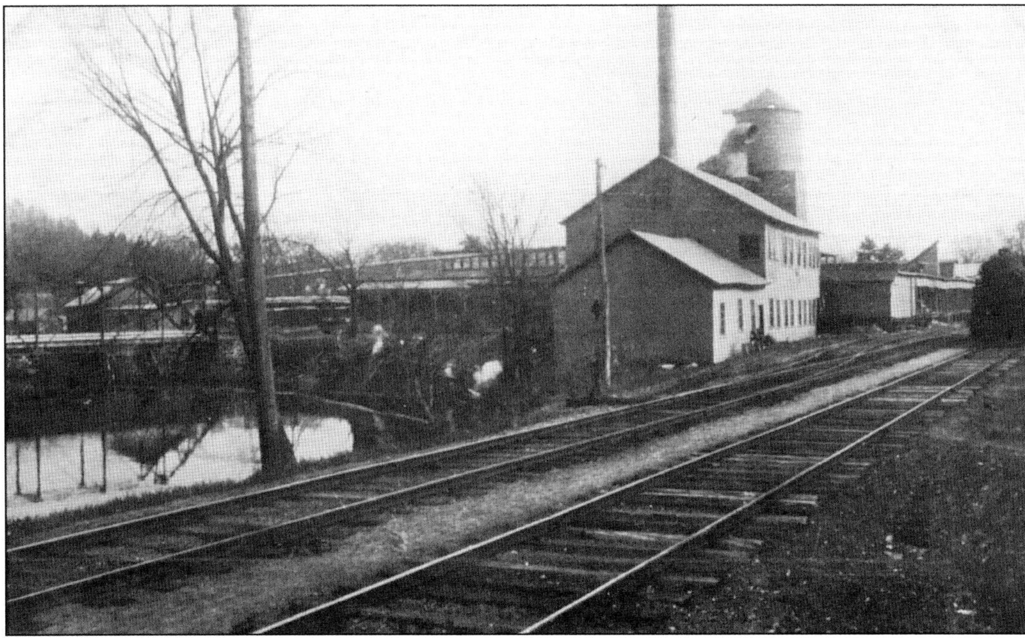

The New England Box Company was located in close proximity to the factory, the railroad, and the river.

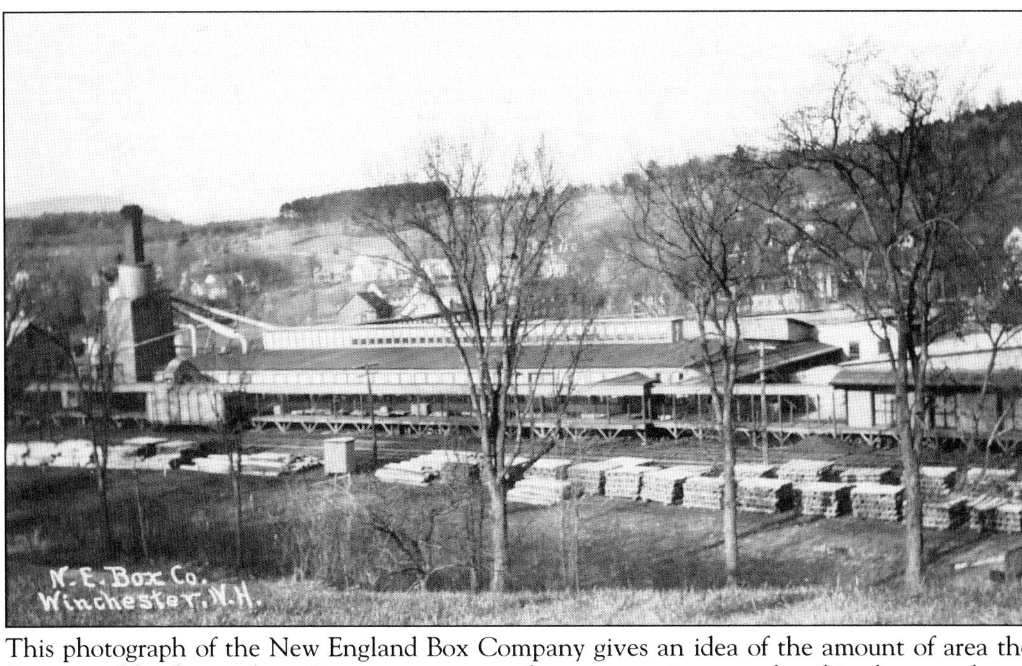

This photograph of the New England Box Company gives an idea of the amount of area the factory and lumber took up. It is not surprising that twenty-six years after this photograph was taken, a flood caused a major lumber jam.

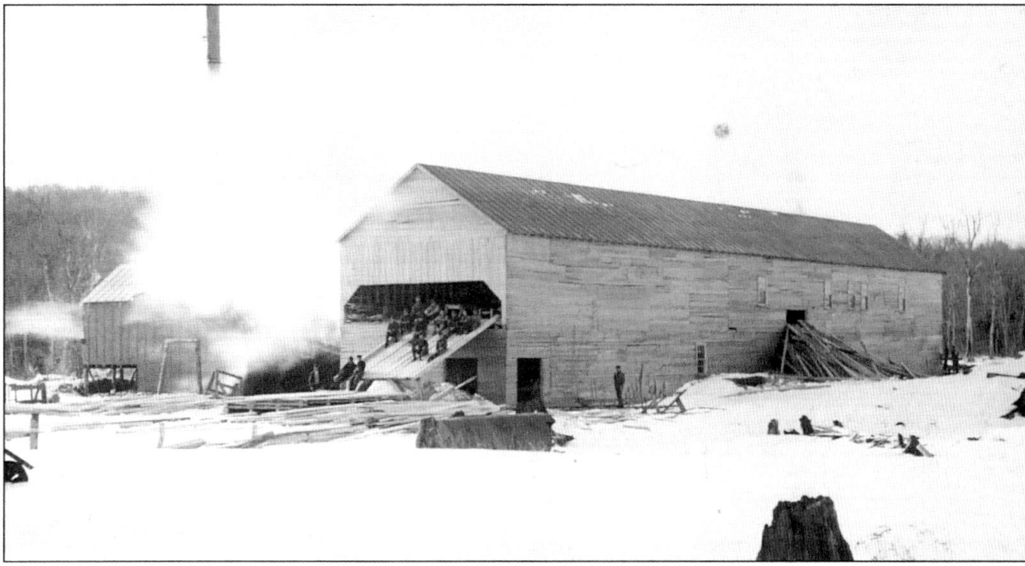

Working conditions could not have been pleasant for employees of the box factory in the middle of a cold, snowy winter.

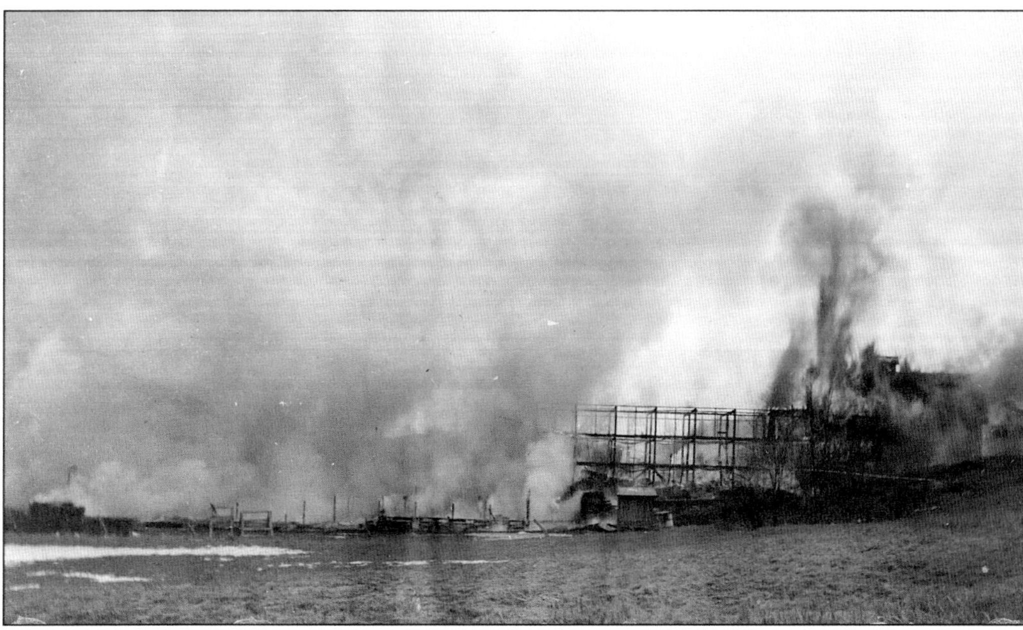

Fire was a major hazard in early Winchester, especially around factories where chemicals and flammable items were being used. The tannery burnt in 1909, leaving many people unemployed. The writer of this postcard wrote that "it is much worse than it looked."

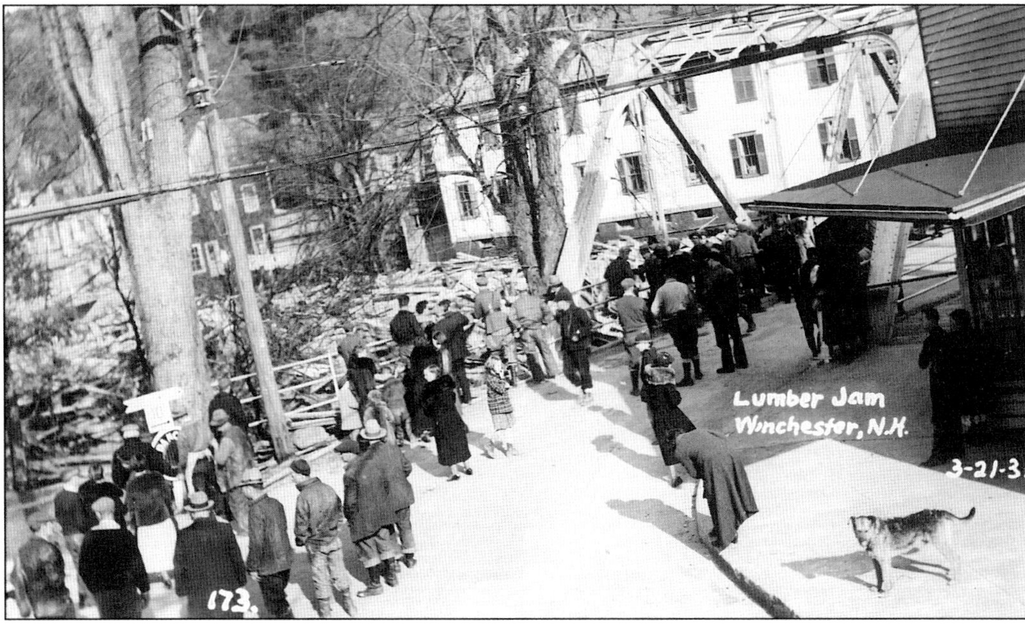

The lumber jam was such an aberration, an incredible phenomenon, that as soon as it was feasible people flocked out to look at the effects of the flood and discuss it with their neighbors. Much of the lumber was salvaged.

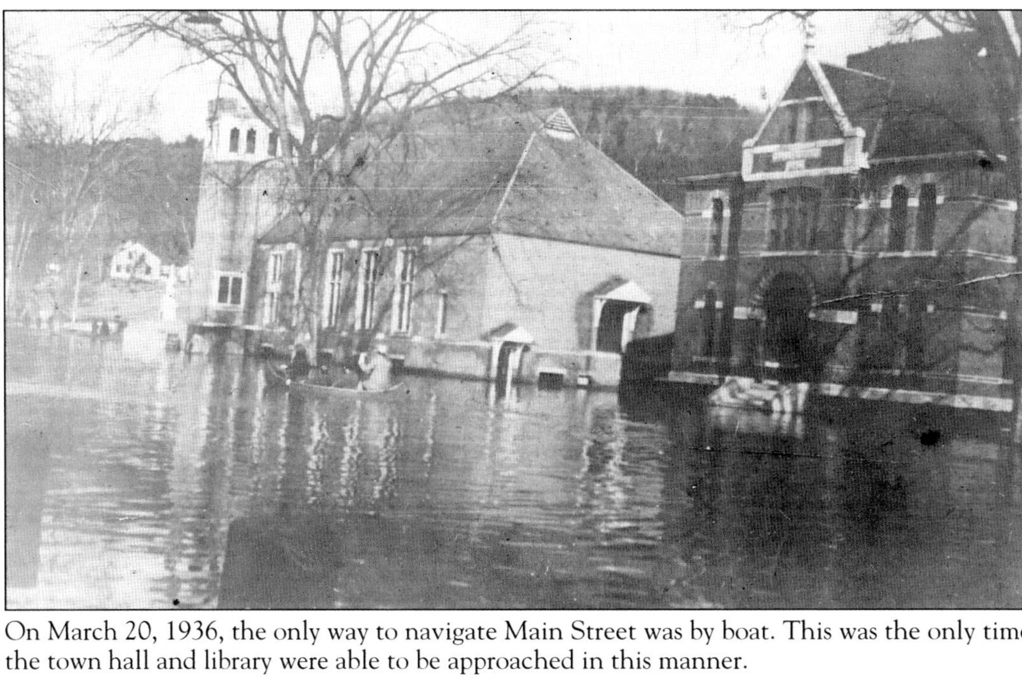

On March 20, 1936, the only way to navigate Main Street was by boat. This was the only time the town hall and library were able to be approached in this manner.

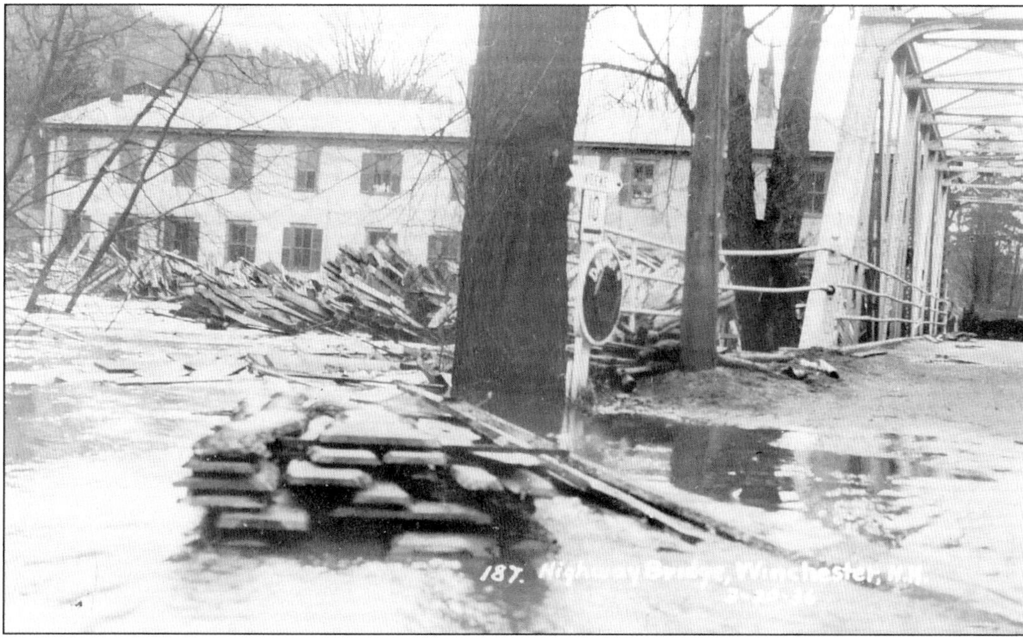

During the jam, lumber was swept with careless abandon by the river against the base of the highway bridge.

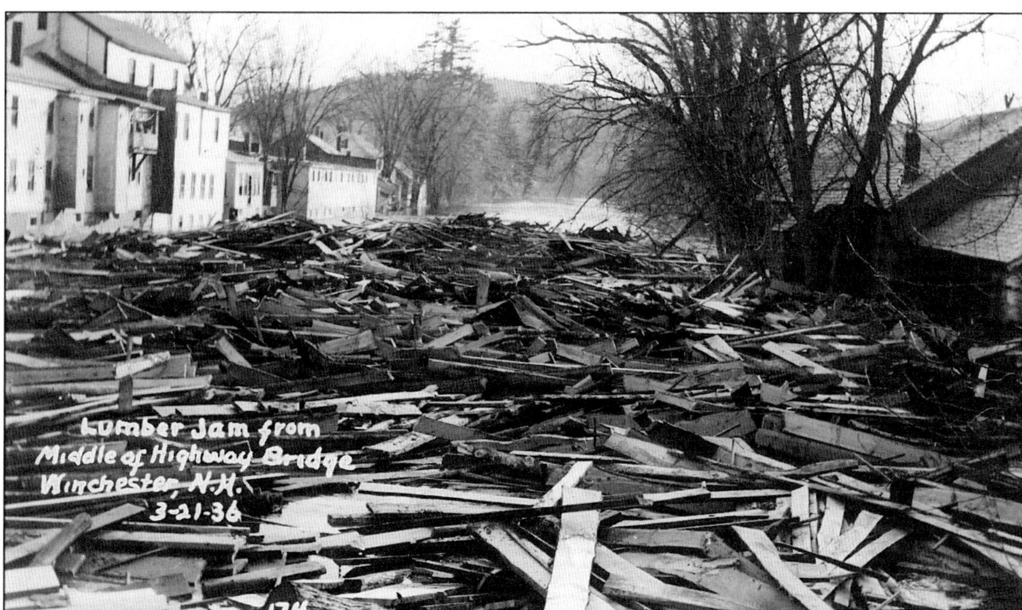

On March 21, the Ashuelot River looked like a lumber pile that could be traversed by foot. This view shows both riverbanks and angry waters in the distance that are trying desperately to go on their merry way.

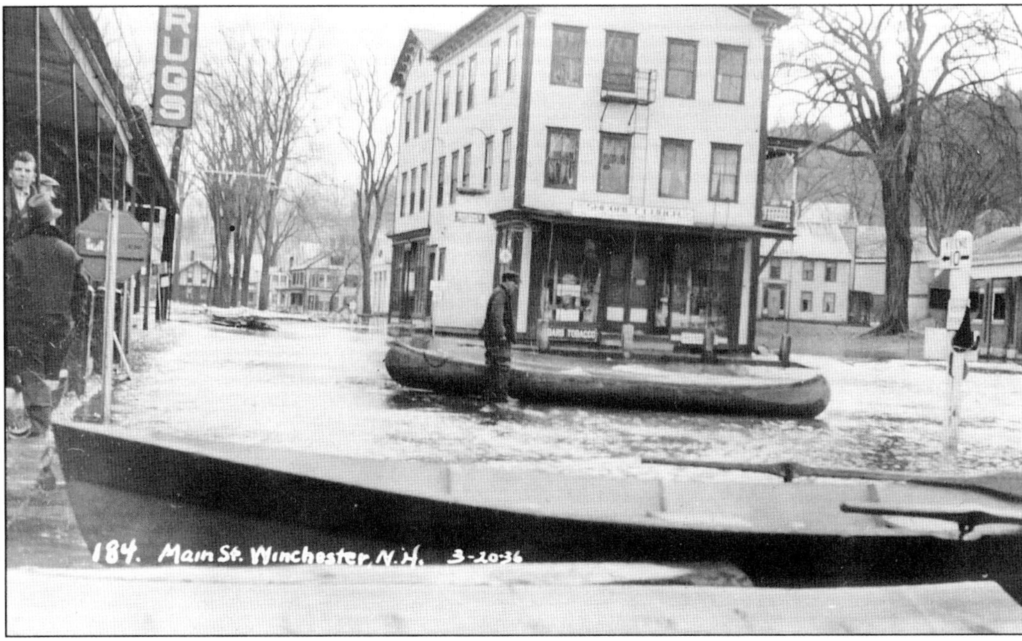

The drug store is on the Ashuelot River side of the street. The water went as far as the bank, flooding cellars and weakening structures.

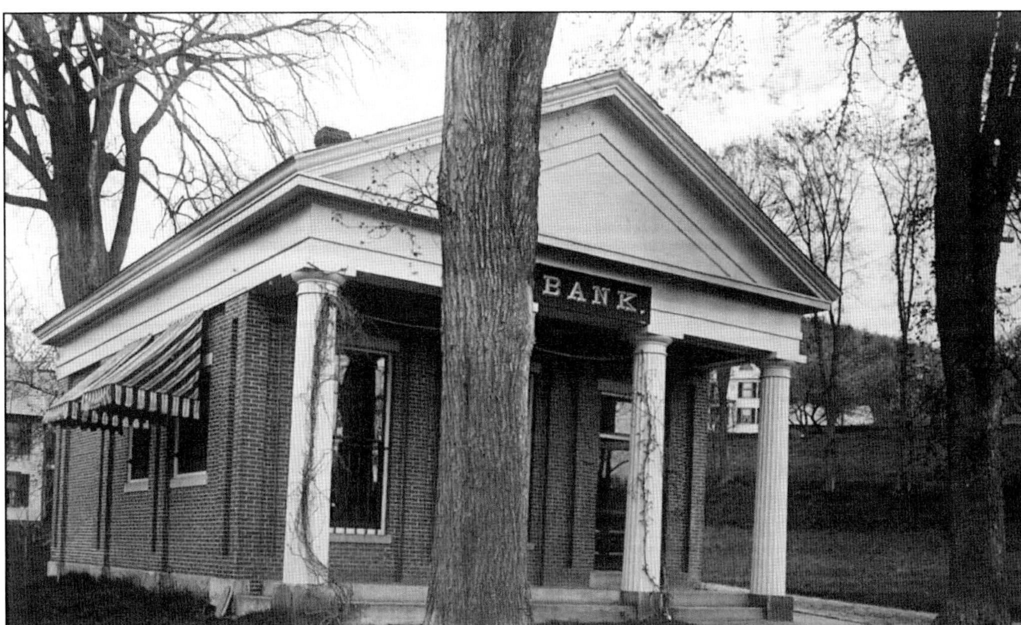

The bank building—which was erected in 1847 and is still standing—was sold a few years ago, leaving the town without a financial institution.

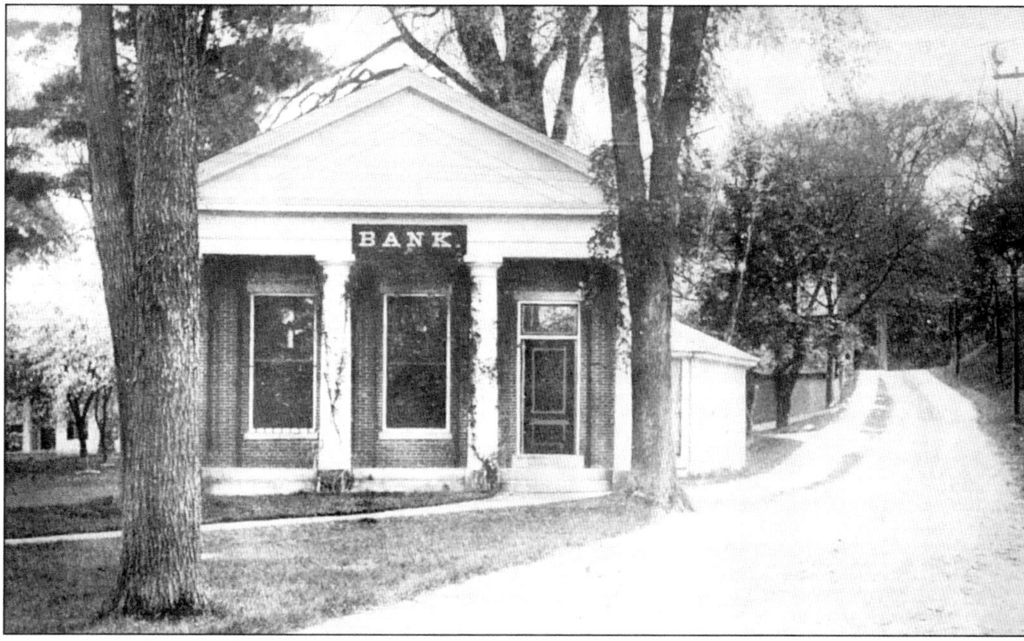

The National Bank building was a proper bank for over a hundred years. It was called the Winchester Bank, the First Bank, etc., depending on who owned it. It sits at the crossroads of Michigan Street, Route 119, and Route 10.

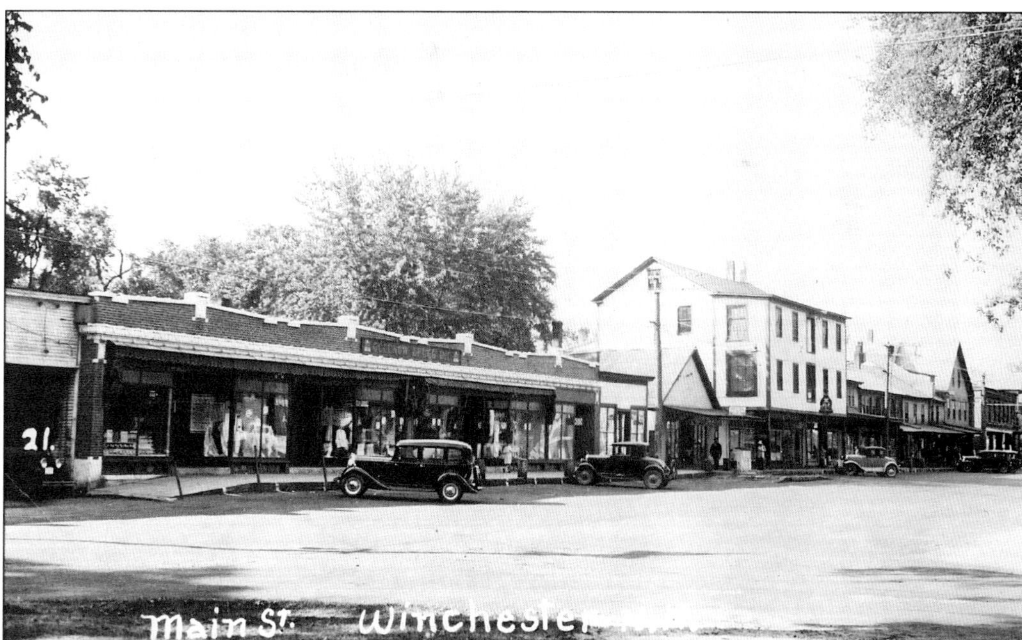

The main street of a town usually shows more evidence of change than any other region. It is the business district and the focus point, literally the heart of the town. This picture was taken in July of 1938, two years after the flood. Notice the well-stocked storefronts and the width of the street.

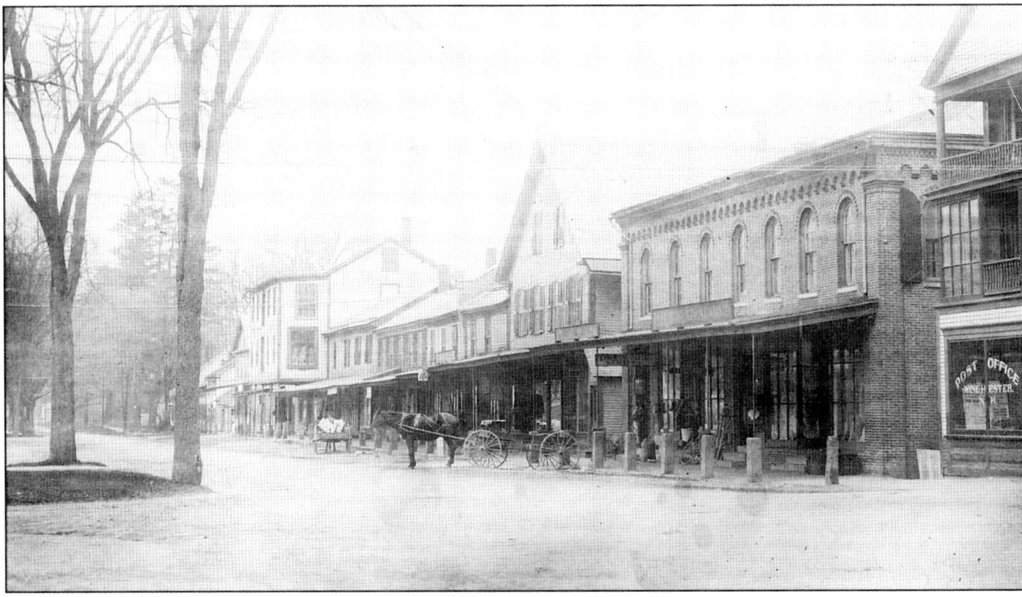

All of the buildings shown in this *c.* 1910 view of Main Street are gone and have been replaced. The post office is now across the street on Route 119. At the time of this photograph, horse-drawn buggies still dominated the roads, and cars were a rarity.

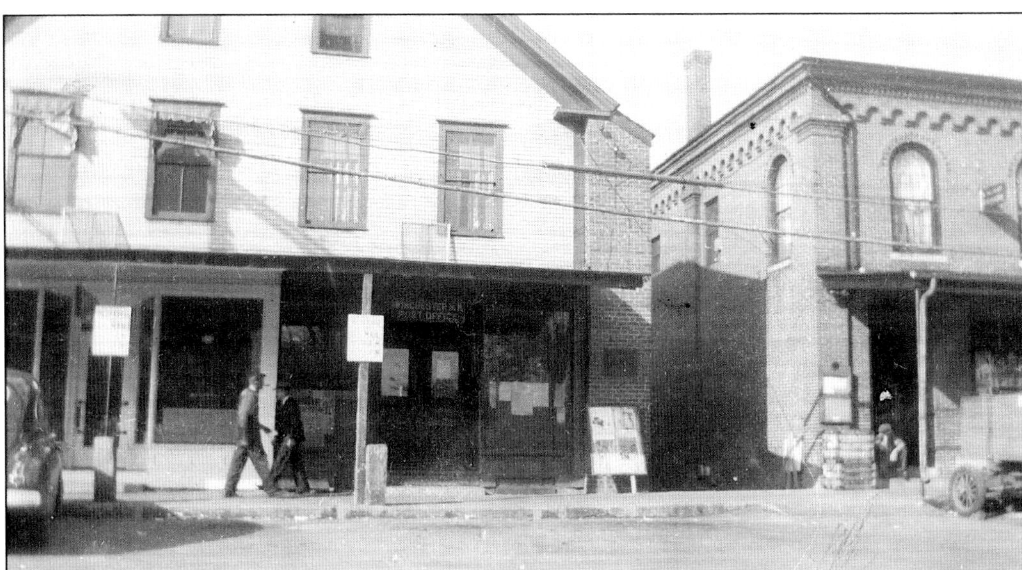

The post office in a small town has always been an important place for congregating and obtaining local news. The railroads would drop off the mail sacks and often people would come into town to collect their mail. This was a time when the mail was delivered three times a day and what was mailed in the morning locally would have been delivered by noon.

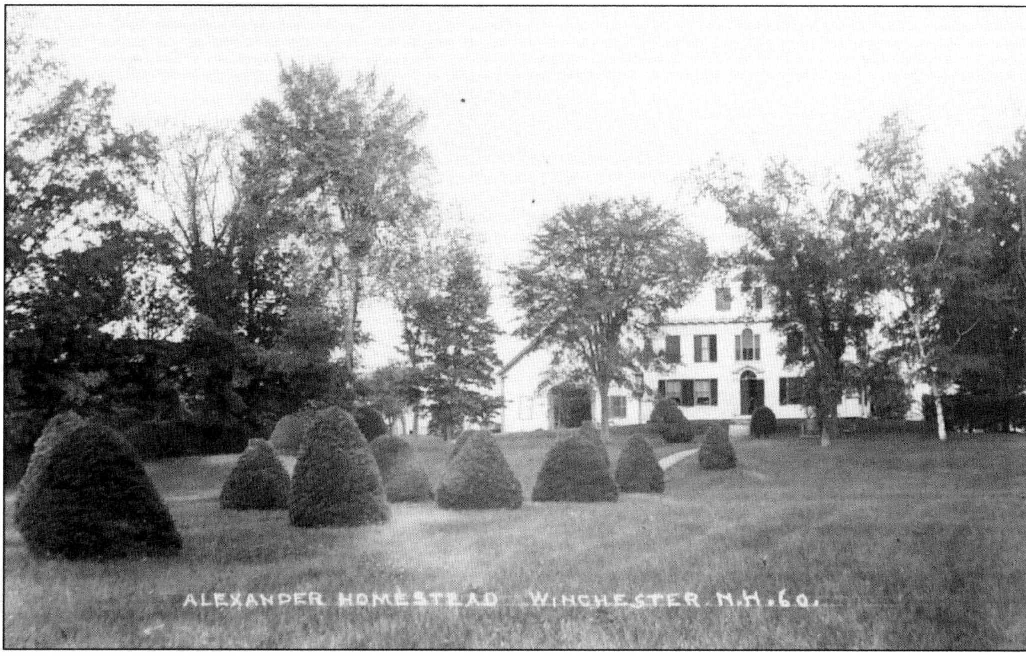

The Alexander homestead was on the 1887 map. The landscaping has changed often over the years, but the house was always strategically placed in an elegant fashion. Today, a small flea market is held during the summer on what was the front lawn.

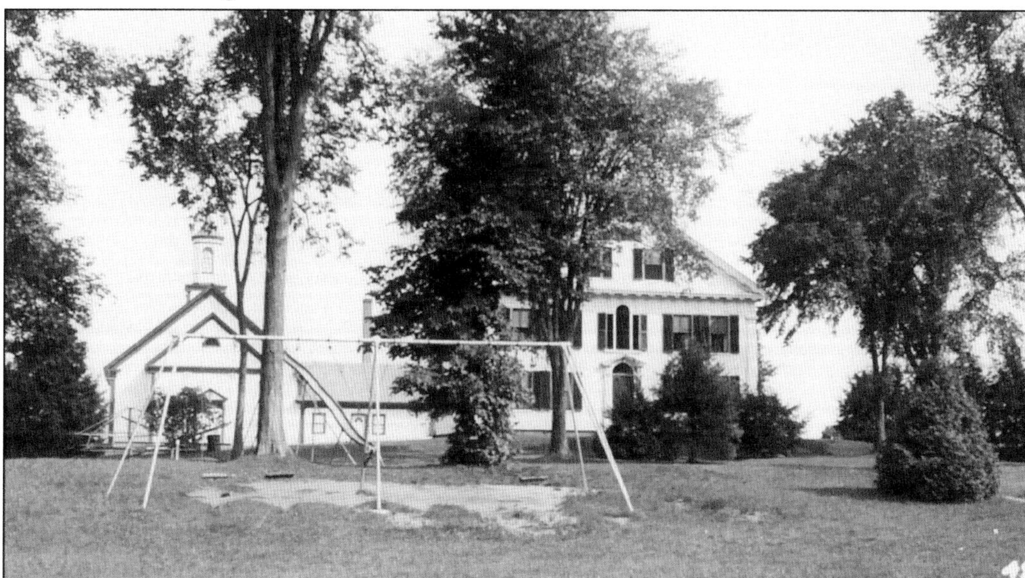

The Alexander homestead became the E.L.M. Hall in 1805, when it was given to the town as a gift by Governor Francis Patrick Murphy in memory of his mother, Ellen Lambert Murphey. Governor Murphey was born at Forrest Lake, and as a child of poverty he admired the Alexander homestead so much that he often "wondered what it would be like to live there and be rich." The E.L.M. Hall, shown here in 1944, is the only recreational facility for the town where plays are enacted, auctions take place, bowling teams meet, postcard shows are held, and tennis and other sports can be played.

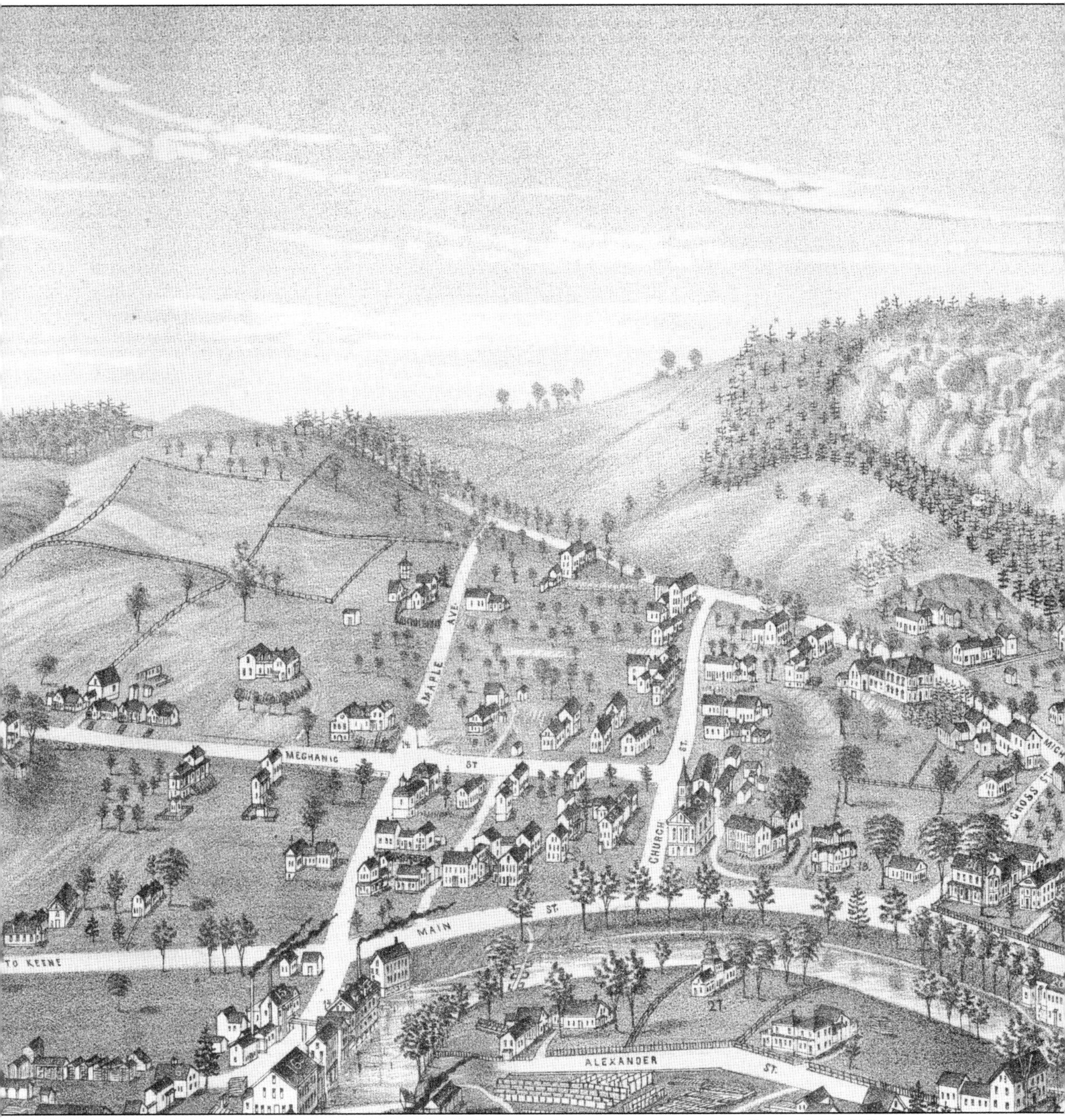

This view of Winchester from Meetinghouse Mountain was created in 1887. This map shows the entire town as it was before the turn of the century, nicely laid out with shops along the

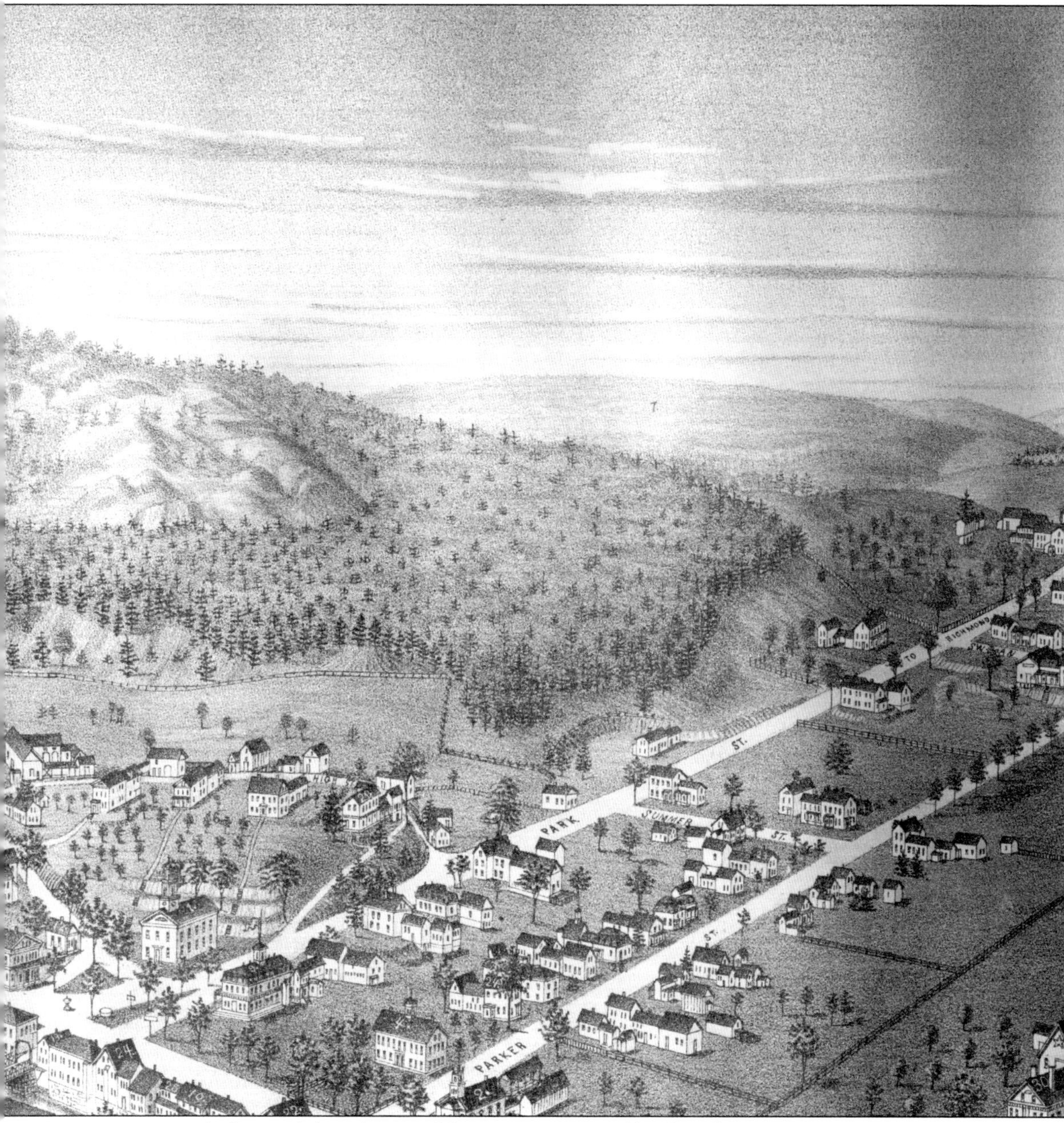

main street, a plethora of churches, and factories strategically placed.

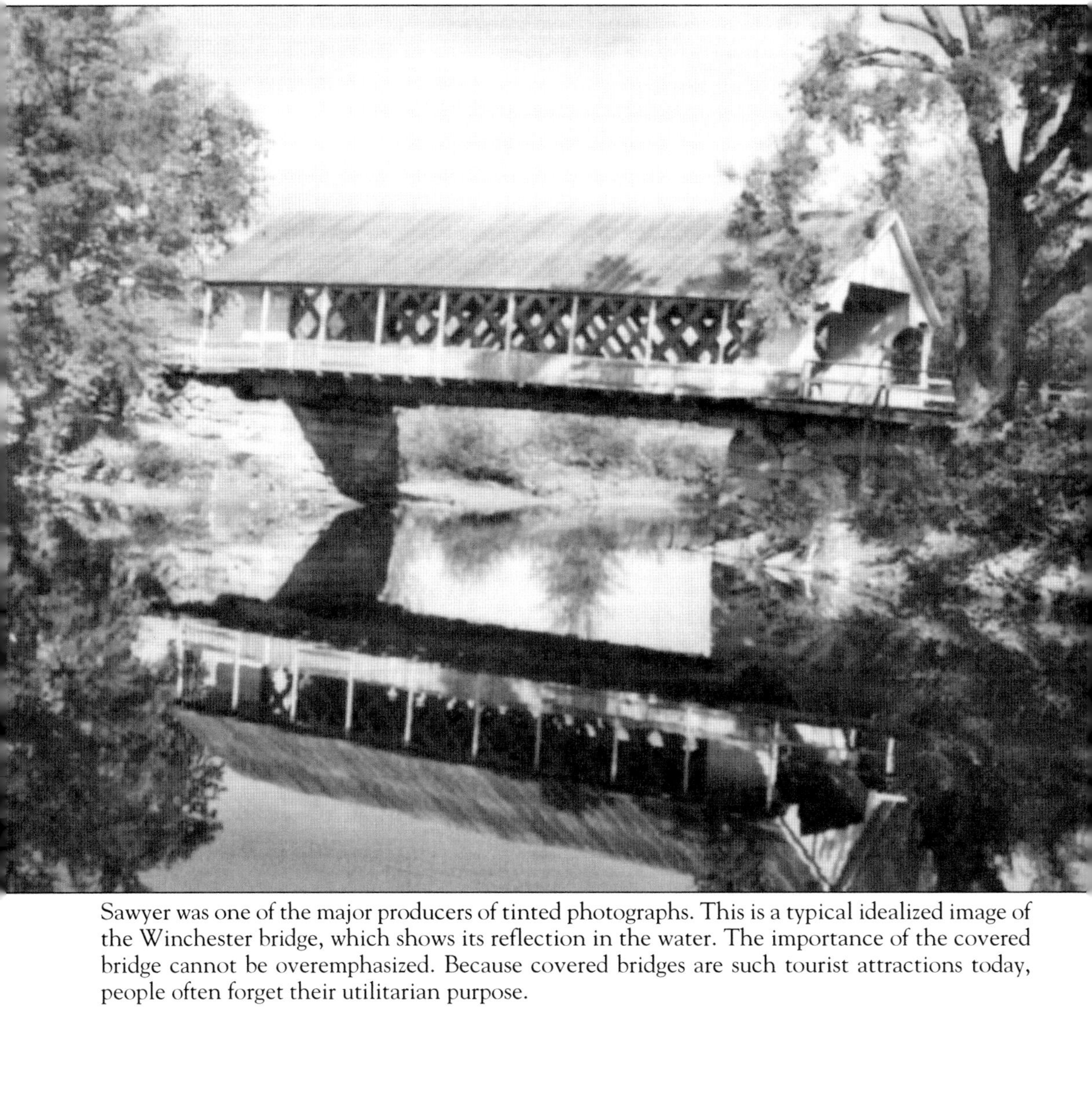

Sawyer was one of the major producers of tinted photographs. This is a typical idealized image of the Winchester bridge, which shows its reflection in the water. The importance of the covered bridge cannot be overemphasized. Because covered bridges are such tourist attractions today, people often forget their utilitarian purpose.

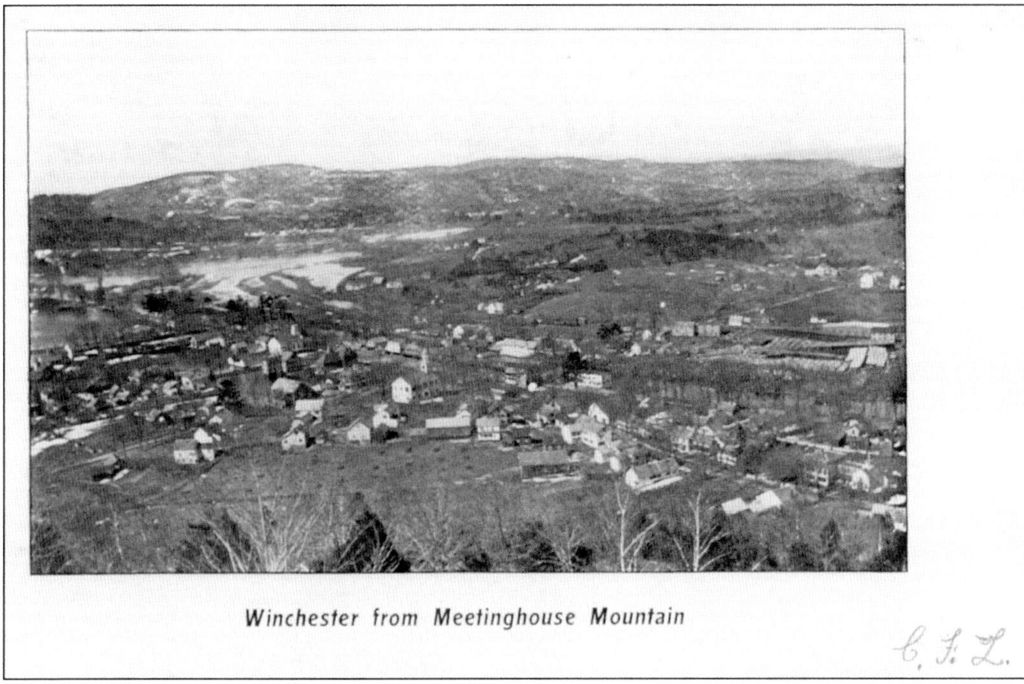

The town of Winchester is shown here *c*. 1910 spread out around Meetinghouse Mountain.

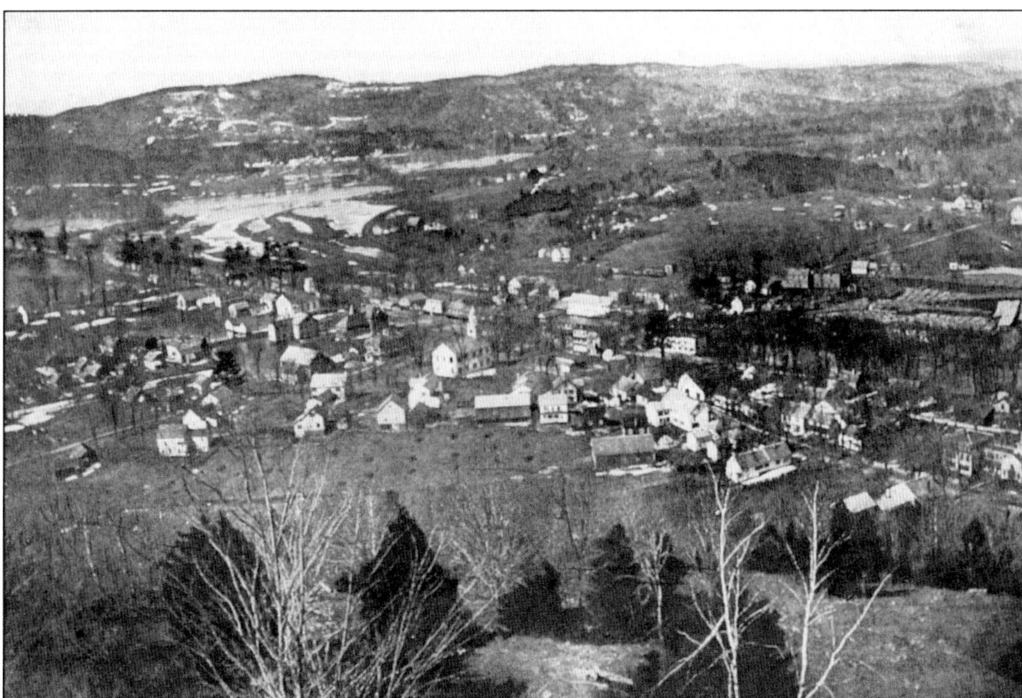

Approximately twenty years passed between the taking of the photograph at the top of the page and this one, and yet very little change has occurred.

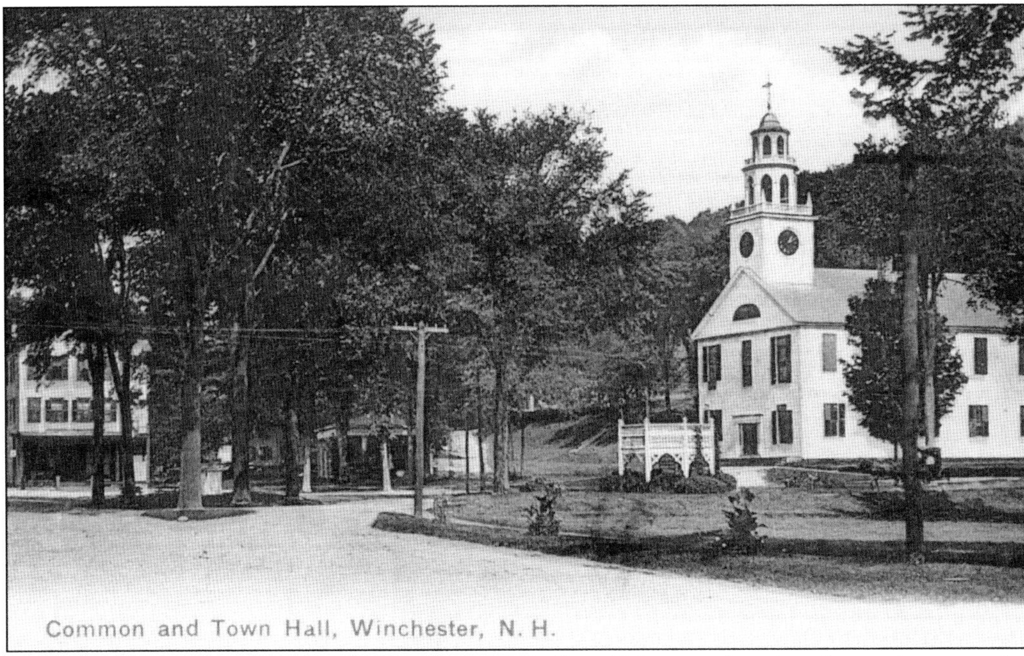

The Winchester Common—including the town hall and Universalist church—is shown in this view, with Meetinghouse Mountain in the background.

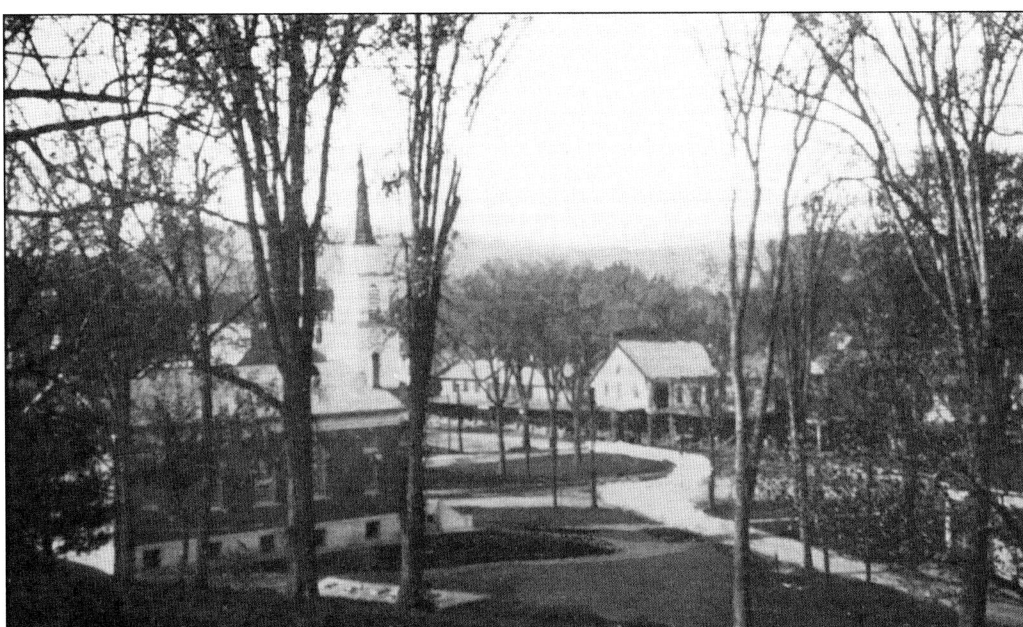

The common is seen here from Meetinghouse Mountain.

The Universalist church and the town hall appear here near the bank, which is tucked in behind the trees. The common's size is noteworthy.

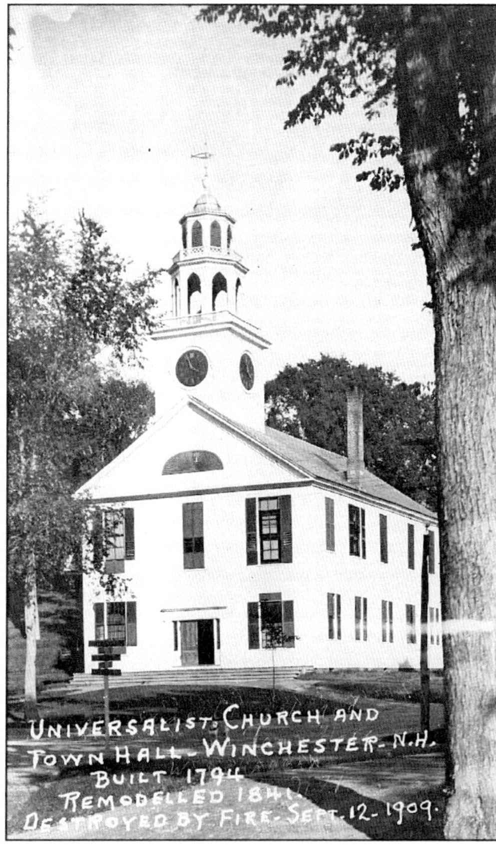

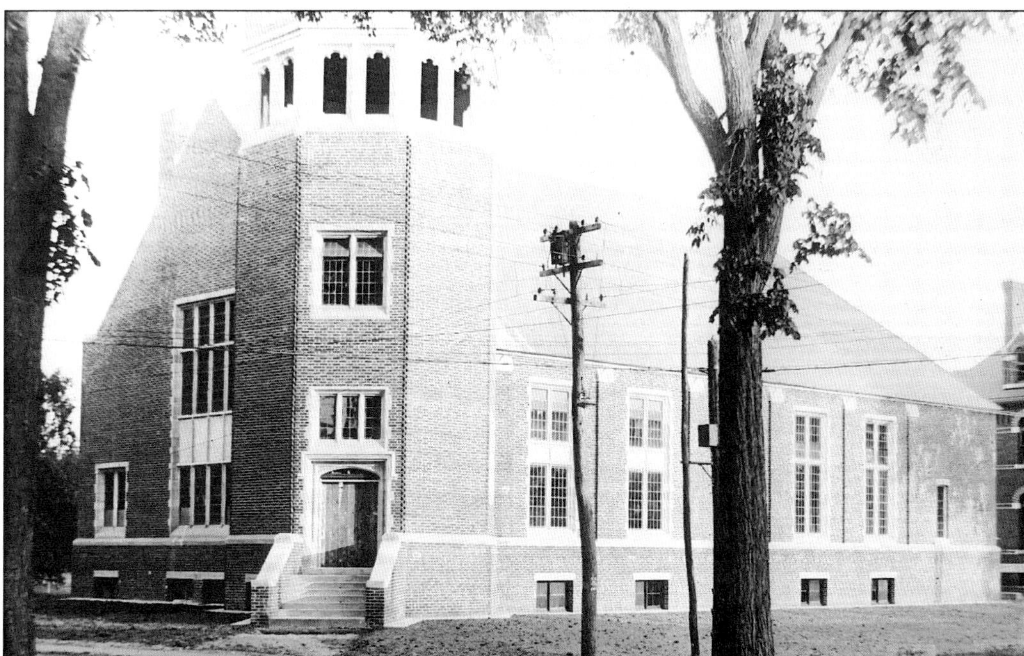

The current town hall and library (in the background) are featured in this view.

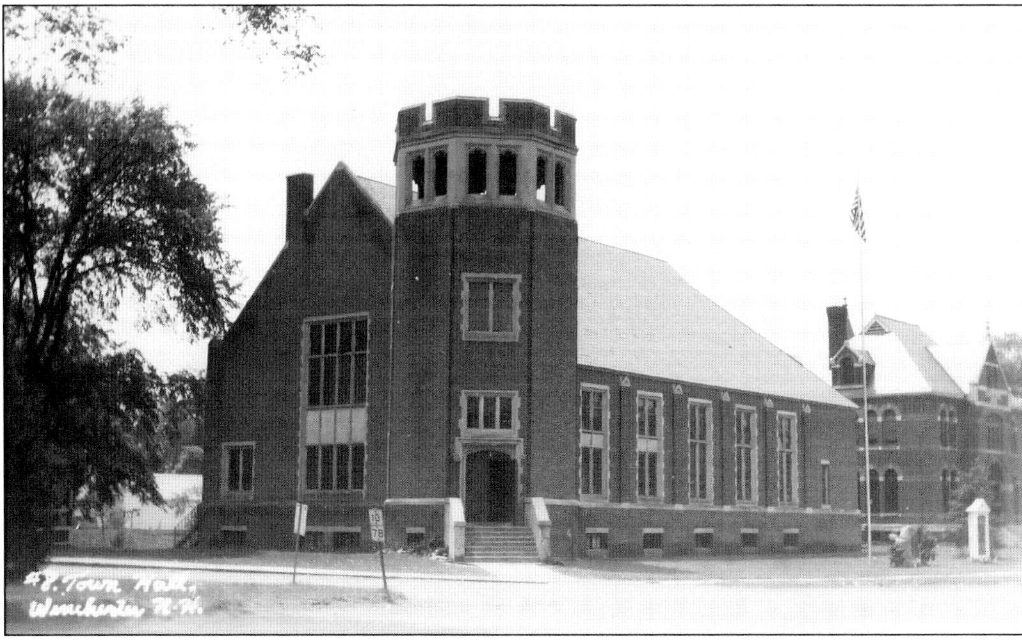

This image of the town hall was captured before the memorial statue was placed in front.

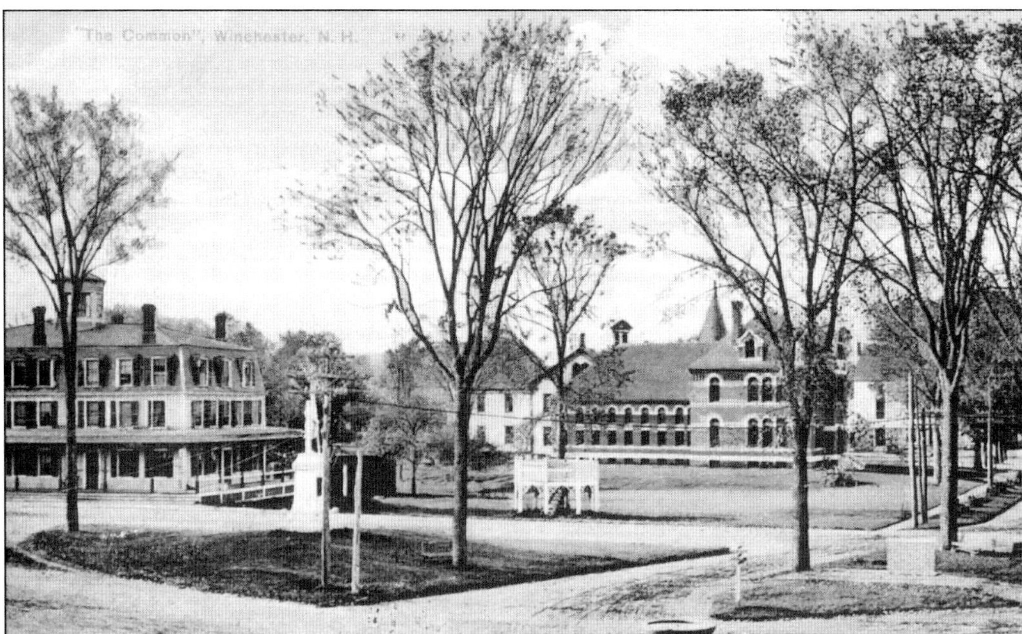

The town hall is shown here with Shipman's Tavern (which no longer exists) and the memorial statue. Notice the distance between them.

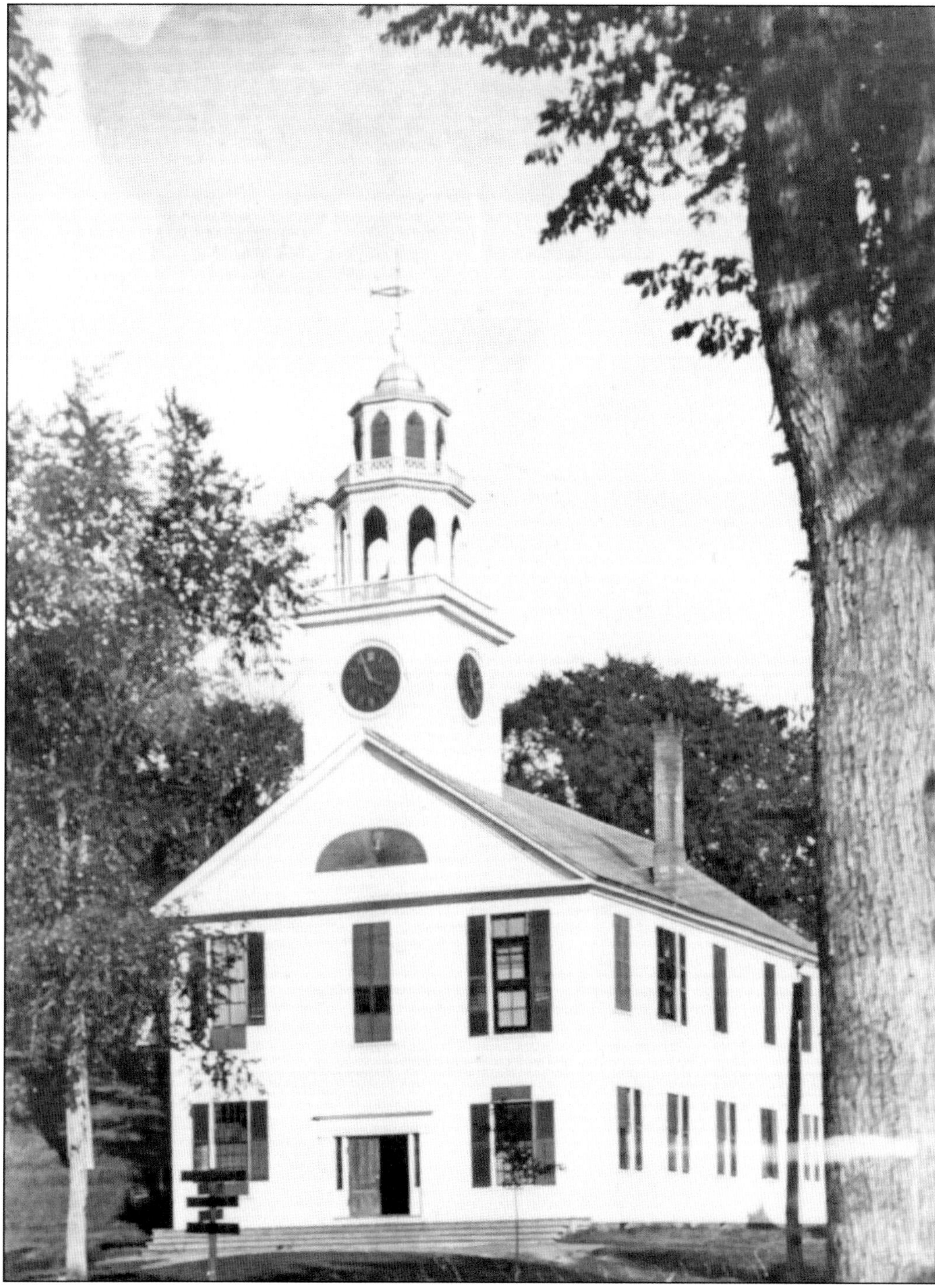

The Universalist church and the town hall were built in 1794, remodeled in 1841, and burned down on September 12, 1909.

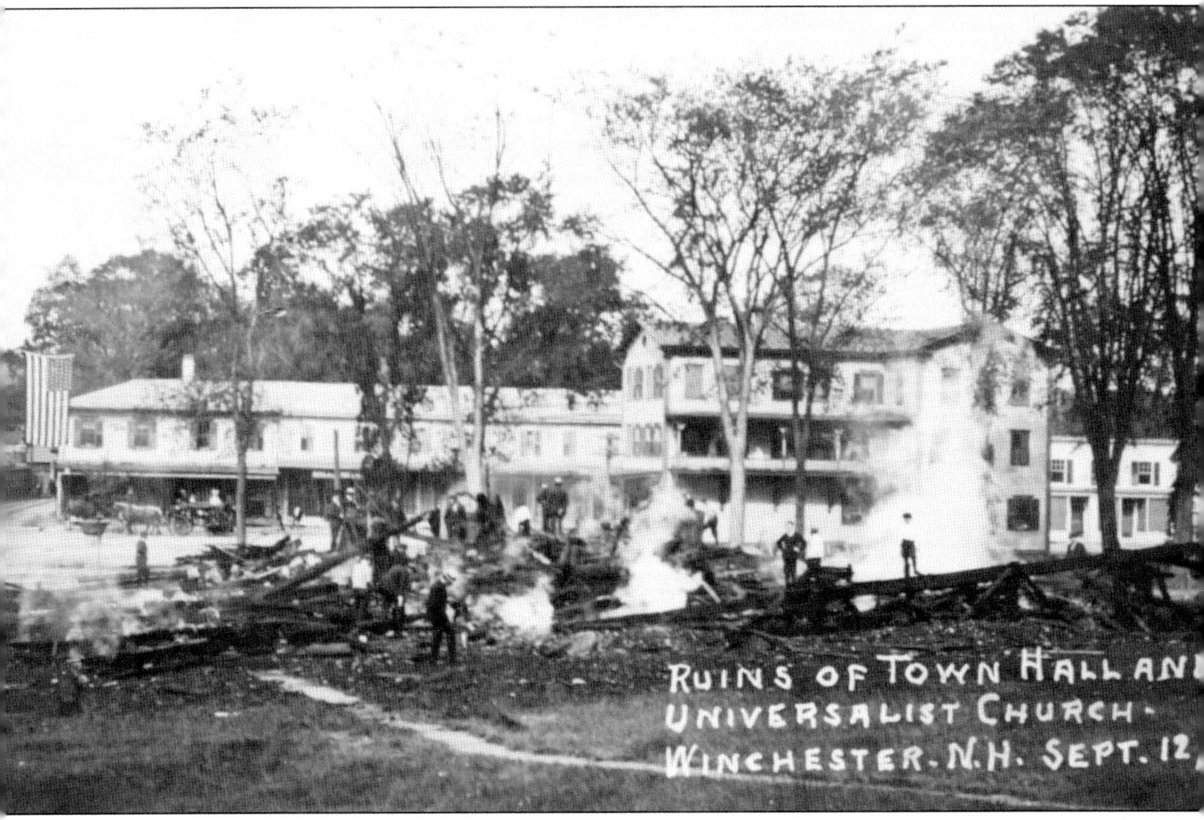

People can be seen here walking through the still smoldering ruins of the Universalist church and the town hall. Notice the flag hanging in the street, which seems to be floating.

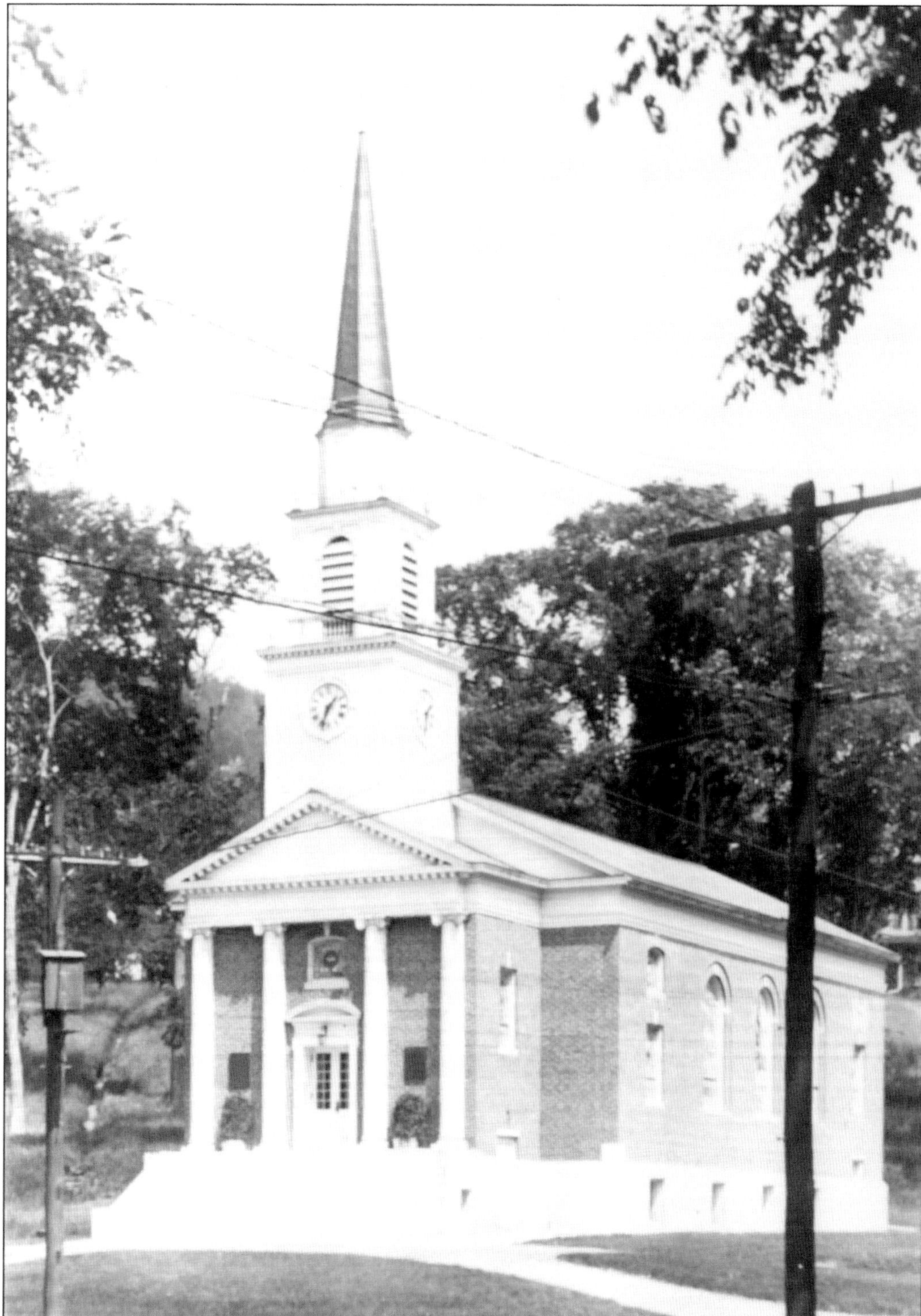

This is how the Universalist church looked in the 1930s. Of note are the clock, steeple, and the different architectural changes visible today in the rebuilt church.

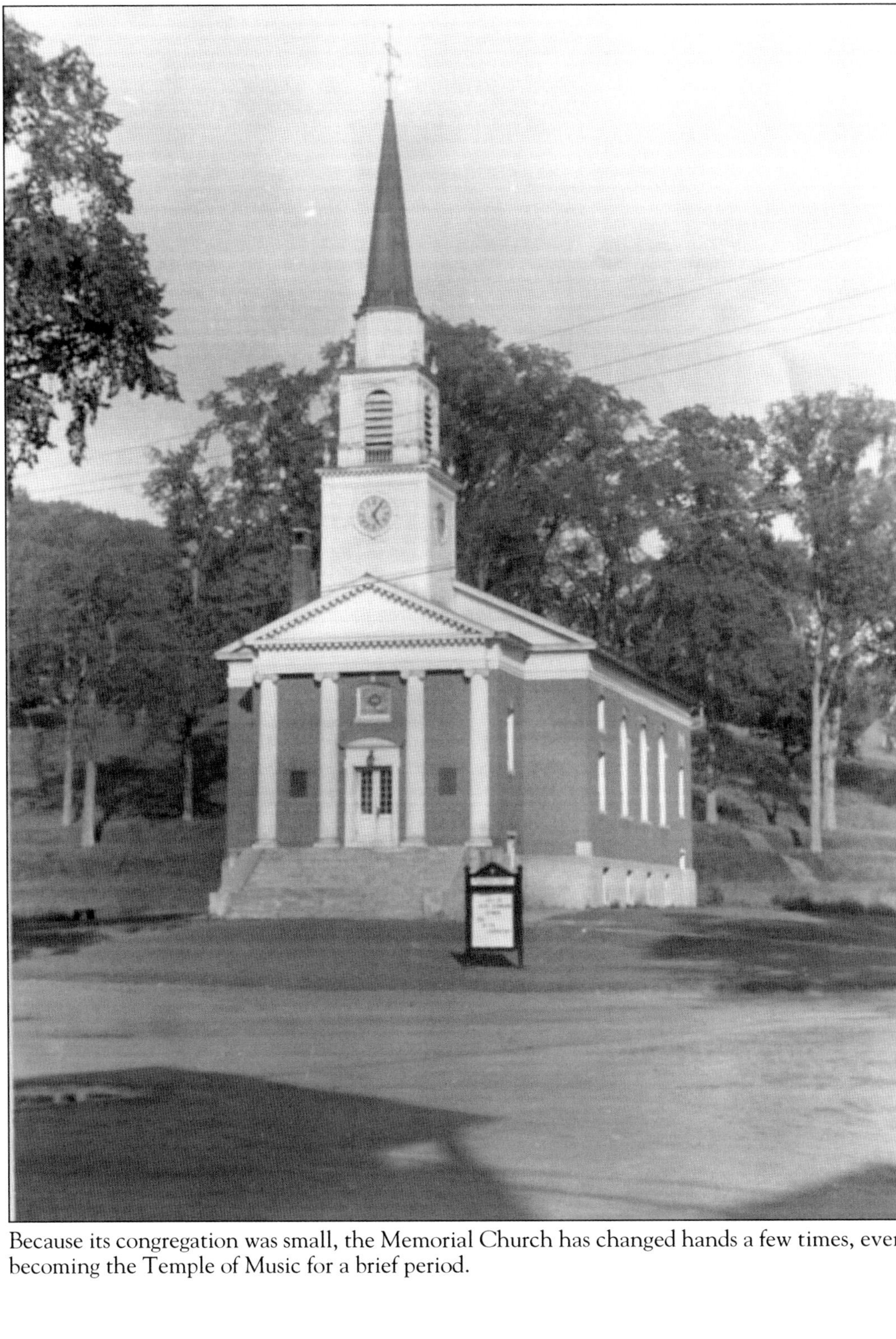

Because its congregation was small, the Memorial Church has changed hands a few times, even becoming the Temple of Music for a brief period.

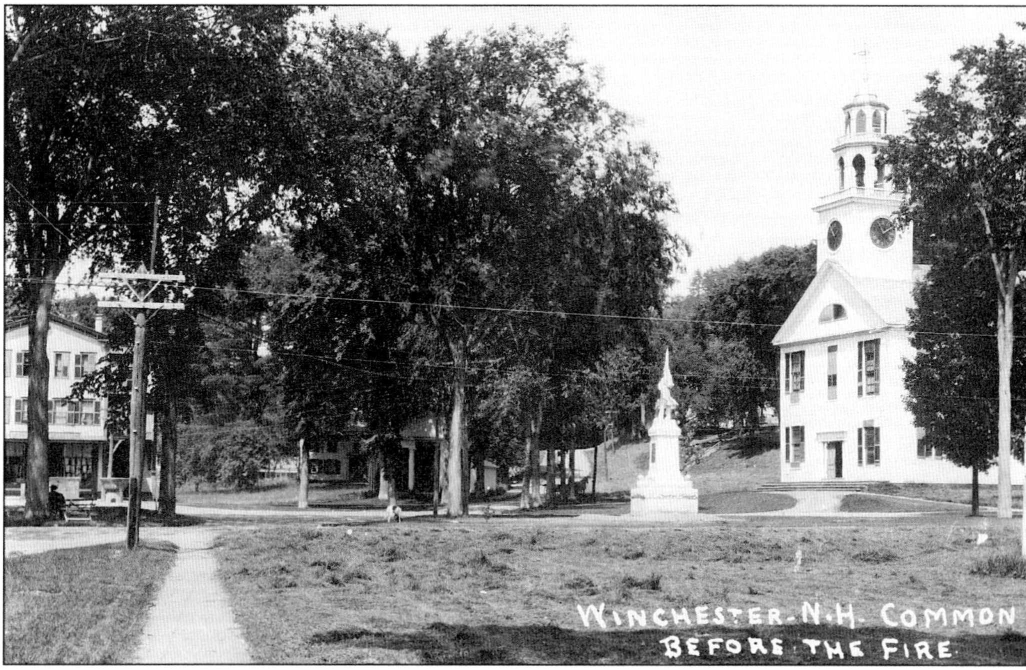

The common is shown here as it looked before the fire. Since that time, the bandstand has been demolished and the monument has been moved. Beside the current church is a life-size crèche that is opened and displayed each Christmas.

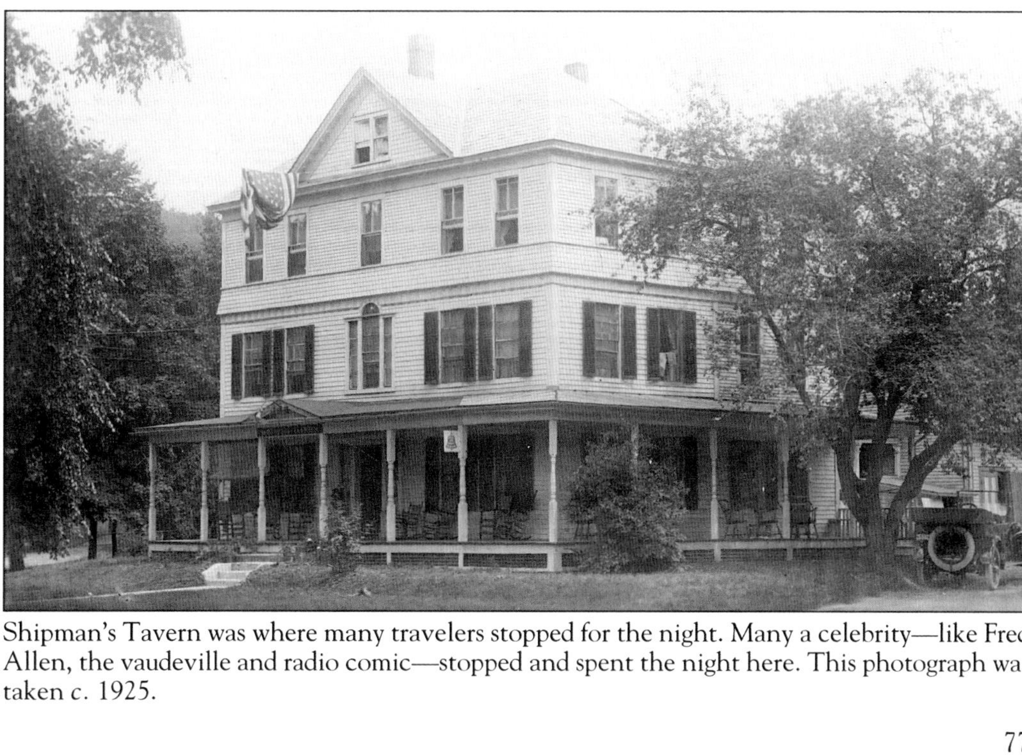

Shipman's Tavern was where many travelers stopped for the night. Many a celebrity—like Fred Allen, the vaudeville and radio comic—stopped and spent the night here. This photograph was taken *c.* 1925.

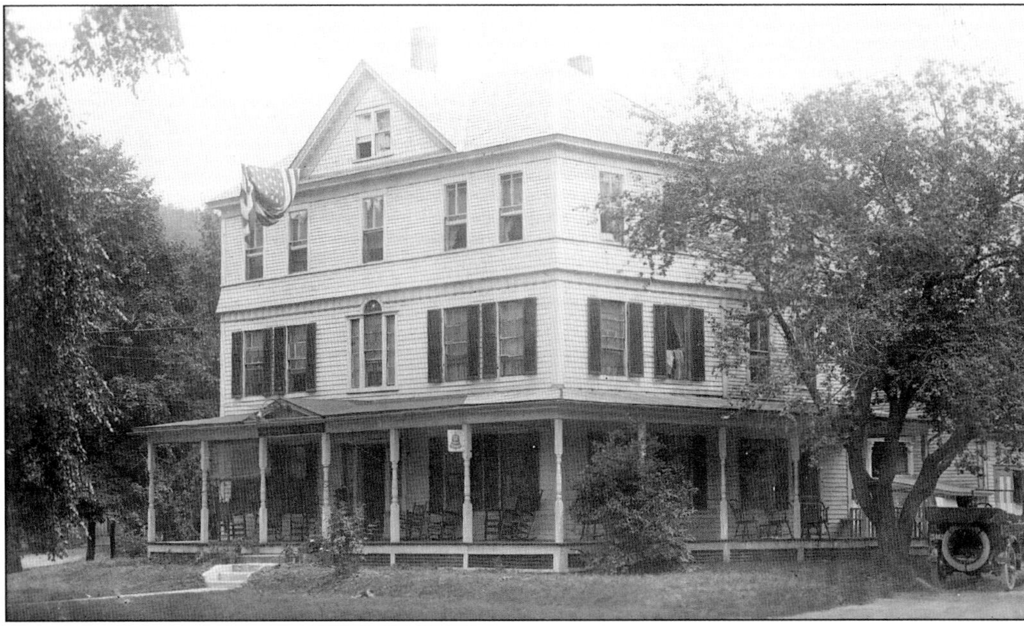

Shipman's Tavern in the 1930s was still a haven for travelers to stop and rest while heading toward recreational areas in the White Mountains and points north and south.

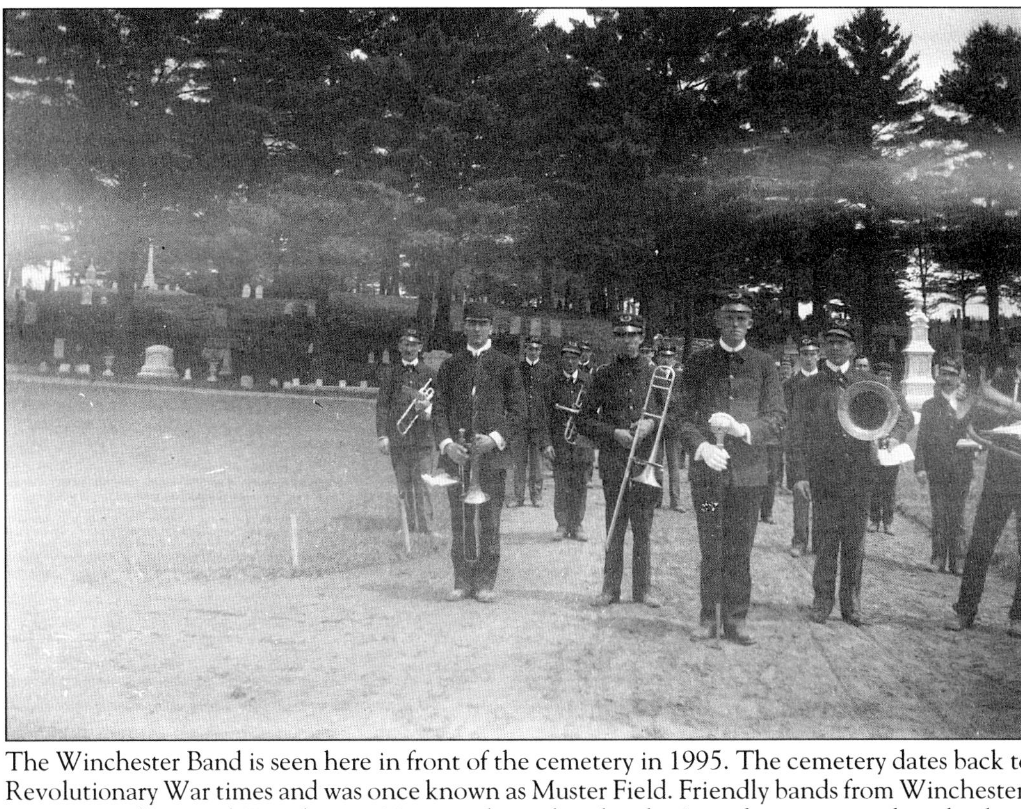

The Winchester Band is seen here in front of the cemetery in 1995. The cemetery dates back to Revolutionary War times and was once known as Muster Field. Friendly bands from Winchester, New Hampshire, and Winchester, Virginia, hosted each other's performances and paid tribute to the victims on both sides in the Civil War.

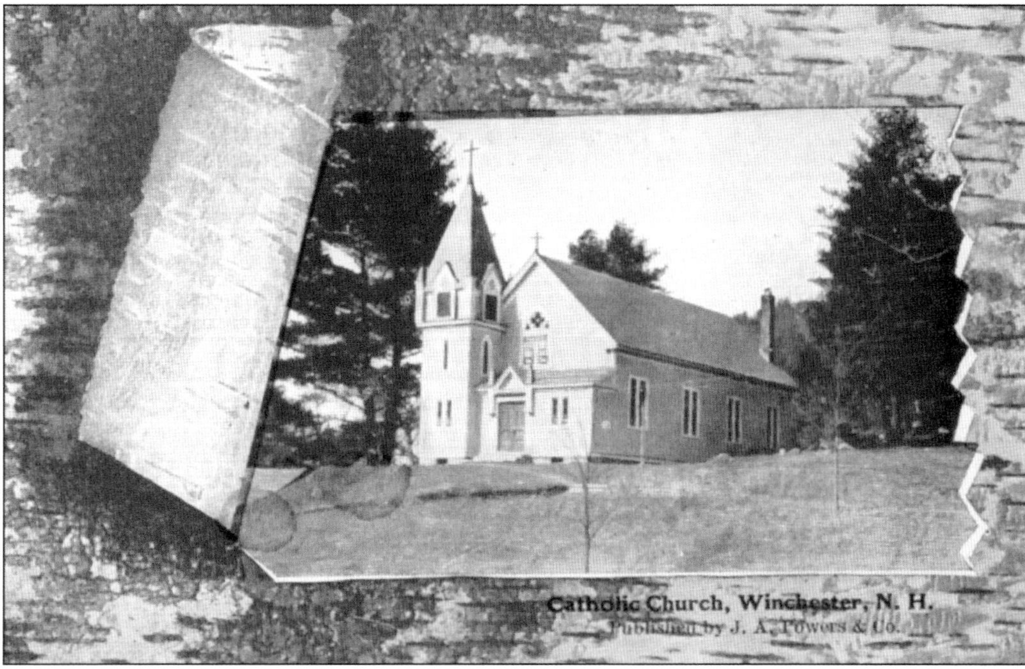

Saint Stanislaus Catholic Church was built at the turn of the century. Mass was conducted in Polish for the tiny congregation.

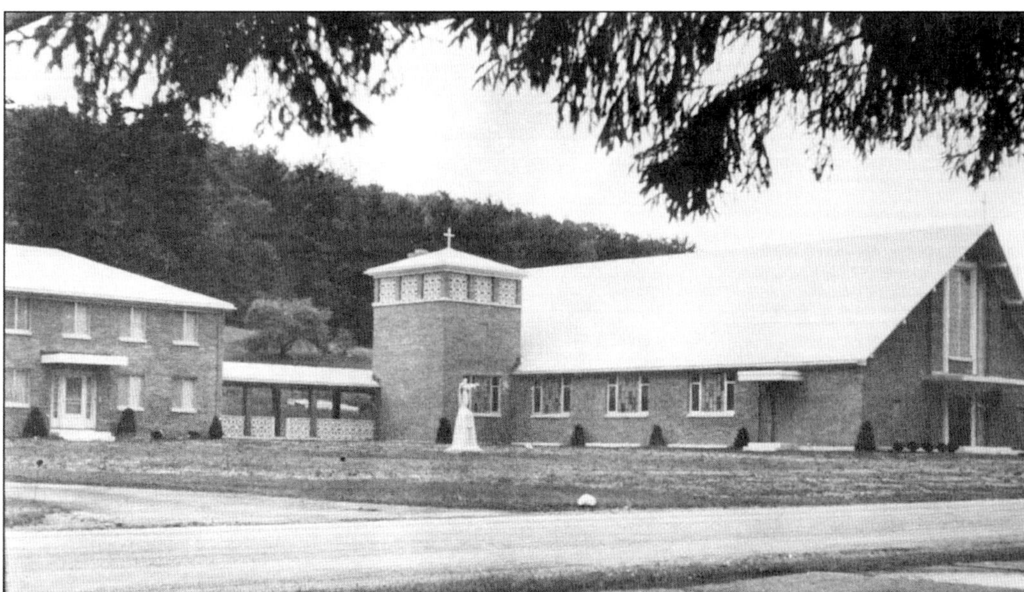
When the parish outgrew the old church in the 1960s, Saint Stanislaus moved a short distance away on Route 119 to larger, more modern facilities.

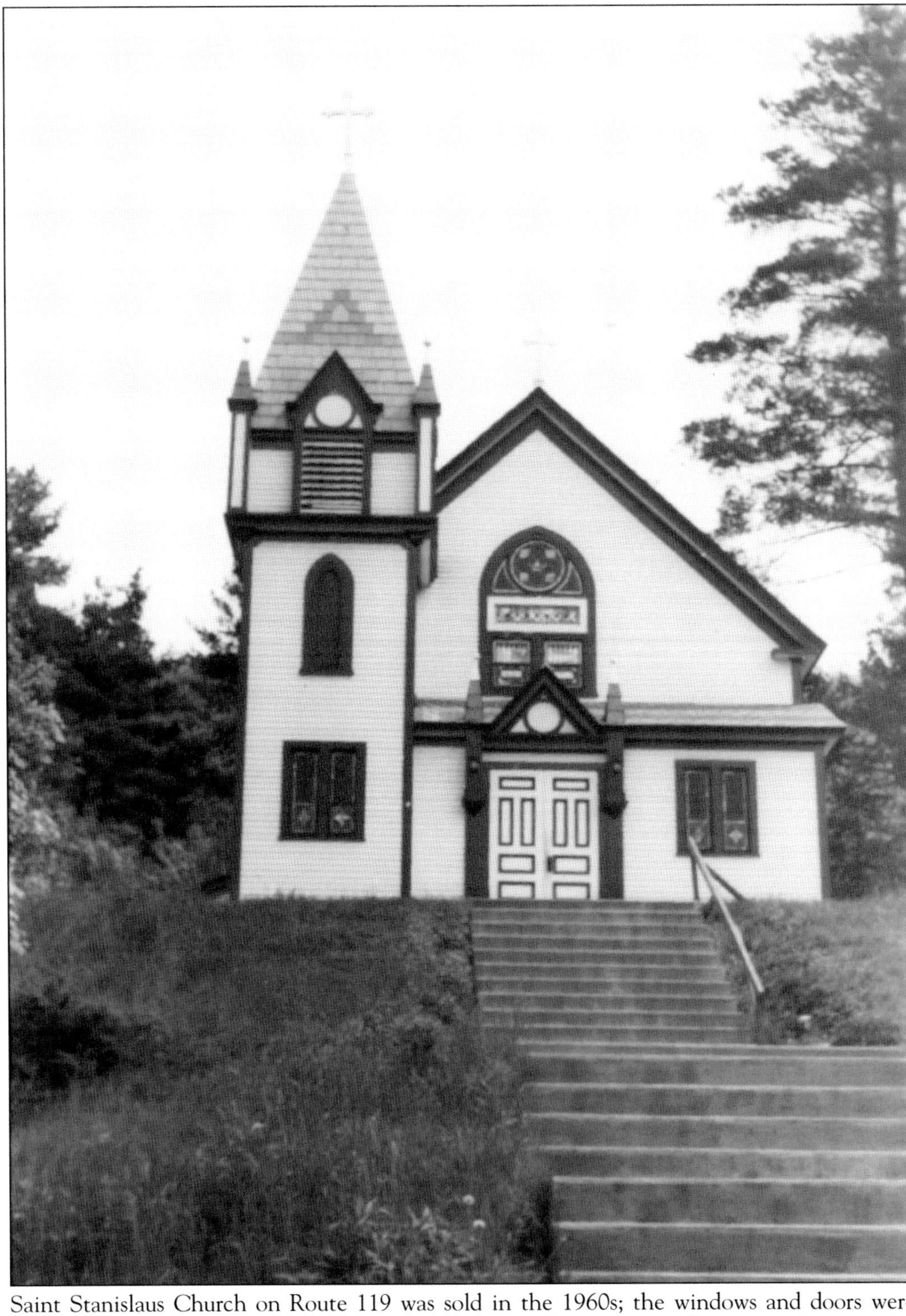

Saint Stanislaus Church on Route 119 was sold in the 1960s; the windows and doors were removed and sold as well. The building served alternately as an art gallery, a residence, and a recreation hall for local youth. It has been the author's home for the past ten years.

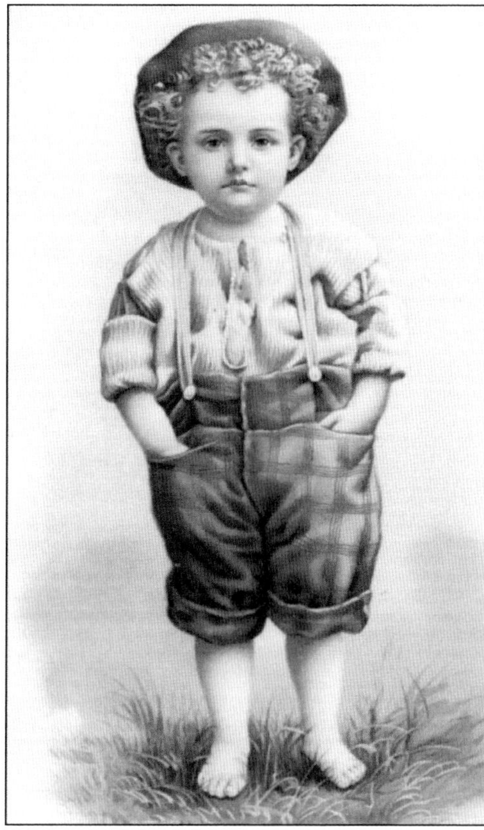

Advertising trade cards were given away in the years between 1870 and 1900 as inducements to purchase products or to patronize the giver. F.C. Thorn Pharmacy on Main Street gave out this one for Hires Root Beer. The card has Thorn's overprint on the reverse where the product advertising is.

The Boy that is robust and healthy is the boy that is capable of enjoying his first pair of suspenders; at this time he thinks he is getting all the pleasure and enjoyment there is in life.

The Child or Adult that drinks

HIRES Rootbeer

is pretty sure to be robust and healthful.

There is perhaps no medicine that will do so much in health giving as

HIRES Rootbeer.

It cleanses the blood from impurities, gives vitality and energy, strengthens and invigorates the whole nervous and physical system. Sarsaparilla Root, Herbs, and Phosphates that go to make up this pleasant and delicious drink furnish muscle, and increases the vigor of the brain and nerve forces, without the injurious effects that narcotics or artificial stimulants produce; but be sure to get **HIRES,** do not take any substitute.

THE CHARLES E. HIRES COMPANY,

PHILADELPHIA, PA.

E. C. THORN.

Pharmacy,

WINCHESTER. NEW HAMPSHIRE,

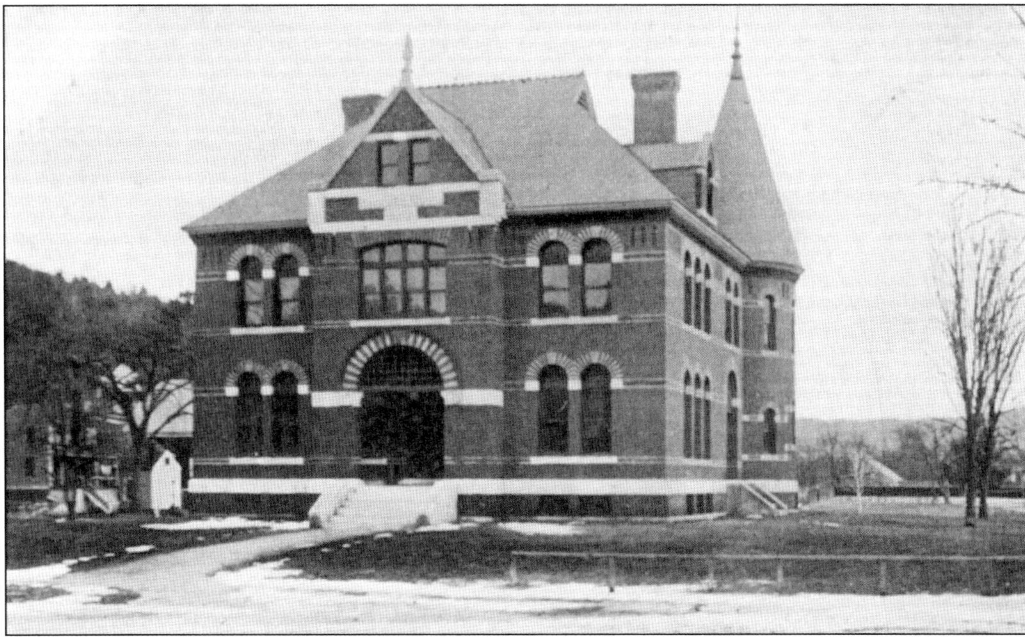

The public library now houses the police station and town hall. Unlike those in larger cities, this municipal complex has limited hours.

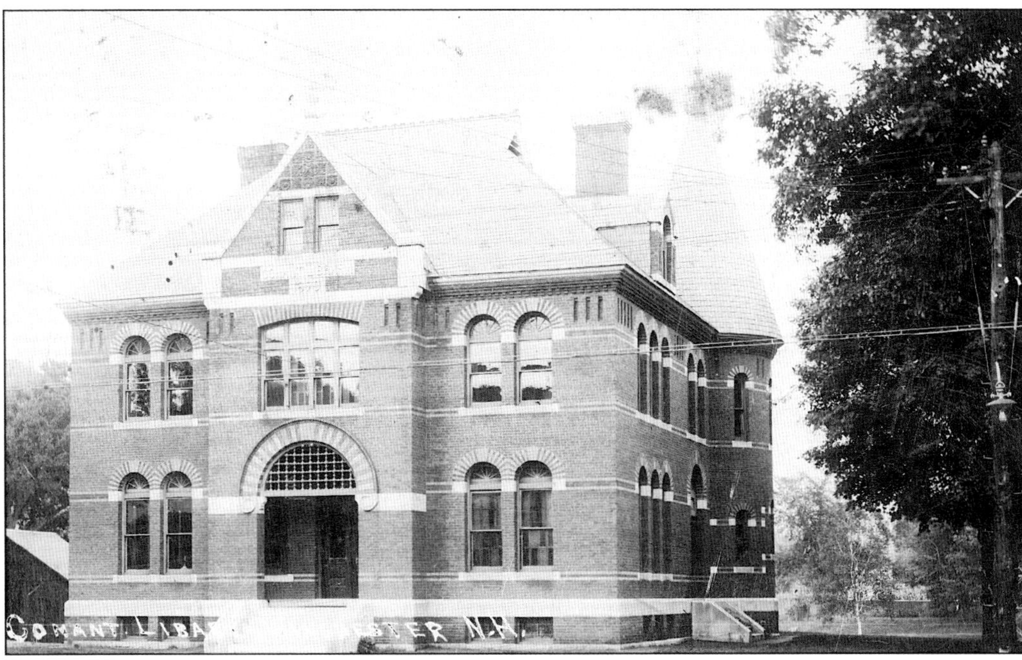

Before the advent of television, the library was an important cultural center for the town. The Conant Library is shown here in 1912.

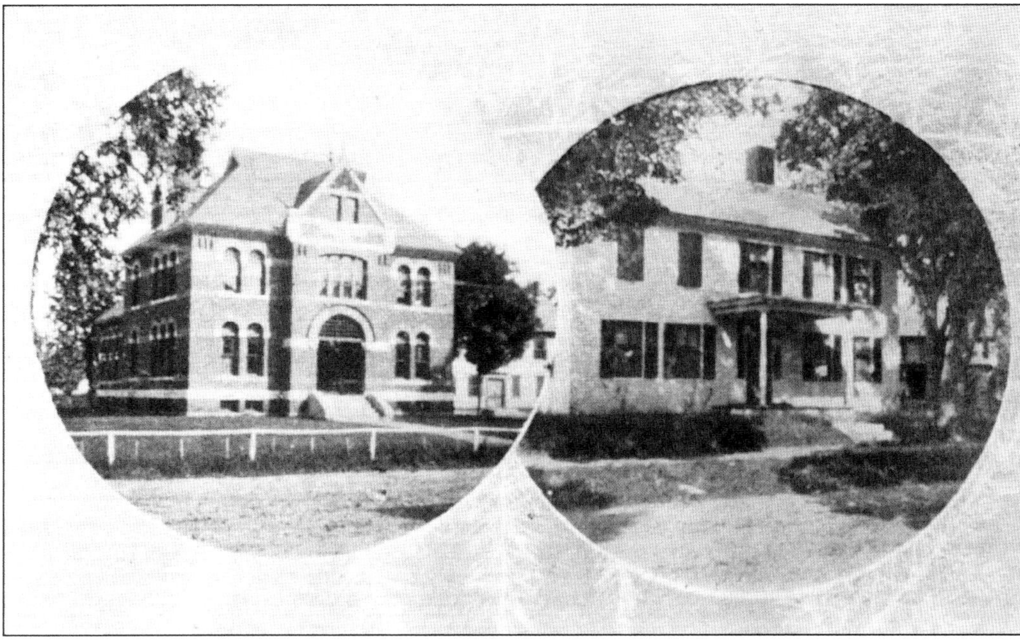

This cameo view shows the two libraries, Winchester's Conant and Ashuelot's Thayer.

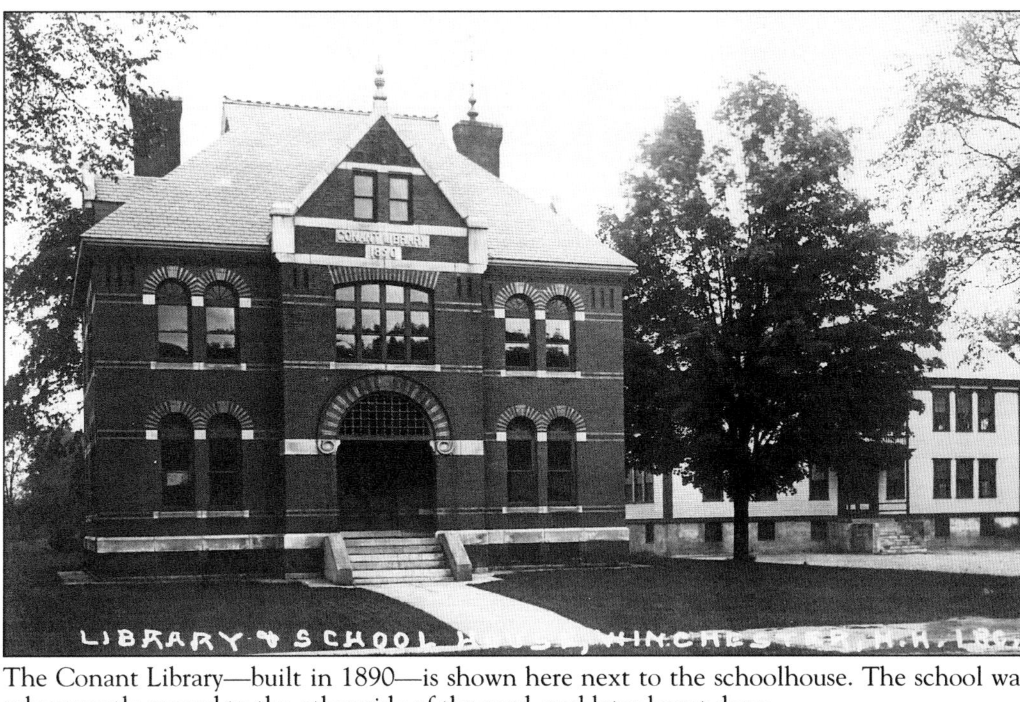

The Conant Library—built in 1890—is shown here next to the schoolhouse. The school was subsequently moved to the other side of the road, and later burnt down.

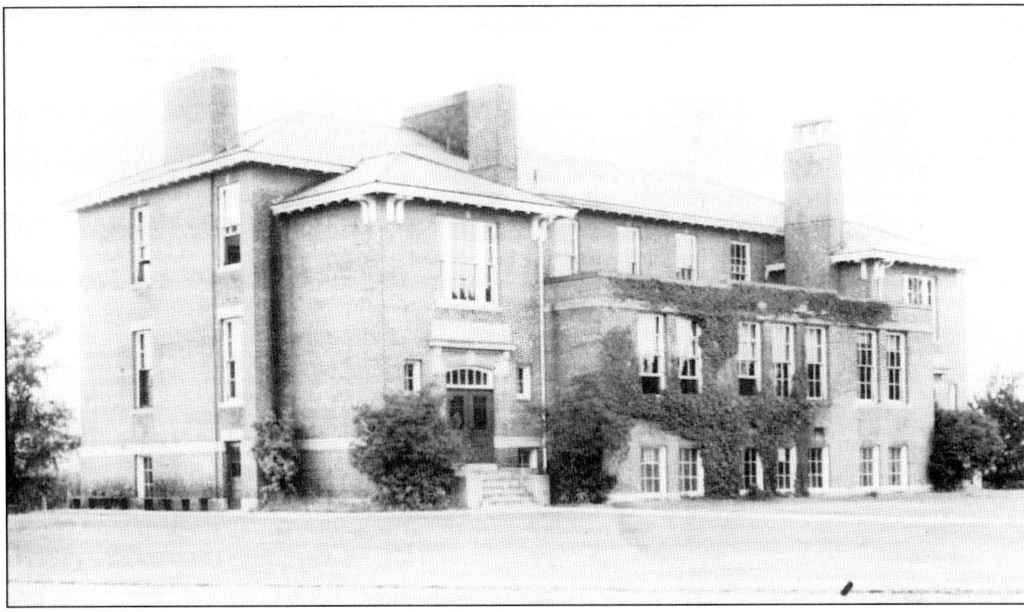

This view shows the Winchester High School.

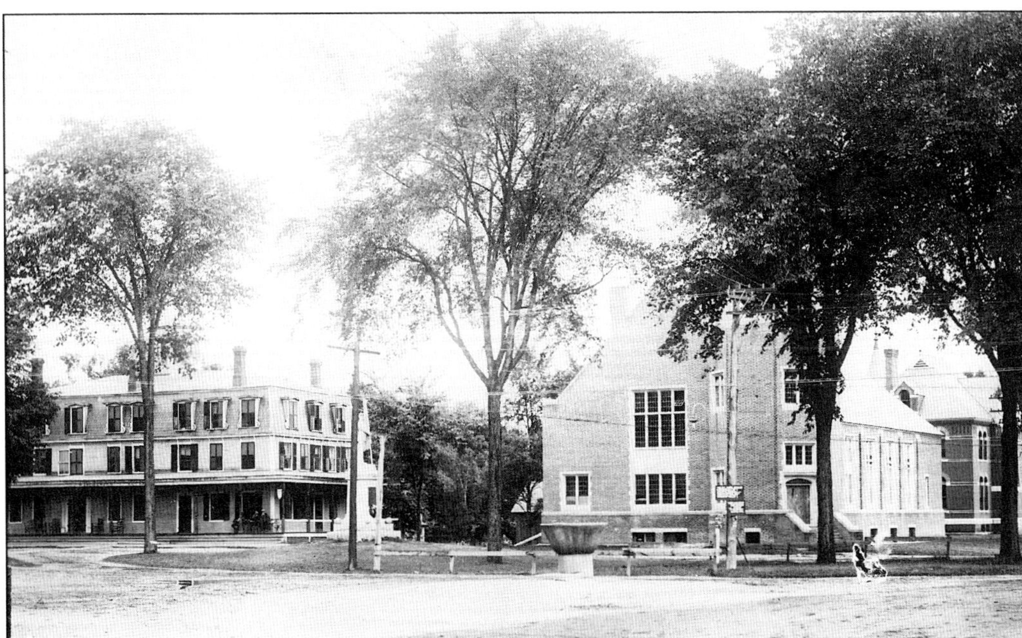

This 1918 shot of Winchester shows the common, Shipman's Tavern, the town hall, and the library (behind the town hall).

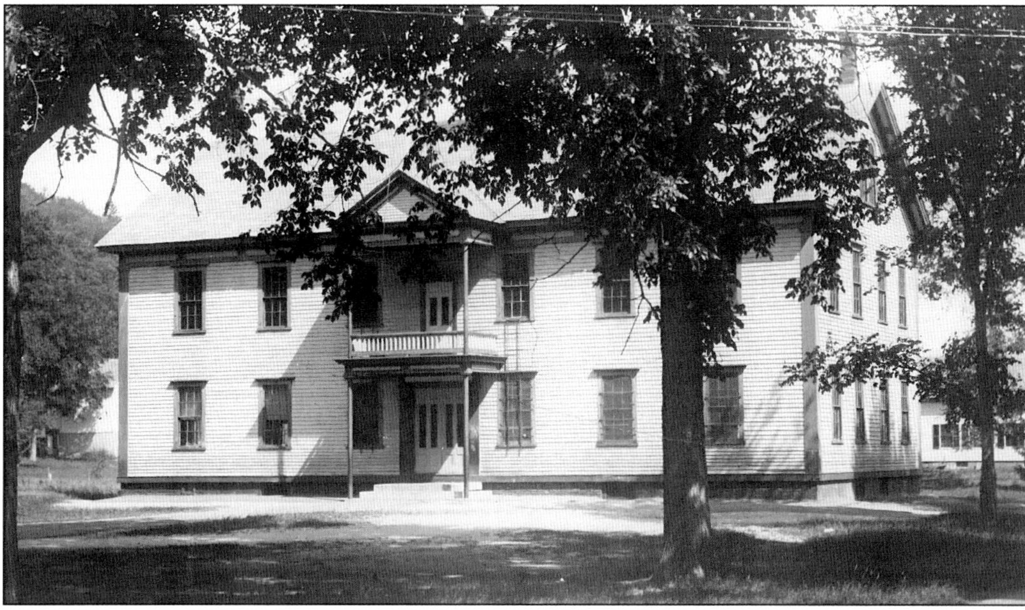

The Center Schoolhouse is shown here in the late 1930s; it was removed in 1971.

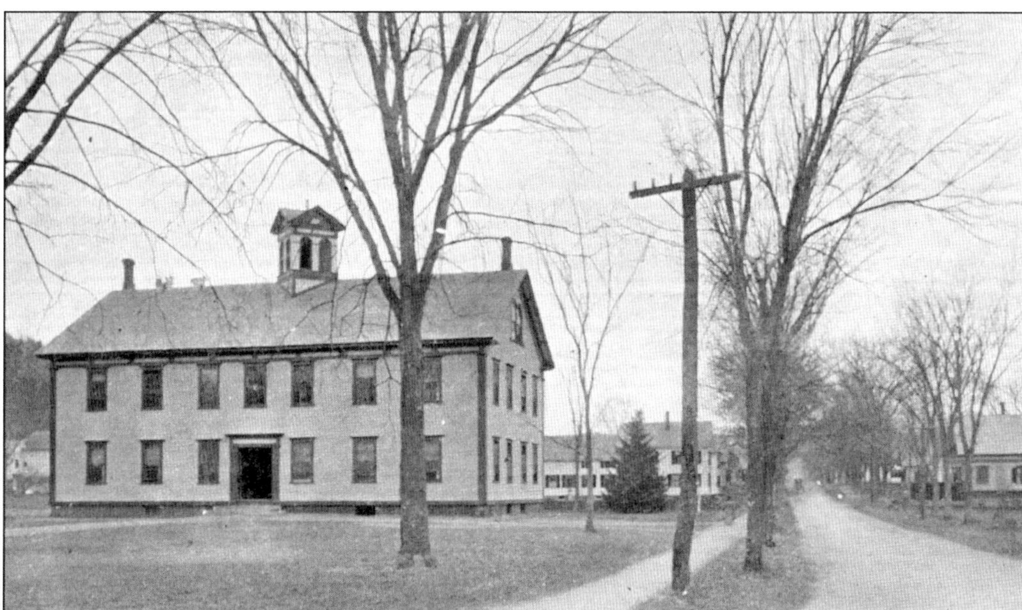

The high school appears here, along with Parker Street.

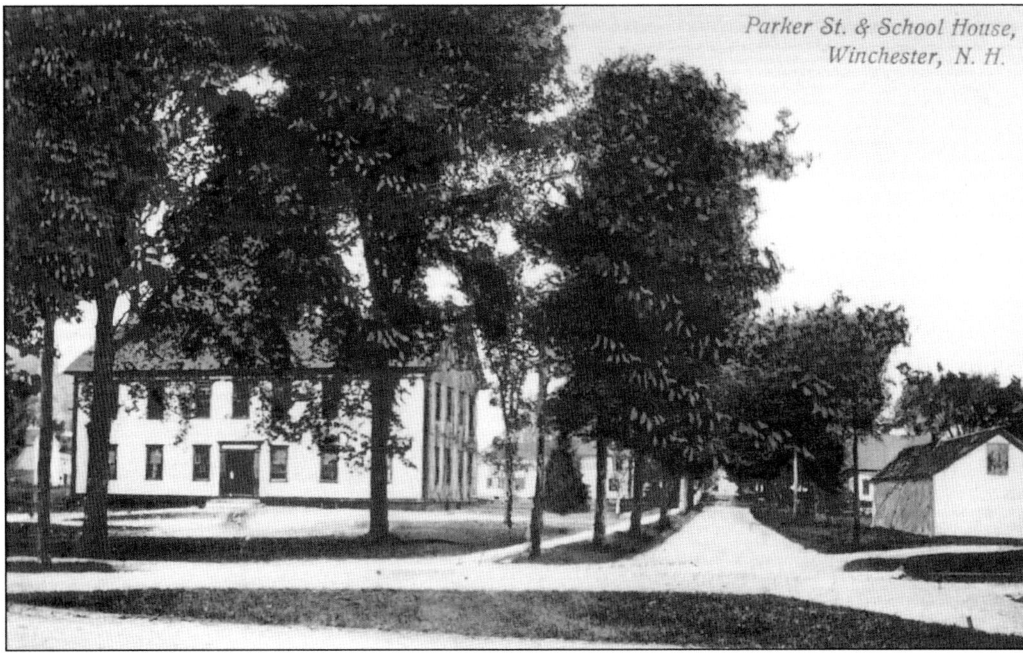

Parker Street and the schoolhouse are featured again in this view taken in May 1908.

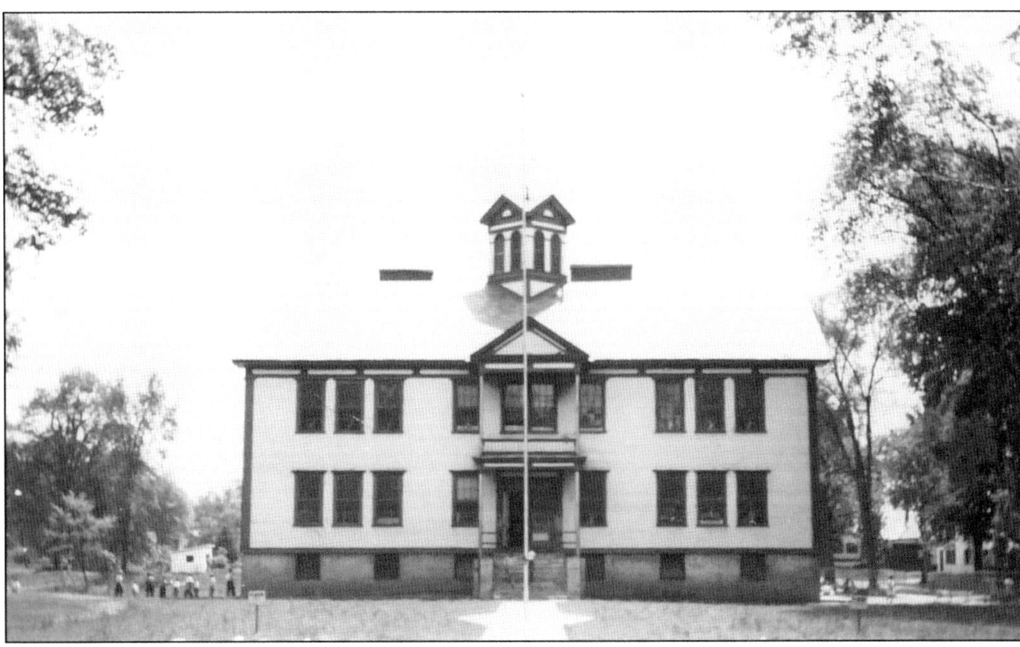

The Center School is the focus of this image.

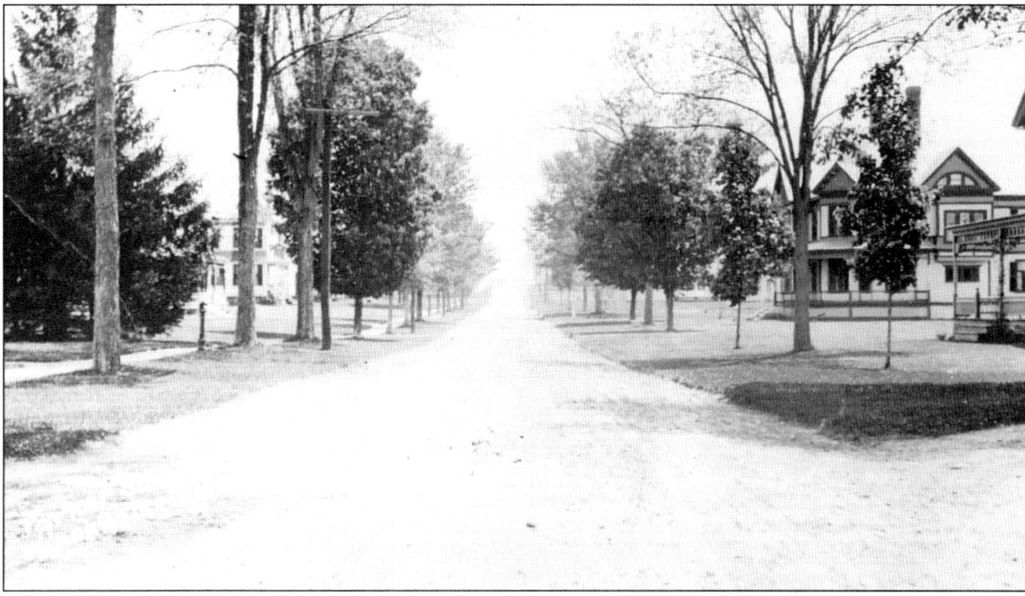

Lovely old Victorian homes appear here on Parker Street, a short road. Today the police and fire station are at the route end and the school is at the far end.

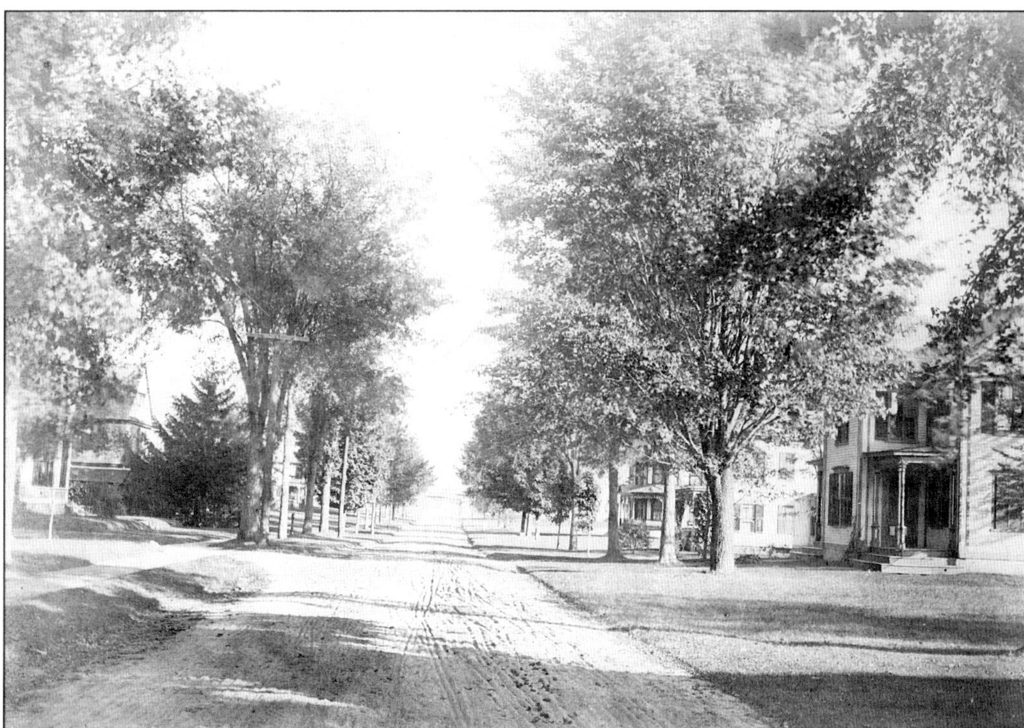

Parker Street was lined with trees and large homes in 1908.

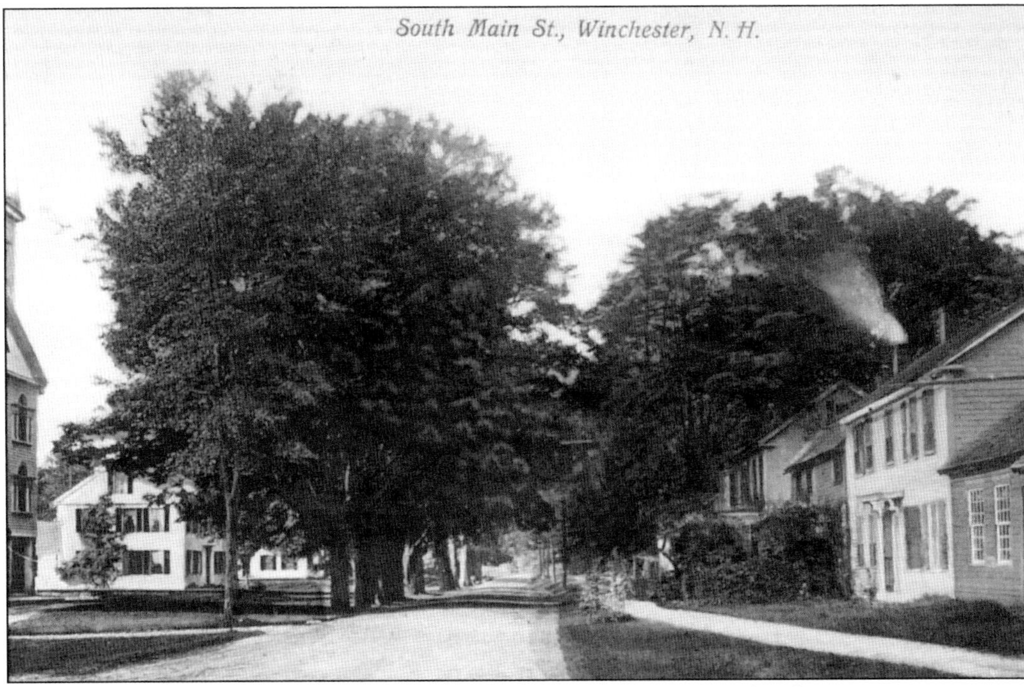

Today the small shops along South Main Street include Amarosa's hardware store, a gourmet coffee shop, a diner, and an Italian restaurant. This picture was taken in 1909.

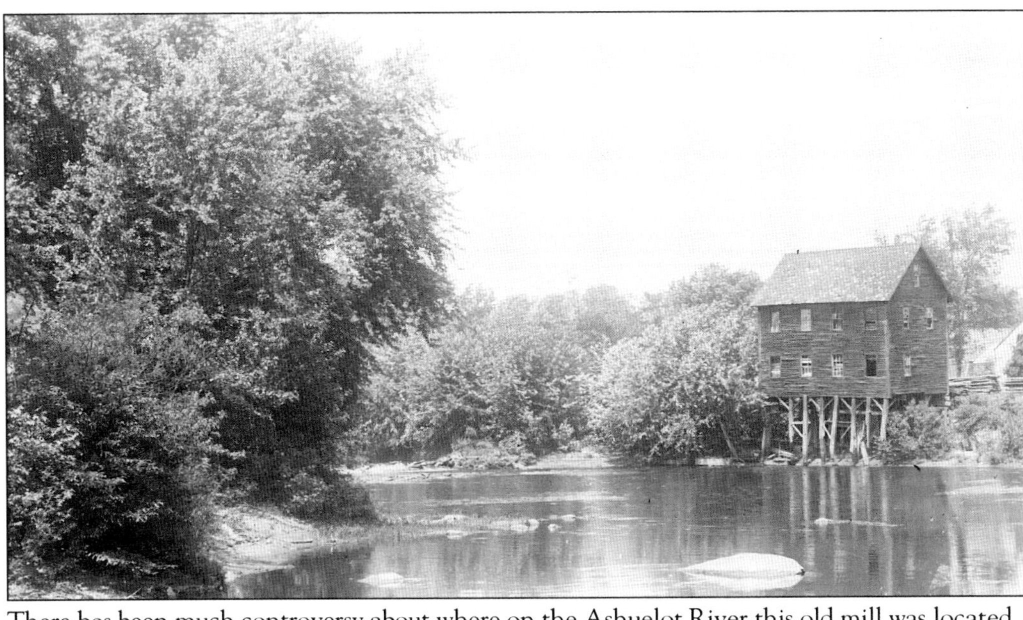
There has been much controversy about where on the Ashuelot River this old mill was located.

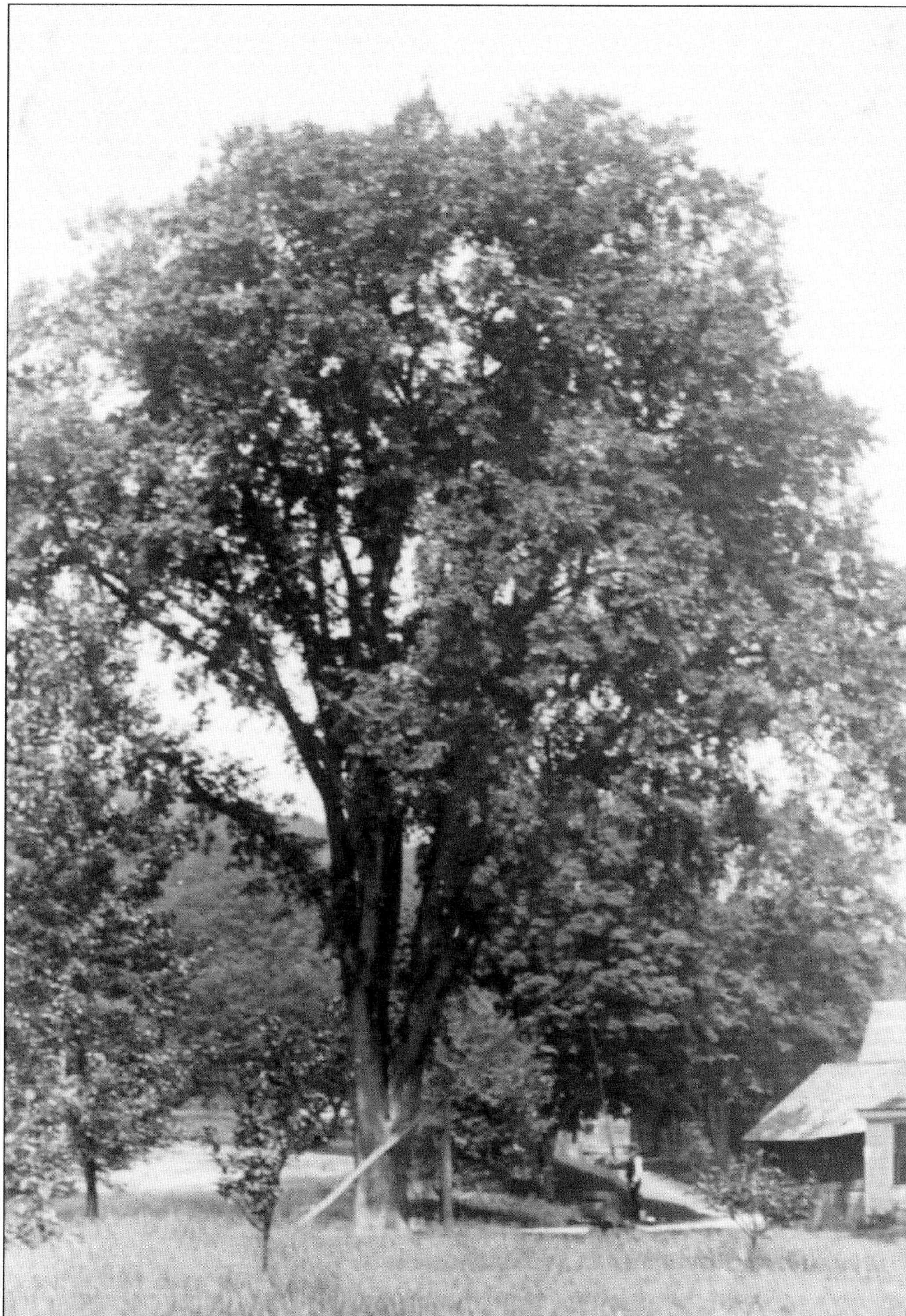

This print features "The Old Oaken Bucket"

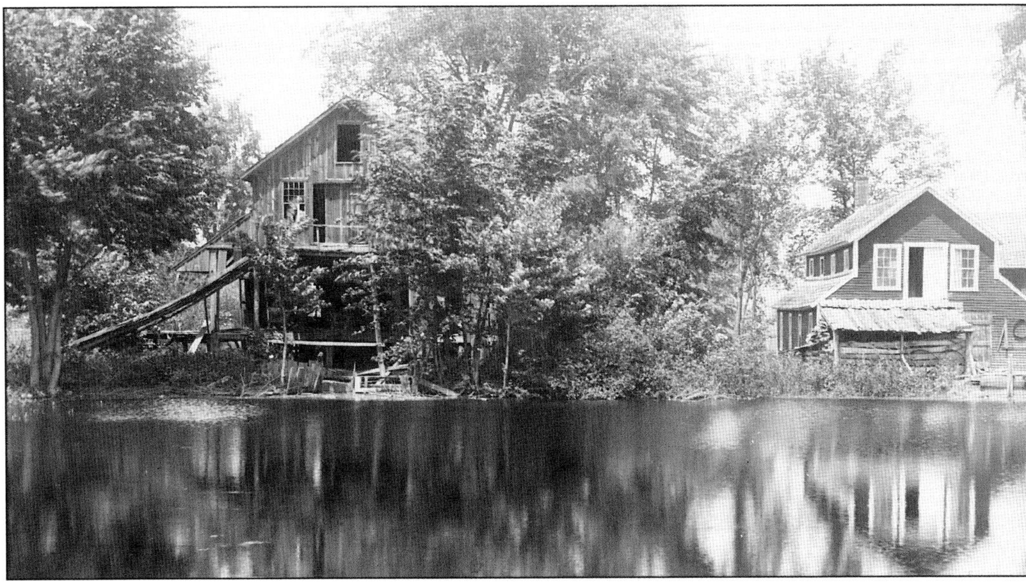

The idyllic Mill Pond, Forrest Lake, until 1883 known as Humphrey's Pond, is shown here. Governor Francis Patrick Murphy was born at Forrest Lake and, as a child of poverty, he admired the Alexander homestead.

Gardner Mountain is depicted here in its all its majesty.

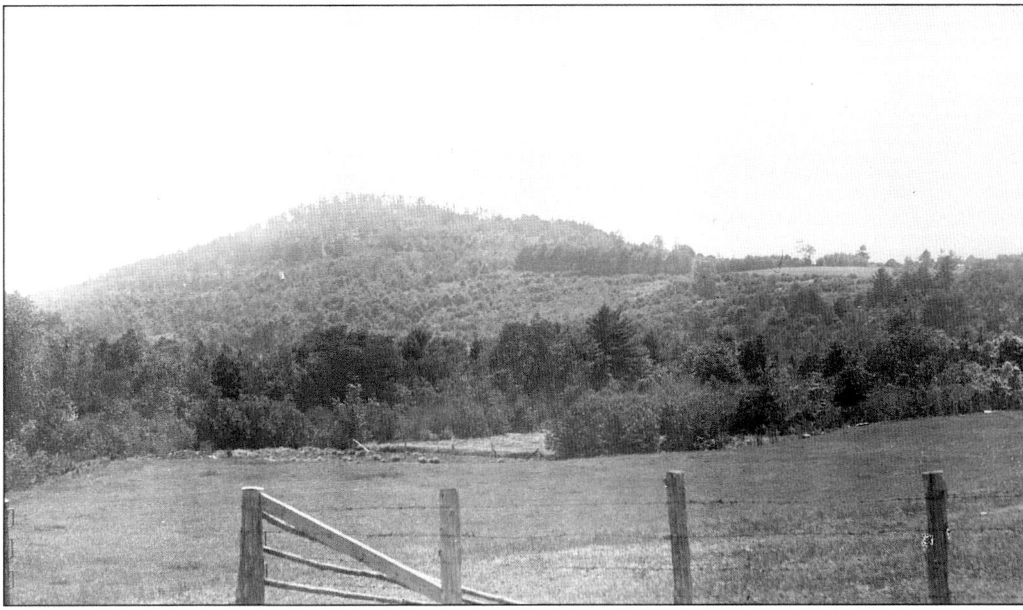

Meetinghouse Mountain is shown here from the headlands. The old Saint Stanislaus Catholic Church was built on the side of it.

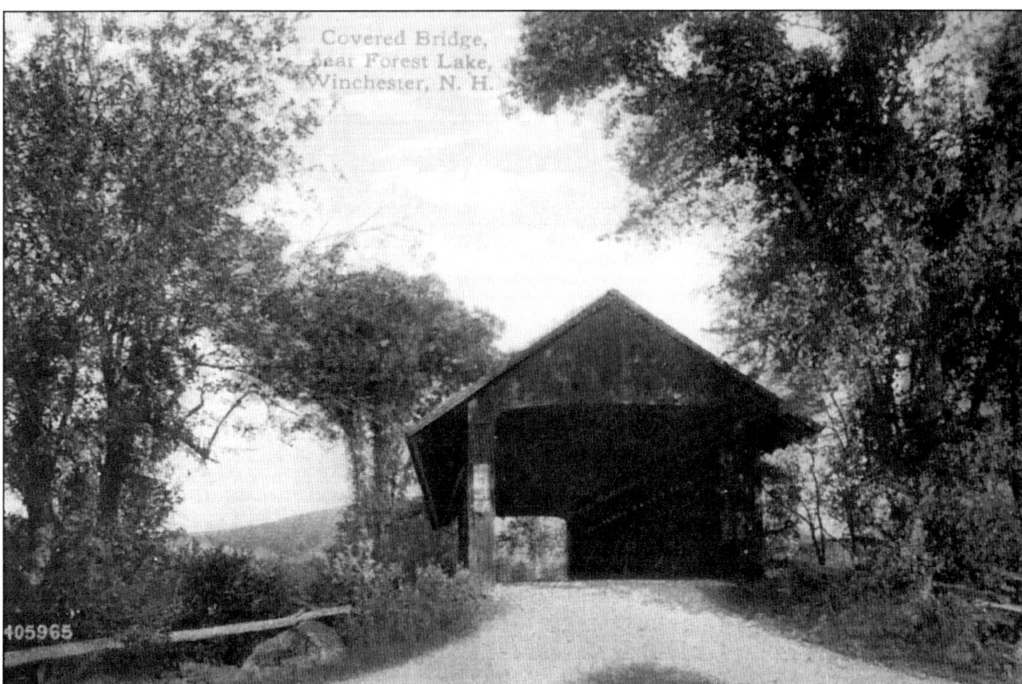

This covered bridge near Forrest Lake provided safe passage for many travelers.

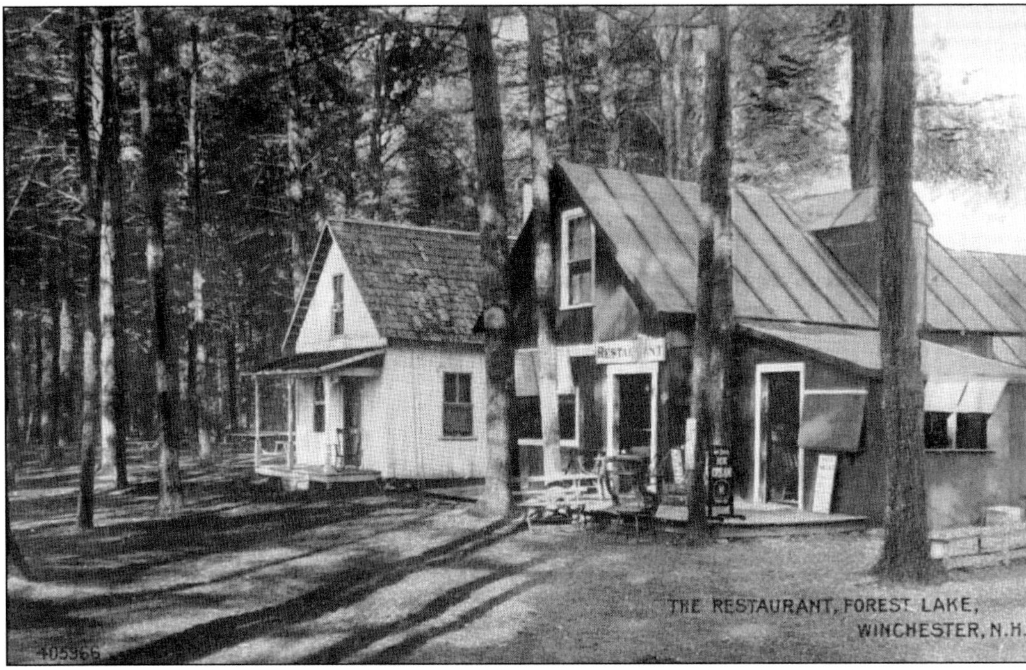

This 1912 view features the restaurant at Forrest Lake.

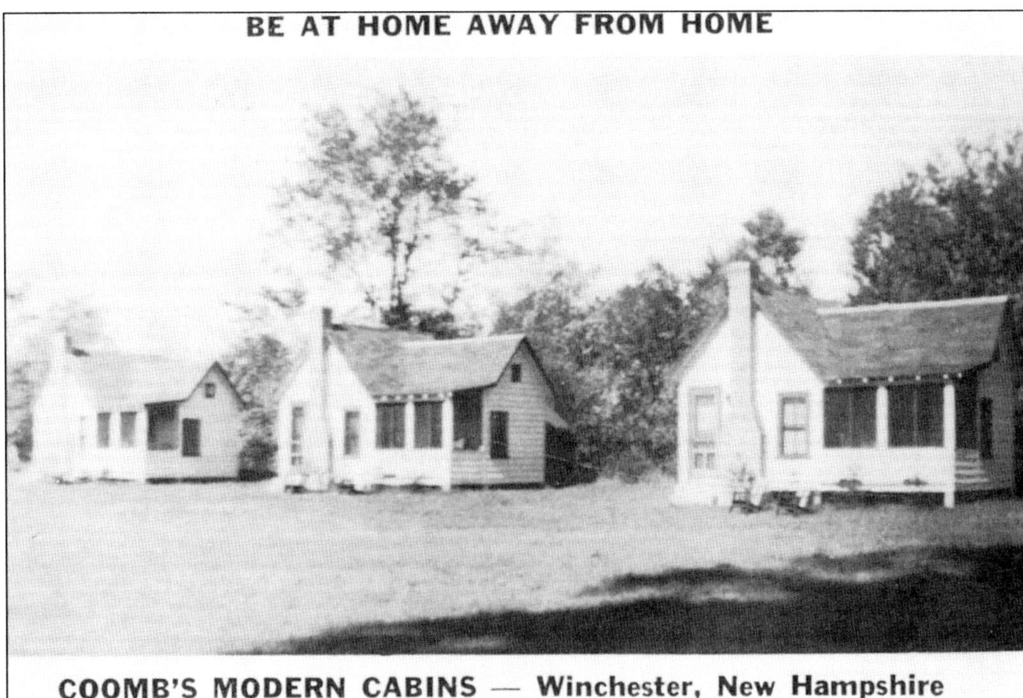

Forrest Lake cottages are shown here in 1931.

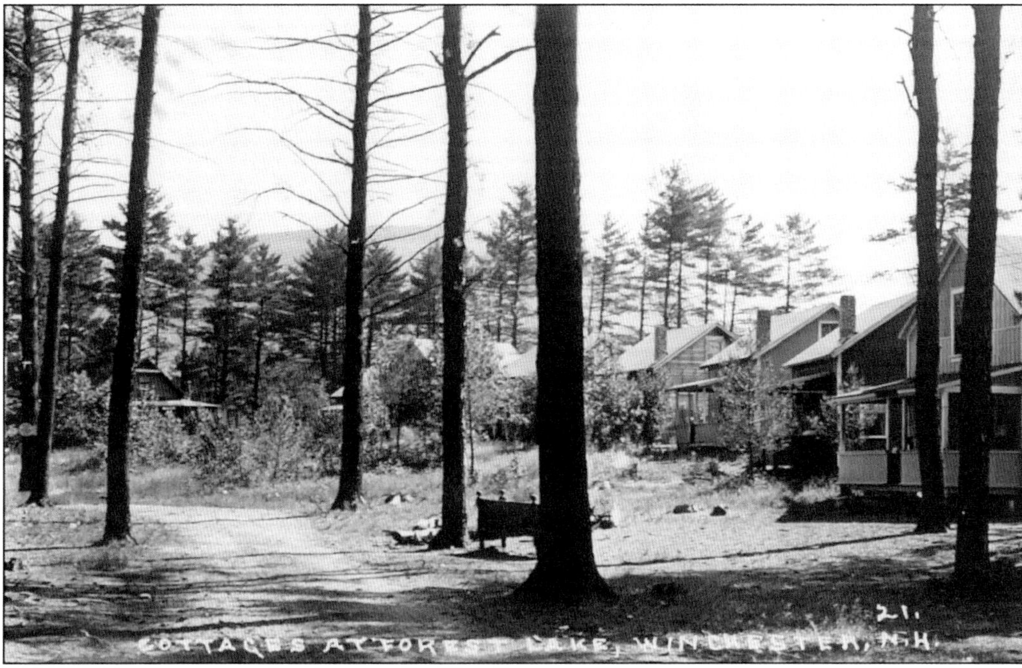

These cottages at Forrest Lake were nestled within a grove of pine trees, *c.* 1931.

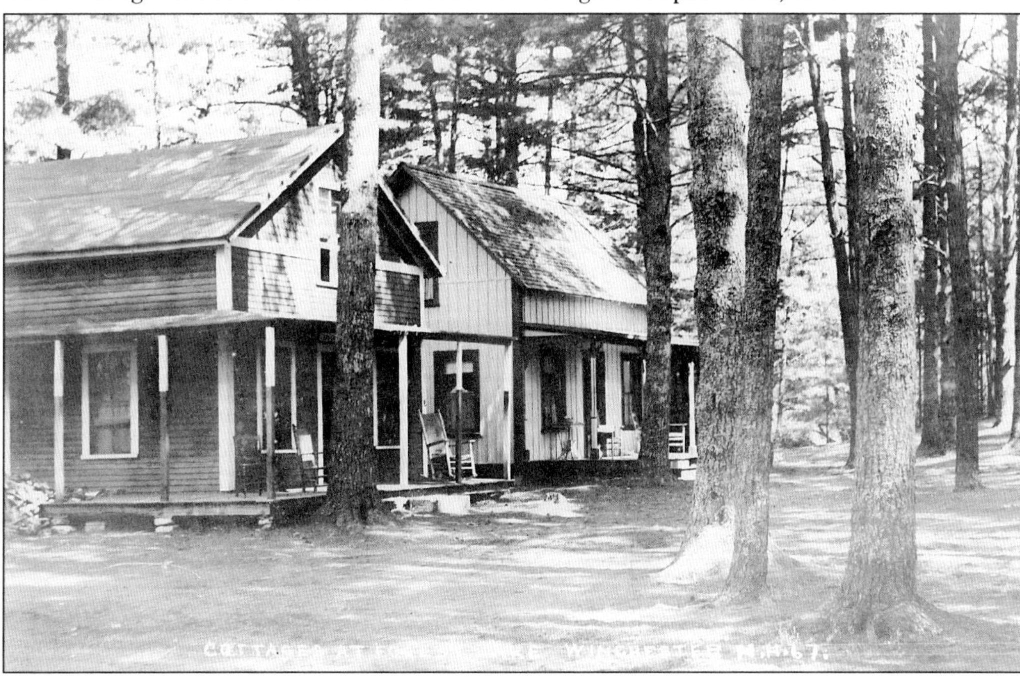

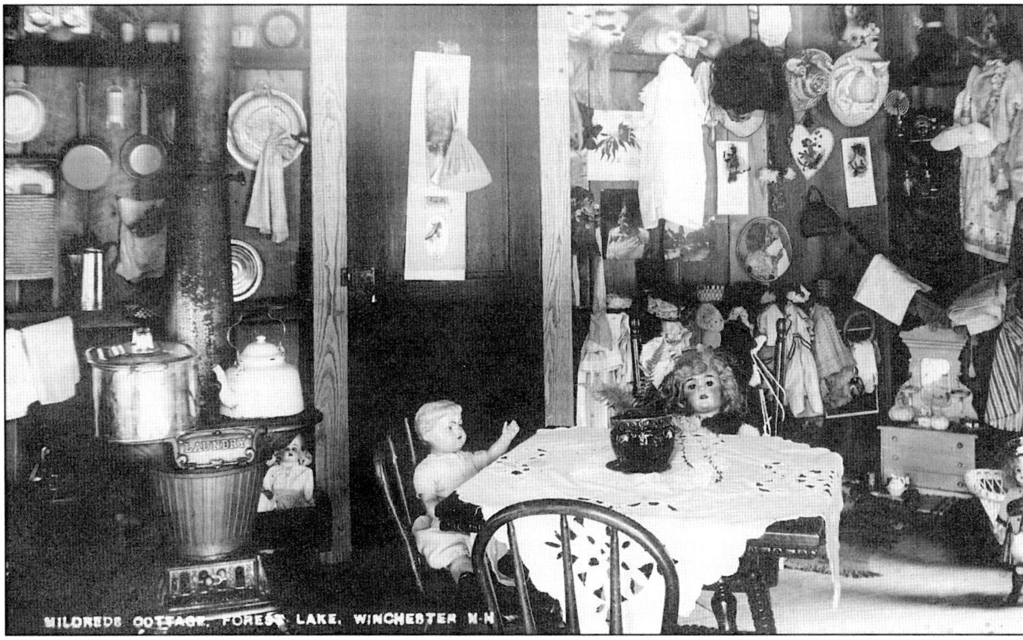

Mildred's Playhouse at Forrest Lake was a child's dream come true. Inside the life-size doll house, she played and entertained both her human and toy friends. The house contained a working wood stove, from which she could make tea and obtain heat. Two of the three dolls shown here are bisque.

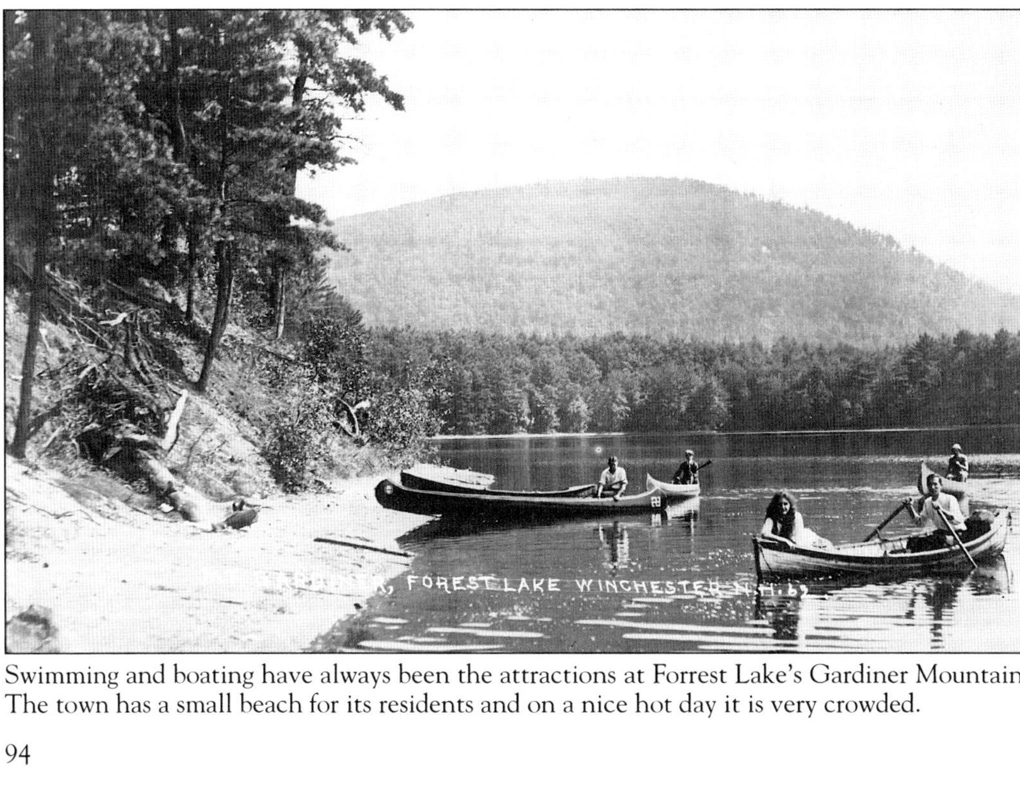

Swimming and boating have always been the attractions at Forrest Lake's Gardiner Mountain. The town has a small beach for its residents and on a nice hot day it is very crowded.

Four

RICHMOND

Richmond is often referred to as the "Four Corners," even though the junction is not the center or downtown area. The town is actually situated on a section of hilly land, which gives it a very pretty appearance. Like its neighbors, Richmond devoted its early years to agriculture and box, pail, saw, and lumber mills. In 1884 the population was 669. The old Richmond Inn with its great ballroom is still standing; it houses memories of romances and dances of days gone by even though it is currently being used as a residence. Camp Takodah is located in Richmond and is probably one of the best-known camps in New Hampshire due to its longevity and the fact it is a YMCA camp used by the entire county. President James Garfield's mother, Eliza Ballou Garfield, was born in Richmond, and the Universalist church began here as well. Some of the oldest houses in the area are located in Richmond.

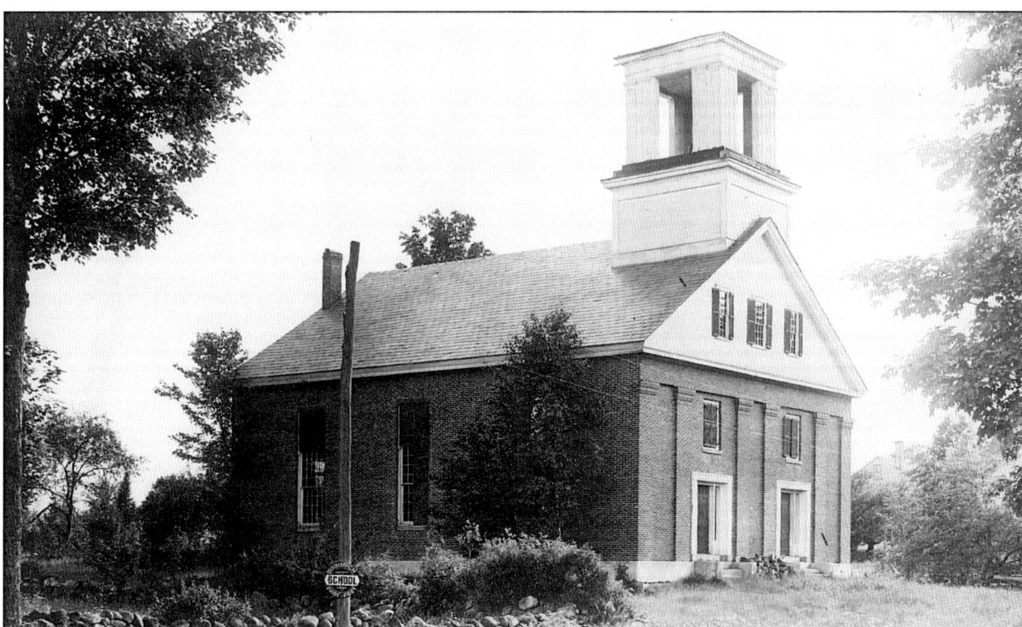

This church, built by Thomas Pickering, started life housing a Unitarian congregation, was later bought by the Baptists, and is currently occupied by a Methodist group. It was built of brick in 1837 for a cost of $2,957, including the stove and bell.

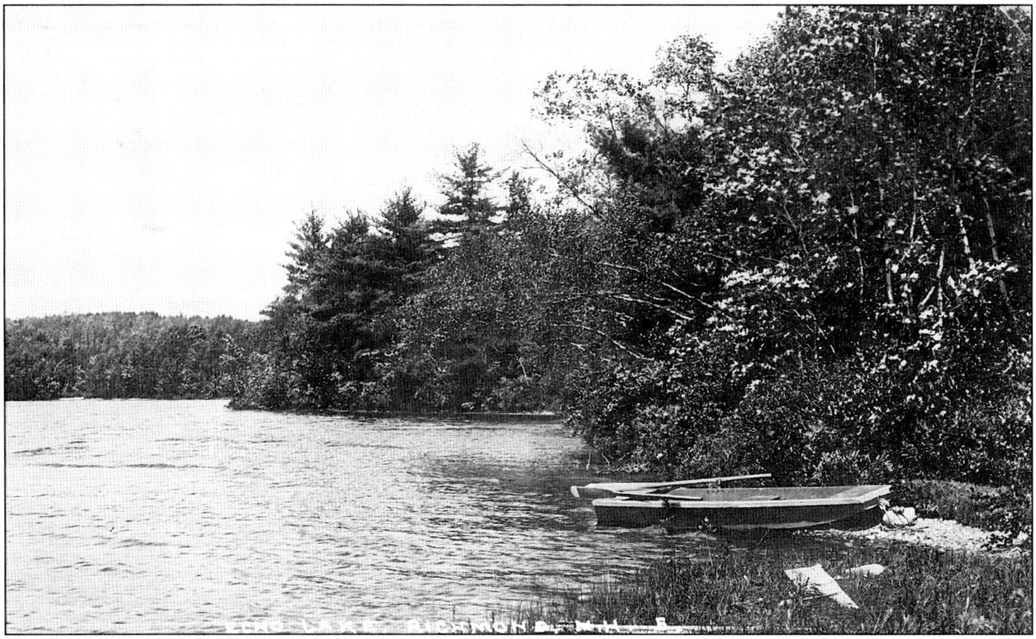

Echo Lake is a recreational site with camps and cottages dotting its shoreline.

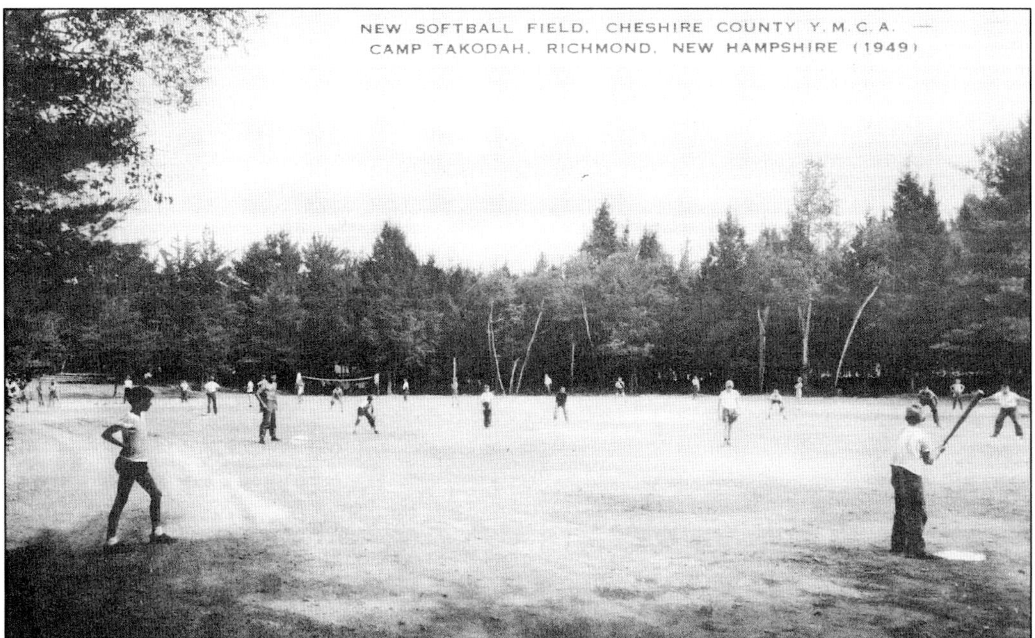

This shot of the Camp Takodah softball field was taken in 1941.

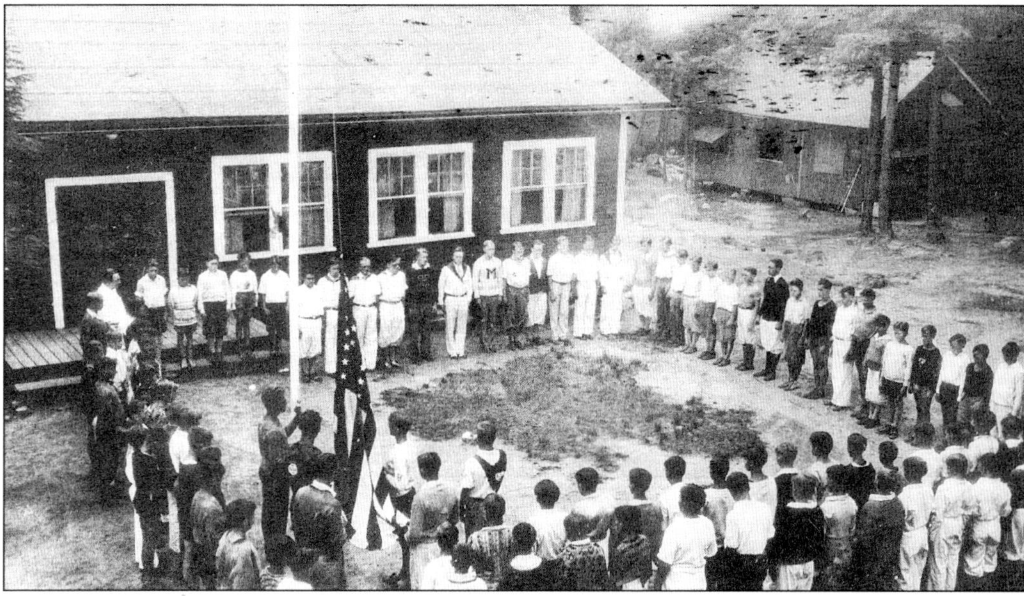

A flag-raising ceremony at Camp Takodah, the Cheshire County YMCA camp, is shown here in 1932. The camp has been running continuously since 1921.

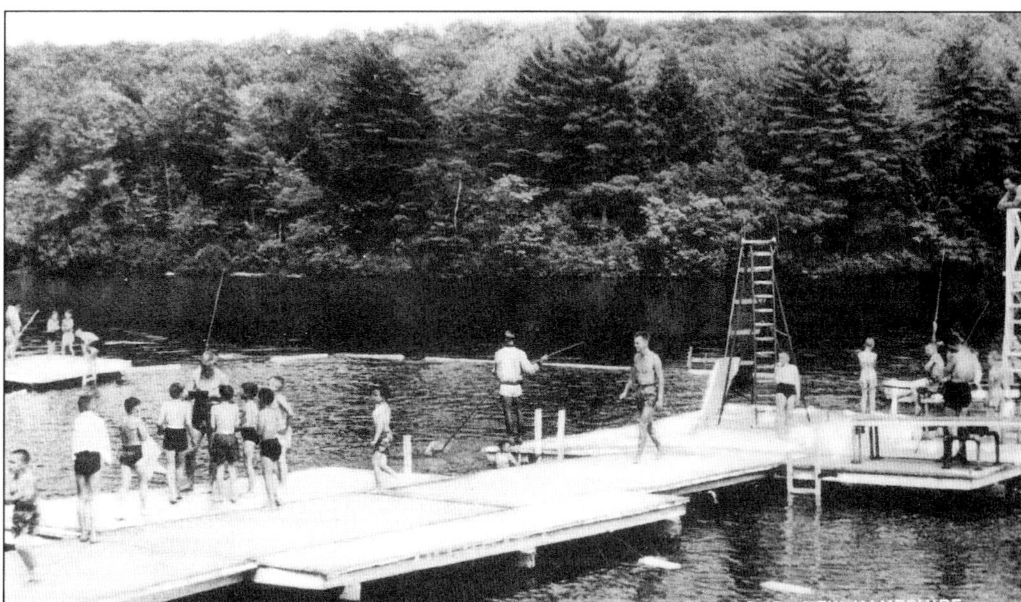

The waterfront area of Camp Takodah is accompanied by a well-supervised swimming dock. The camp has separate facilities for male and female campers.

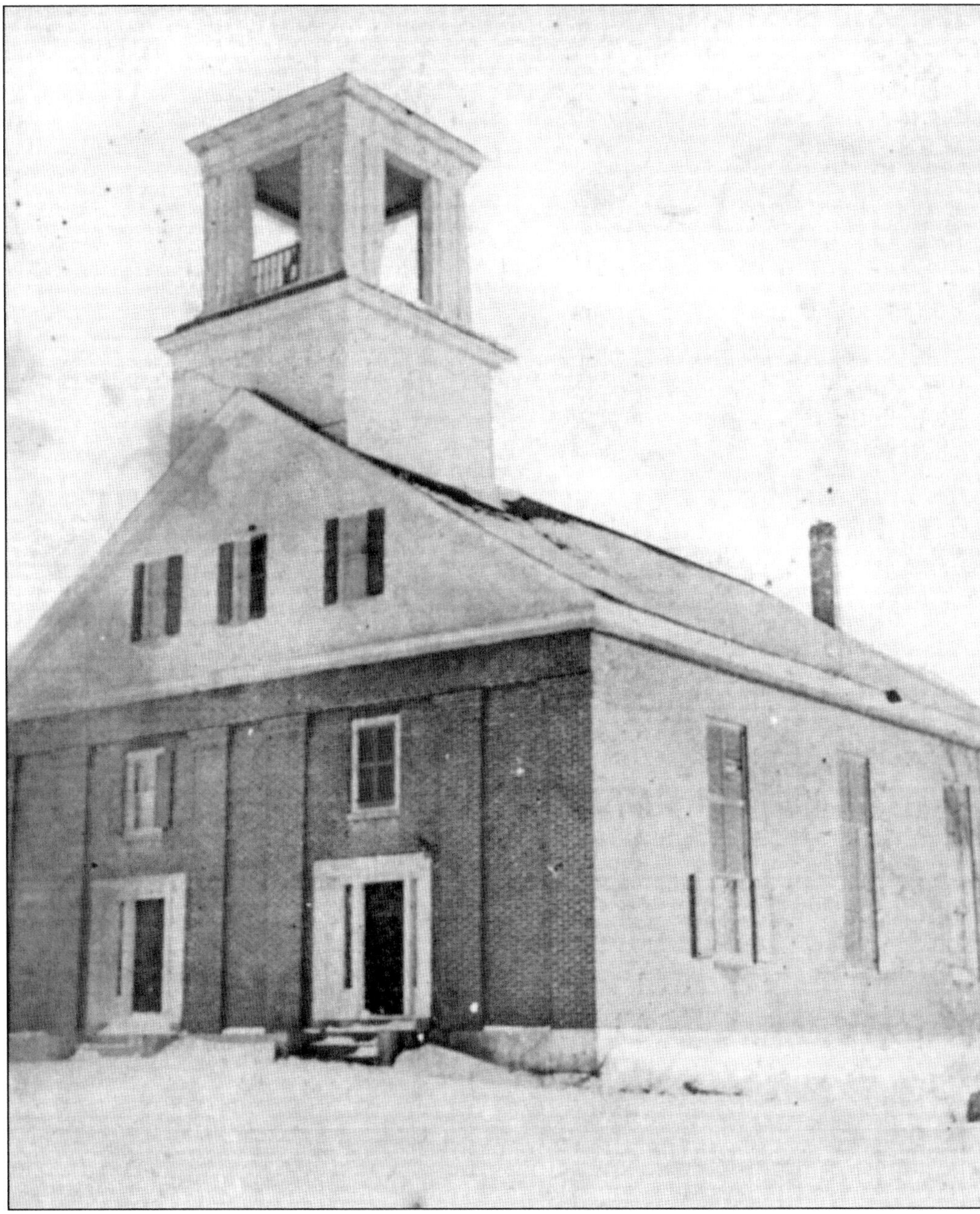

Brick churches like this one in Richmond became fashionable because they were less prone to fire.

Five

FITZWILLIAM

Fitzwilliam and Fitzwilliam Depot share a history similar to that of southwestern New Hampshire towns. The industries that built the town were agriculture and the manufacture of boxes, pails, and furniture. Fitzwilliam also had a granite quarry, which is no longer operational. The depot section grew up with the arrival of the train and was an important means of transporting one's products to market.

Fitzwilliam, at 1,201 feet above sea level, has one of the highest altitudes in the state. The town center is built around the common, with churches, the town hall, homes, and the Fitzwilliam Inn composing a picture-postcard image of this typical old-fashioned New England town. The tavern has always been a meeting place and stopover, and still is a running concern. Antique and rare book shops have opened in some of the larger houses, in keeping with the old-world image of the town.

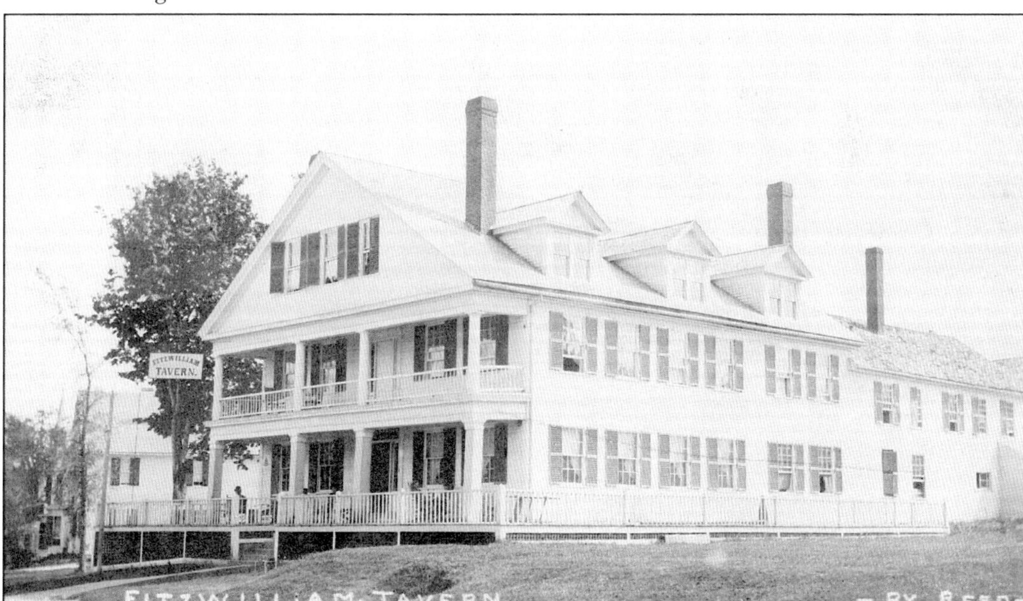

The Fitzwilliam Tavern is shown here as it looked in 1908. The inn is two hundred years old and still retains the stenciling and decoration of many years ago. Slight renovations have occurred, but most of the building is true to its original period.

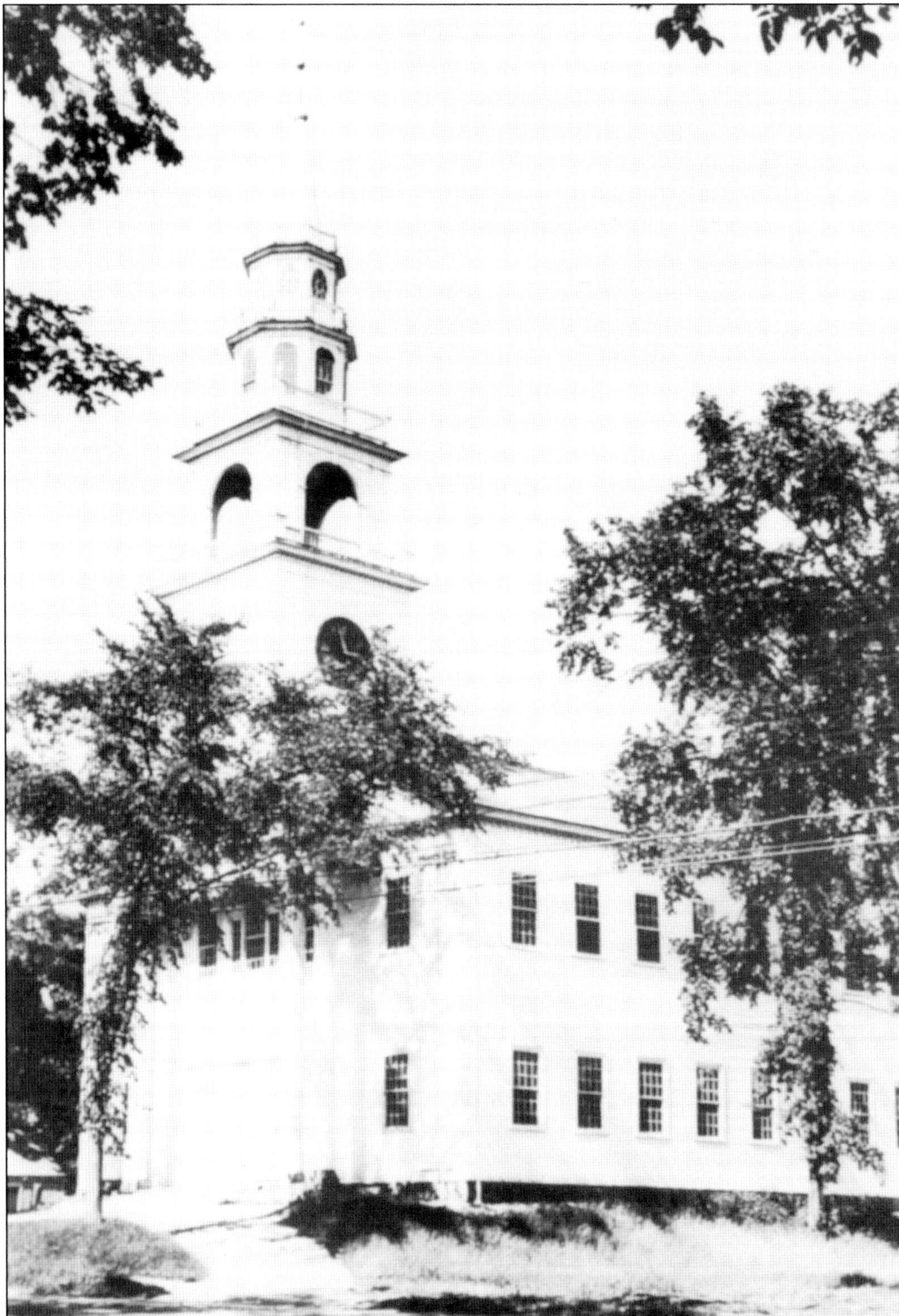

The town hall overlooks the common.

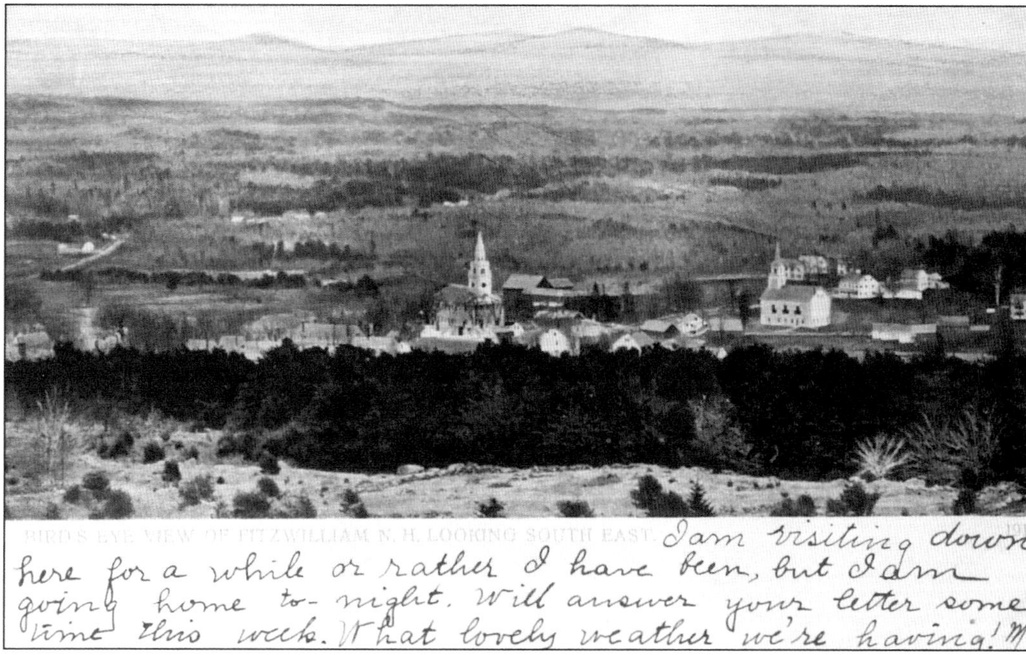

This bird's-eye view shows the town from the southeast.

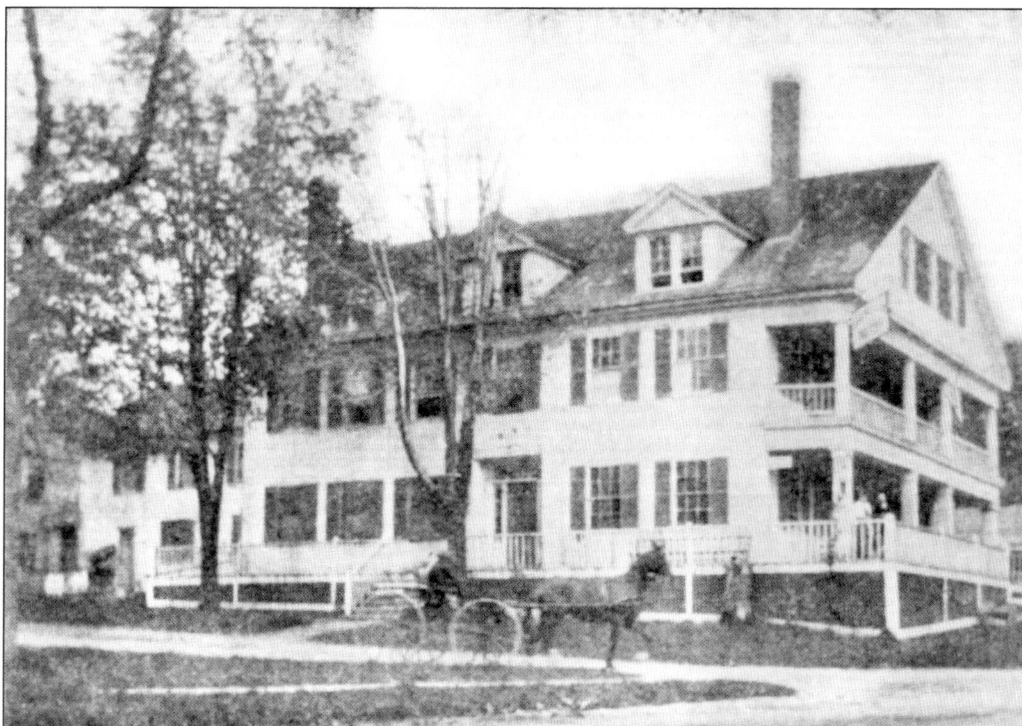

The Fitzwilliam Inn was at the edge of the common. John Blair was the manager of this lodging house, which offered rates of $4 per day, in-house telephone and telegraph service, four mail deliveries per day, and newspapers all the way from Boston! The town also boasted uncontaminated water, rare local flowers, and a malaria-free environment.

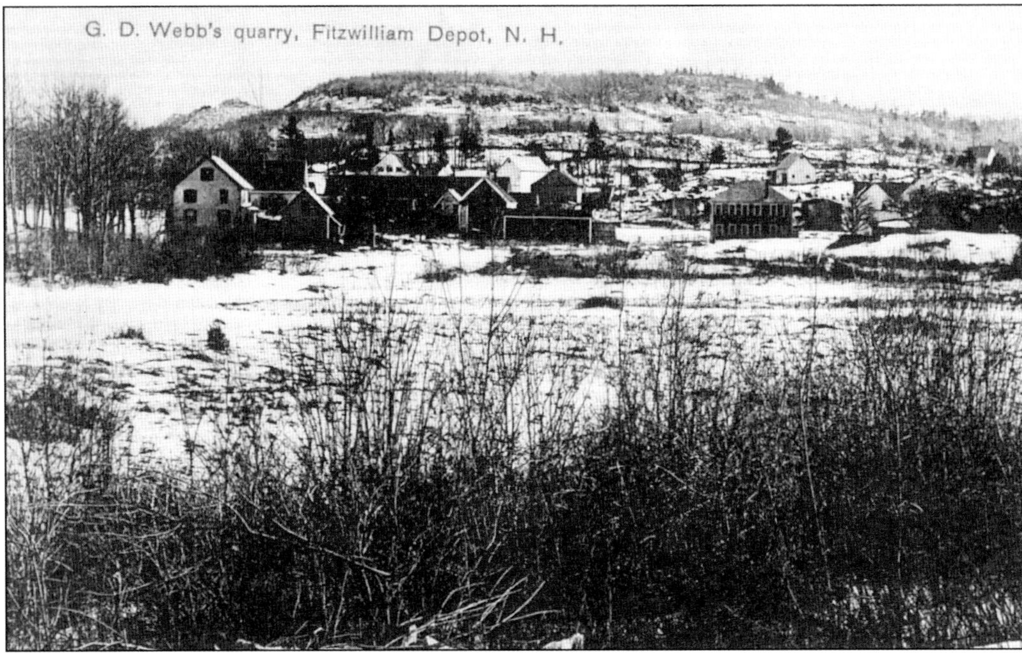

The common is shown here as it looked in 1934.

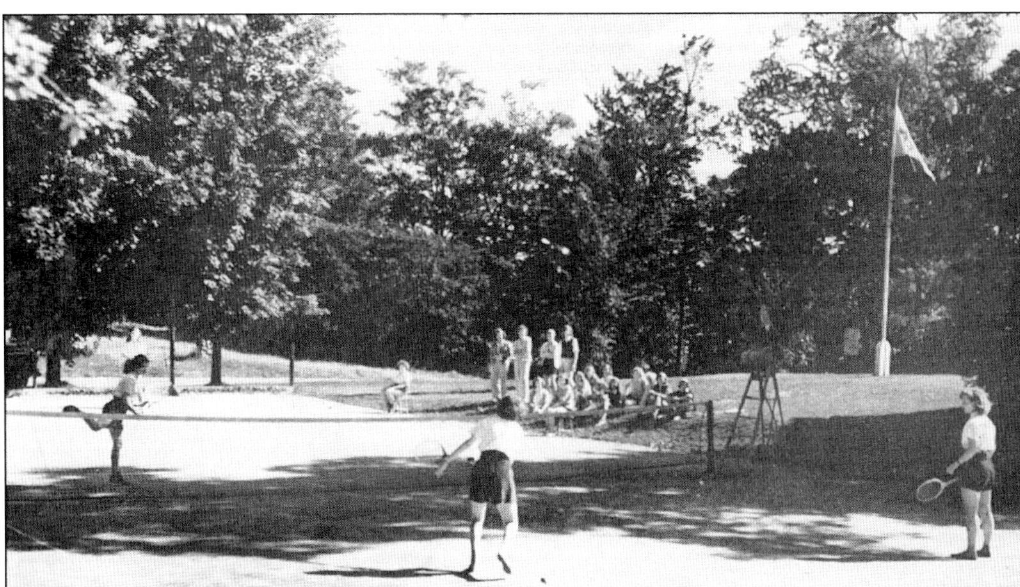
A tennis match is shown here at the Fleur de Lis Camp in 1957.

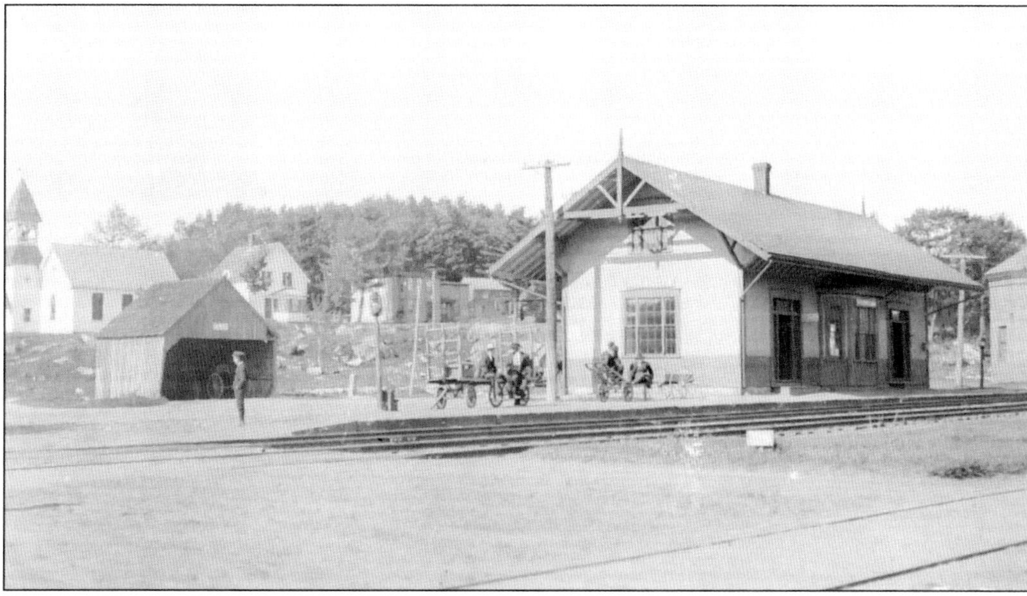

The depot or railroad station was the lifeline to the economy of small towns. The people and vehicles on the side look like employees waiting for the next train to arrive in order to unload something fairly substantial in size.

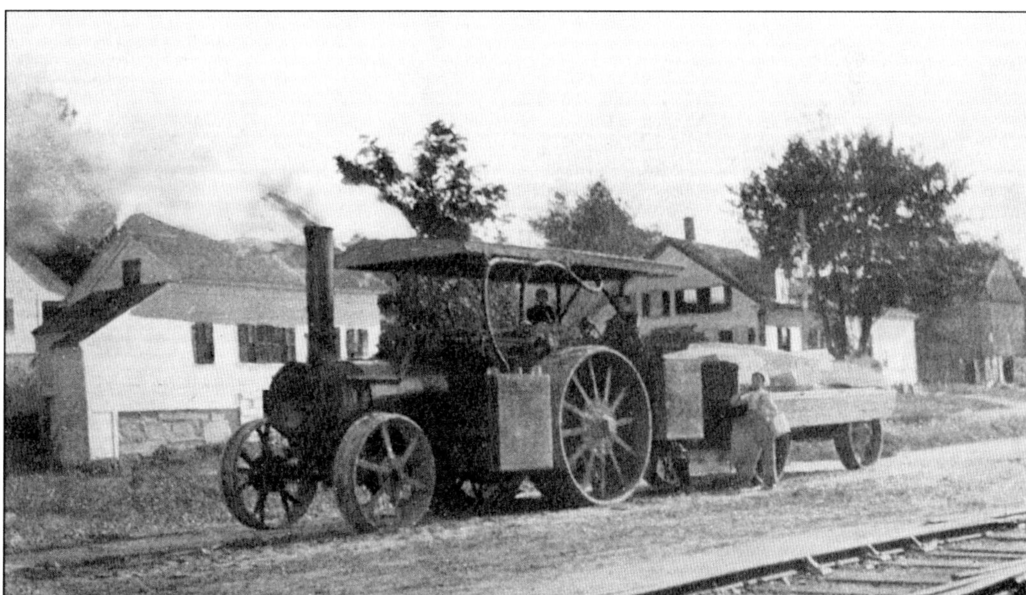

Traction engines were used to haul heavy loads. Note the railroad track in the foreground.

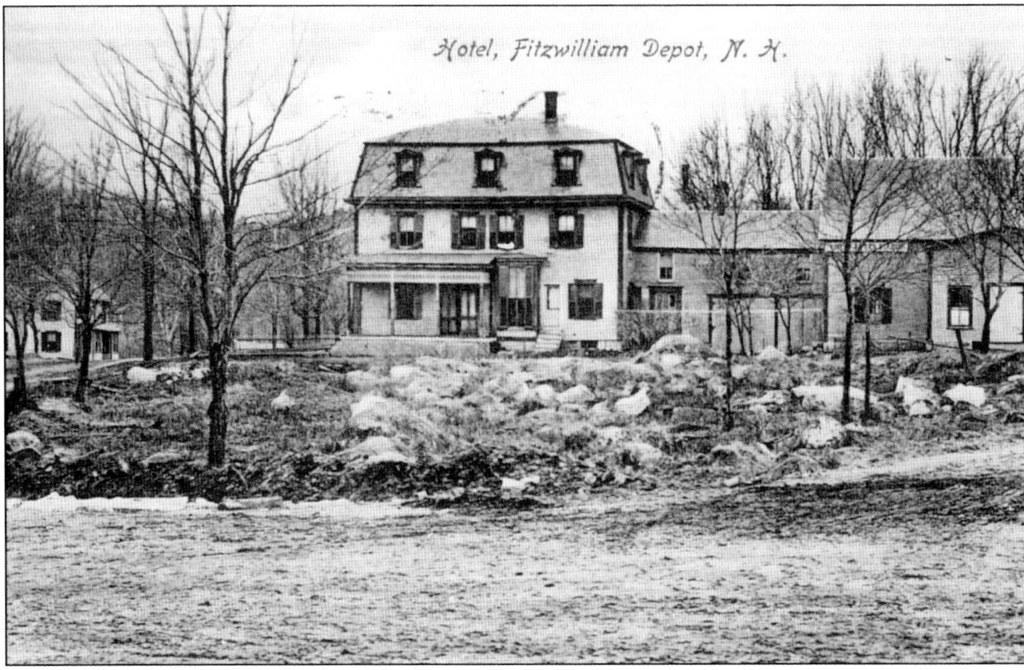

The Hotel at Fitzwilliam Depot was convenient and economical. It was not very posh, but it was comfortable and its location made it easy to catch the train in the morning. Many of the Webb quarry workers resided here. Close proximity to the train was a plus for any company, as it meant employees did not have to travel far to place products aboard.

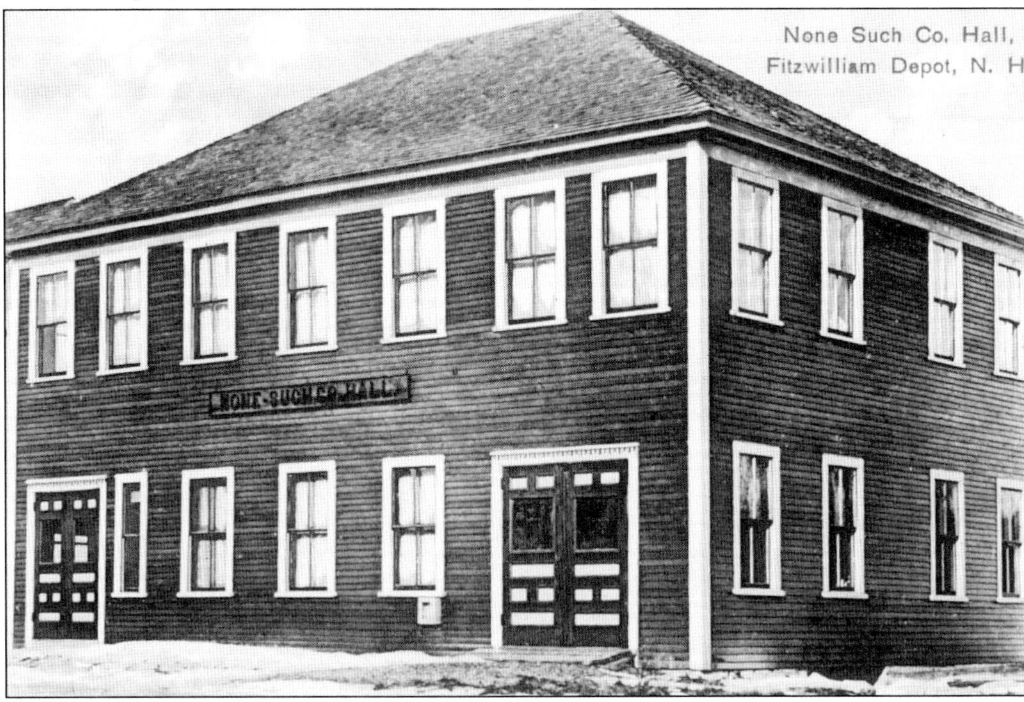

The Non Such Company Hall at Fitzwilliam Depot began in 1903 as a social enterprise for those who liked to play checkers and cards. Shares were sold to the members.

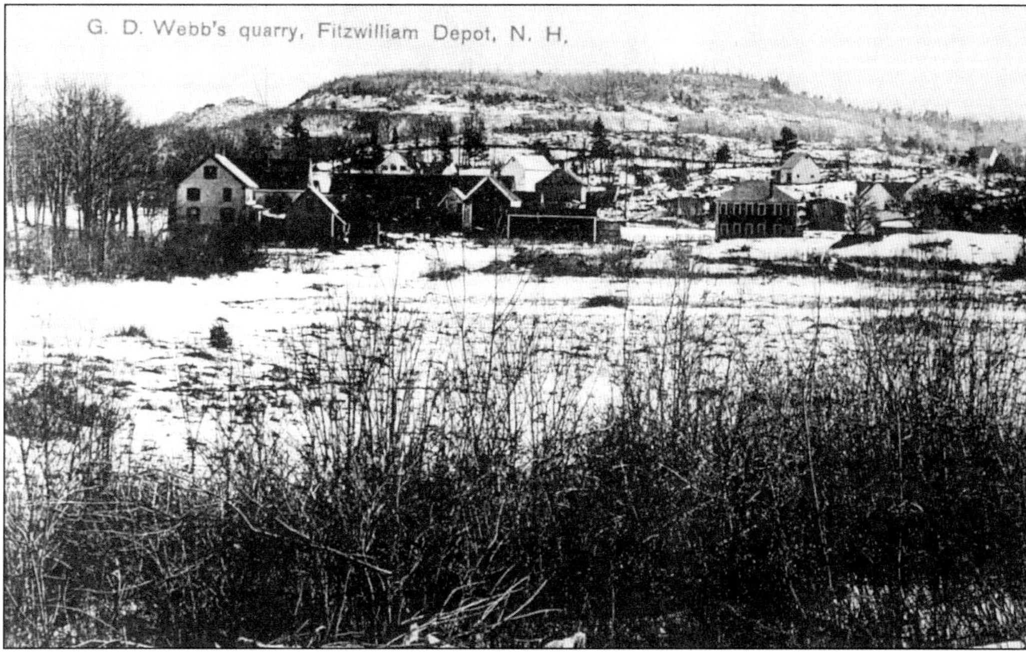

This image of G.D. Webb's quarry at Fitzwilliam Depot illustrates how hilly the land is and the number of houses that were built in the quarry area.

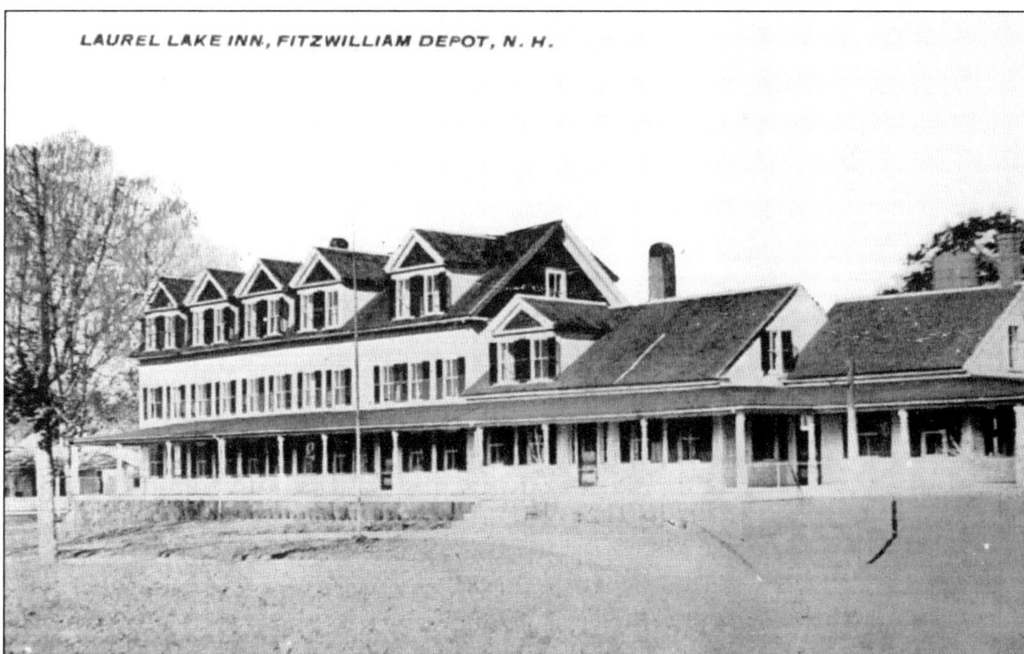

This postcard of the Laurel Lake Inn in Fitzwilliam Depot was sent from an Ohio deltiologist in the 1950s. One can only wonder how and why he or she happened to have the card.

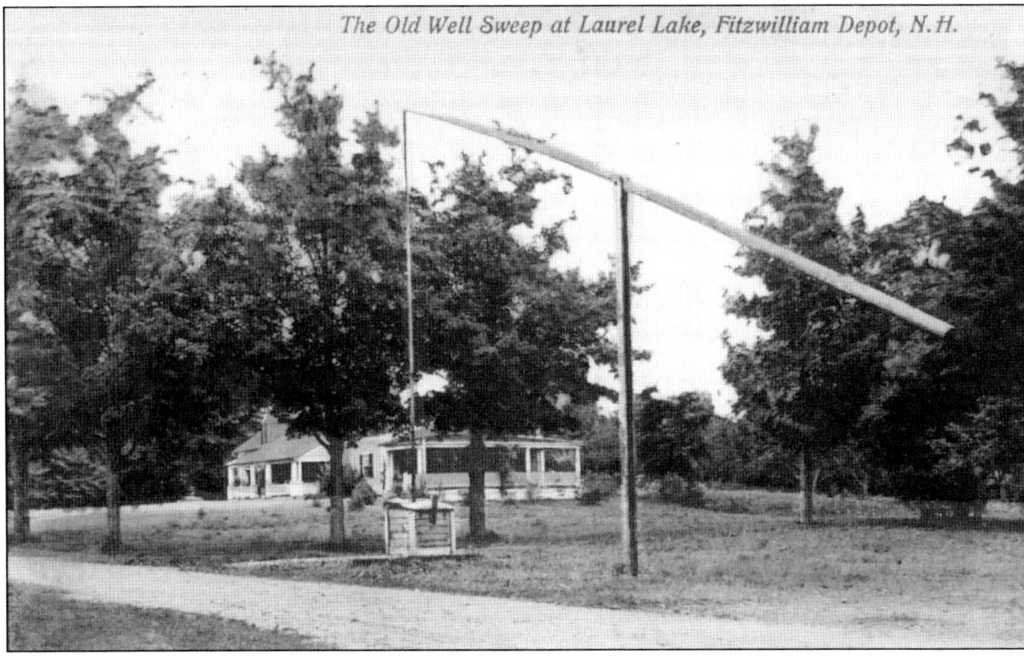

The Old Well Sweep at Laurel Lake in Fitzwilliam Depot is shown here in 1908.

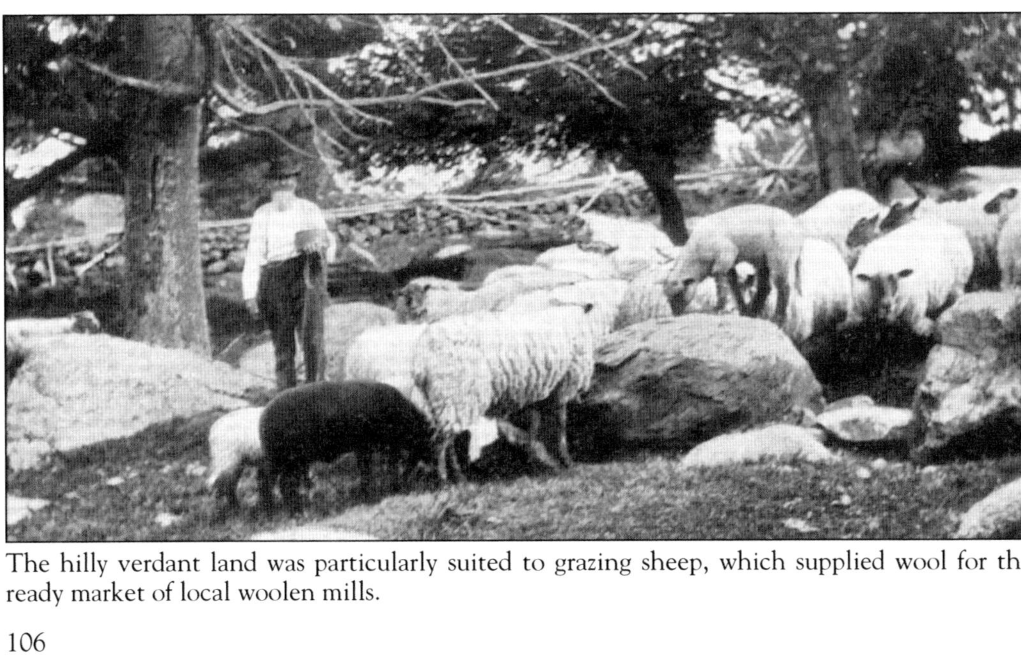

The hilly verdant land was particularly suited to grazing sheep, which supplied wool for the ready market of local woolen mills.

Six

HINSDALE

Hinsdale—named either after the Reverend Theodore Hinsdale or Colonel Ebenezer Hinsdale—has been a manufacturing town for much of its life, although it is also blessed with fertile land, mineral deposits, and two rivers (the Connecticut and the Ashuelot). In 1816 the Hinsdale Post Office opened, and it is the oldest post office in continuous use in the United States. The building of the Vernon or Hinsdale Dam was a major project begun in 1907 and completed in 1909 that changed the tenor of life not only Hinsdale but in surrounding towns in New Hampshire and Vermont.

The town is well known as the home of dog racing; however, for many years the track offered horse racing and drew well-known racers and jockeys from around New England. The mills have deteriorated in Hinsdale as they have in neighboring towns; the abandoned eyesores sometimes create ecological nightmares for residents. Hinsdale is today addressing these problems, and even as this is being written the worst of the mills on the banks of the Ashuelot is being torn down.

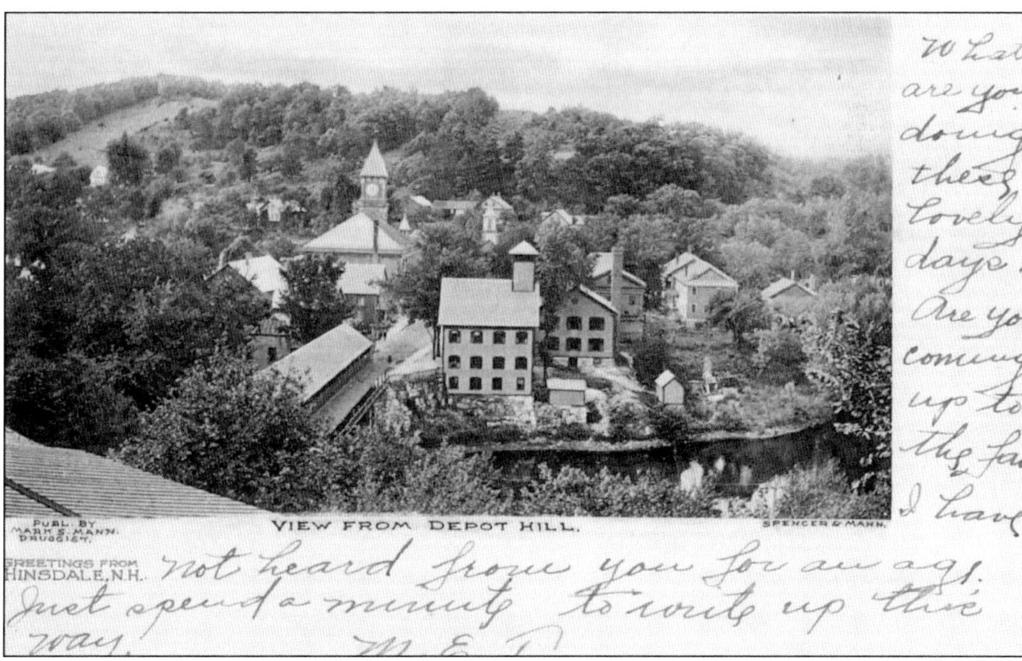

This view from Depot Hill shows the Ashuelot River, the opera house, and the paper mill.

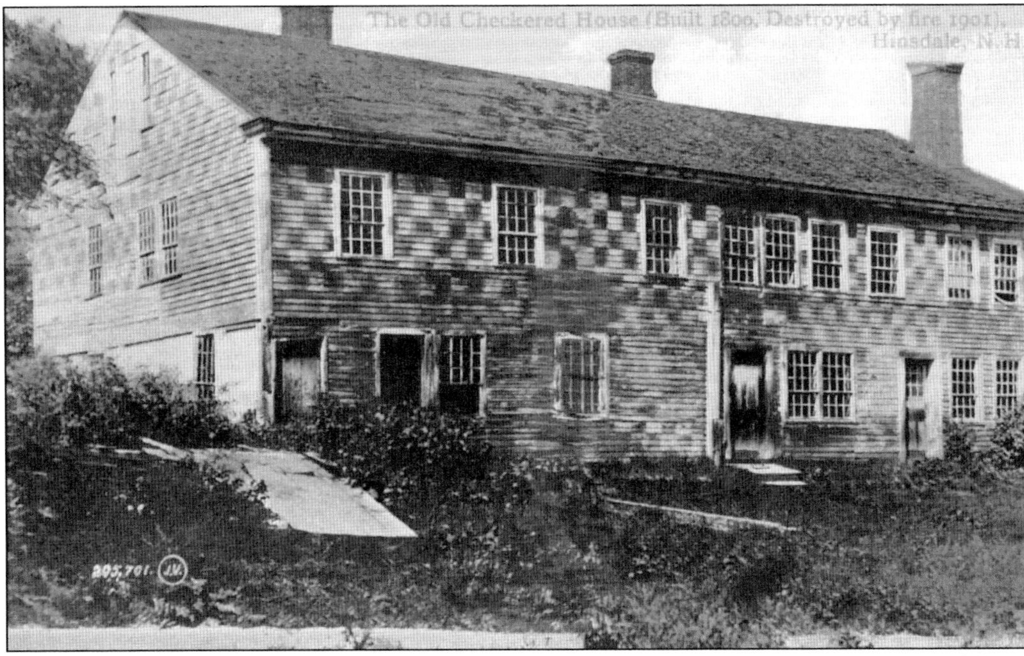

This checkered house, built in 1800, was a local tourist attraction and was much admired for its craftsmanship. It burned down in 1901.

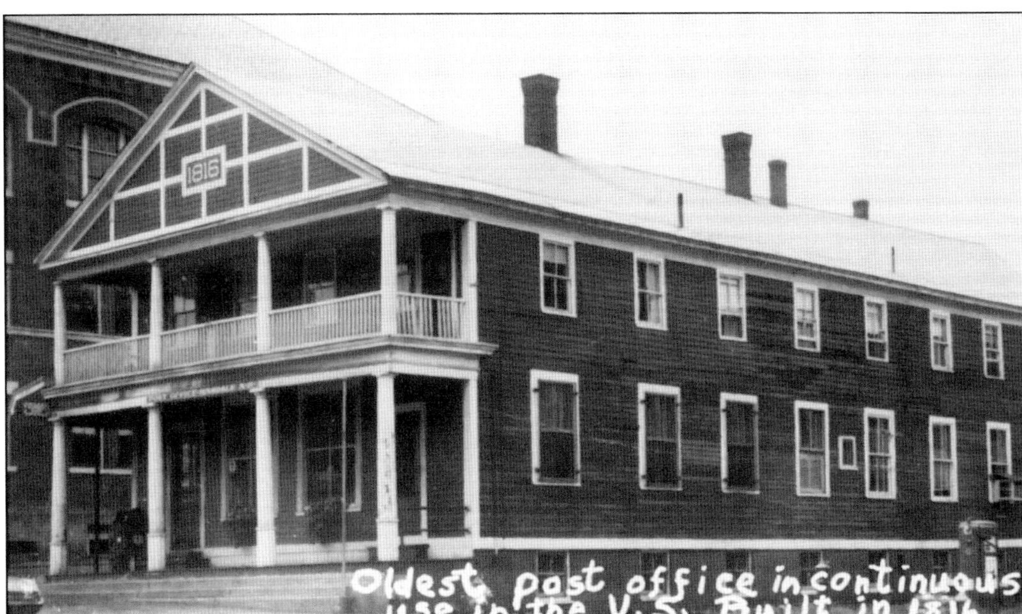

The oldest post office in continuous use (from 1816 to the present) is shown here c. 1950.

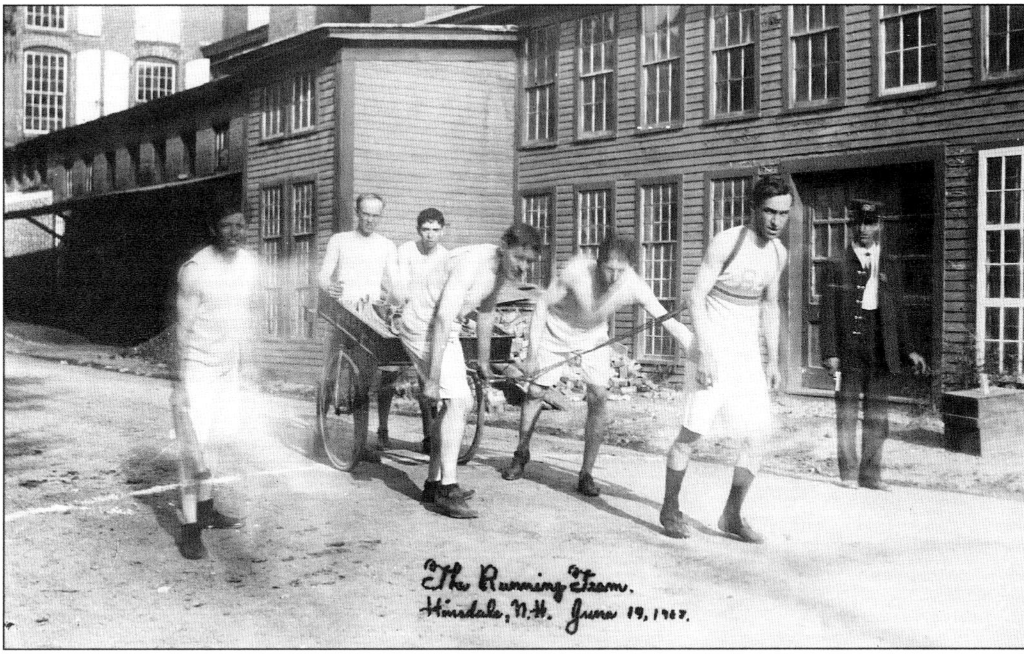

The Hinsdale running team competed on a hot June day in Ashuelot. The team was purportedly from the fire department.

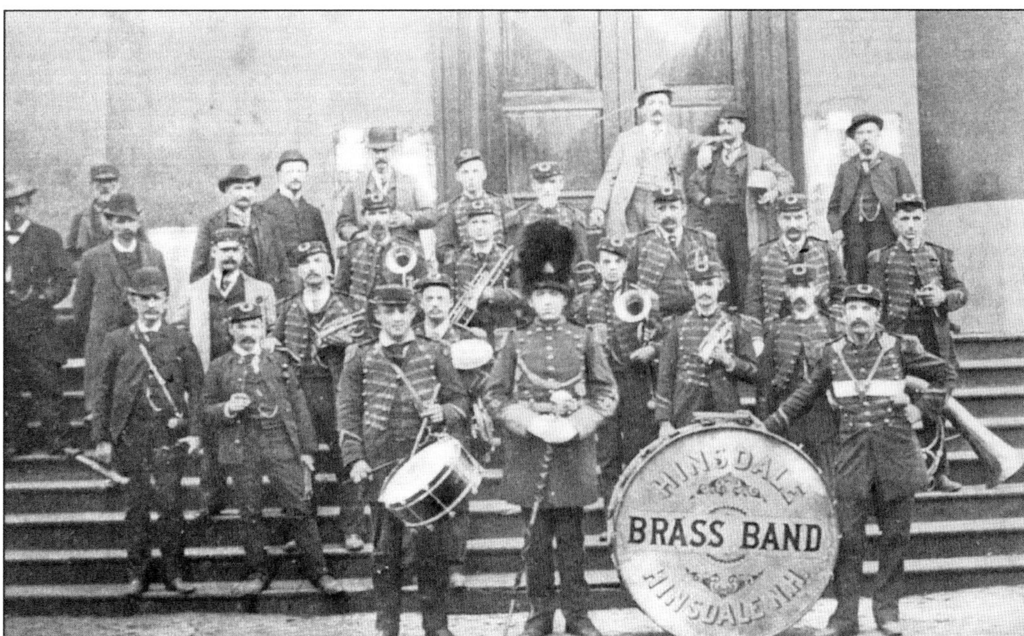

The Hinsdale Brass Band appears here in Winchester, Virginia, in October of 1889. Both the Hinsdale and Winchester bands went to Virginia, and the two towns took turns hosting the Winchester, Virginia, band in post-Civil War years.

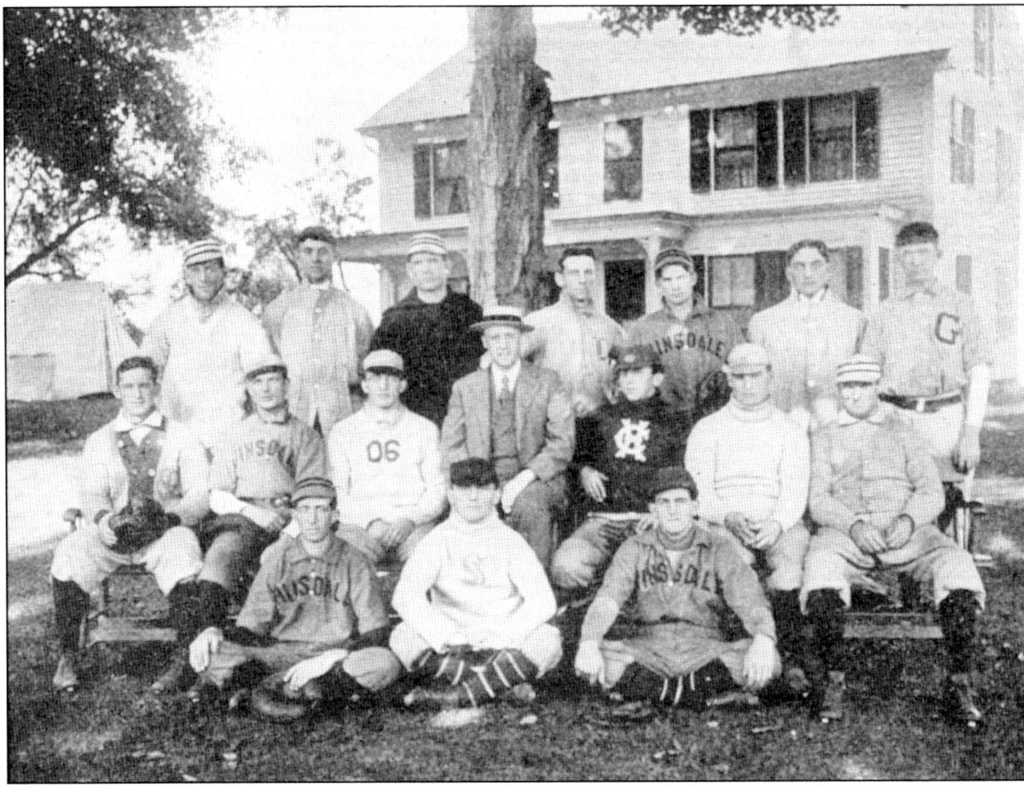

Baseball was a fun, participatory game that was usually sponsored by local businesses and watched by the entire community. The 1904 Hinsdale baseball team is pictured above.

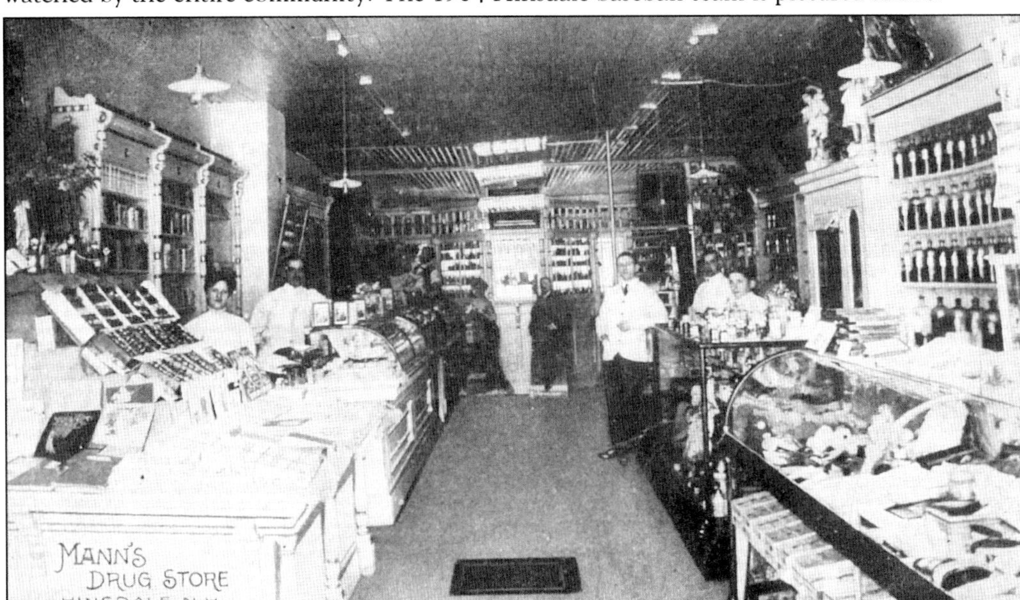

Mann's Drug Store in the Stebbins block was a good place to buy prescriptions, novelties, candies, and fancy goods. The Stebbins block, or the Beehive as it was often called, suffered a very bad fire on March 12, 1891. This image was captured in 1908.

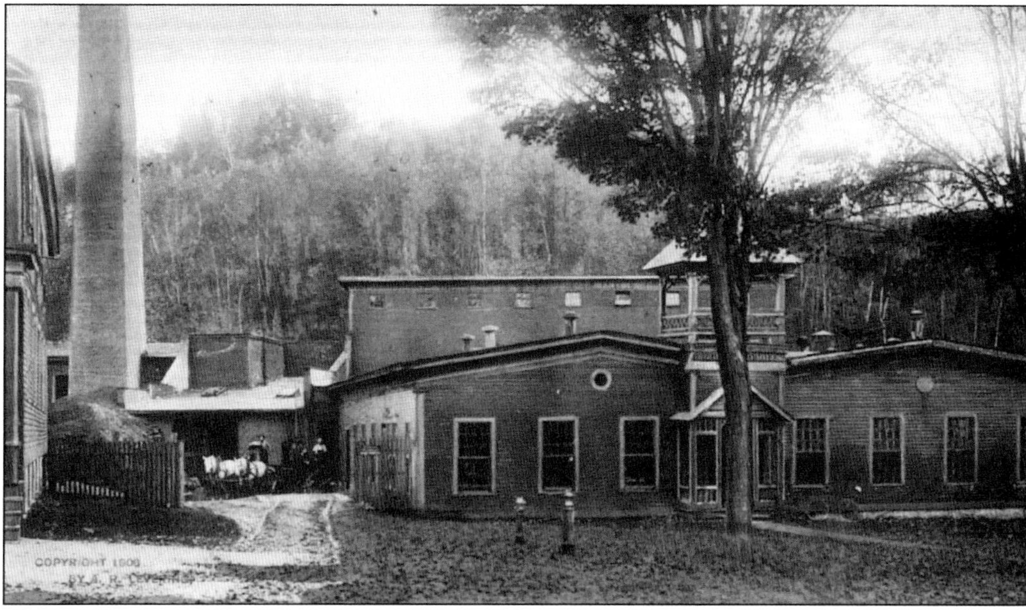

The Fisk Paper Company's mill was made entirely of local lumber and was destroyed by fire in 1911. It was rebuilt as the Brightwood Mill in 1912. Notice the horse-drawn wagon at the rear of the mill in this 1908 photograph.

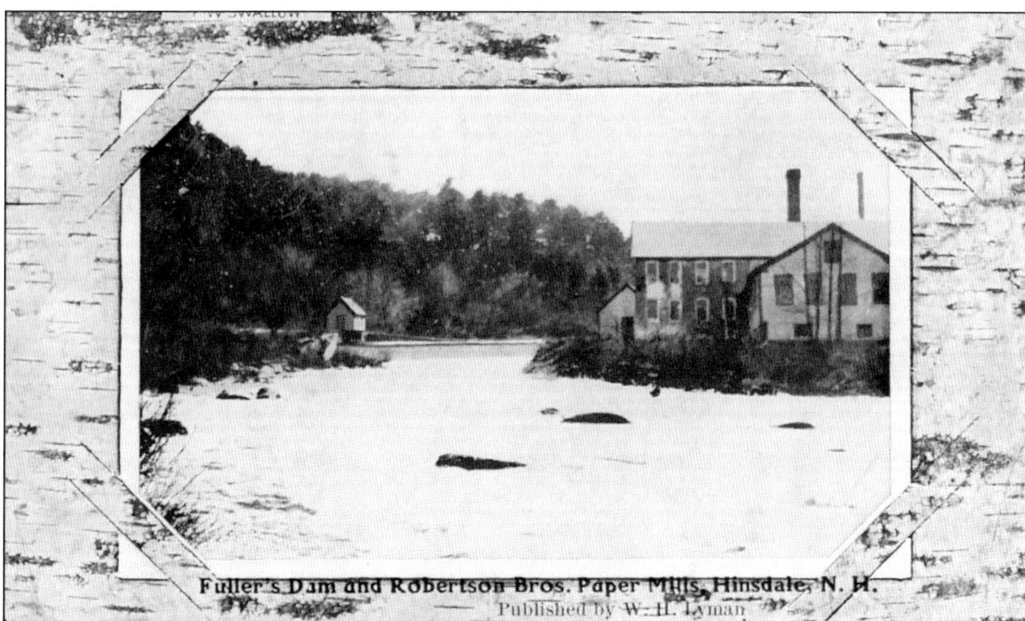

Fullers Dam and Robertson's paper mills—located very close to the river—are the focus of this 1909 printed card.

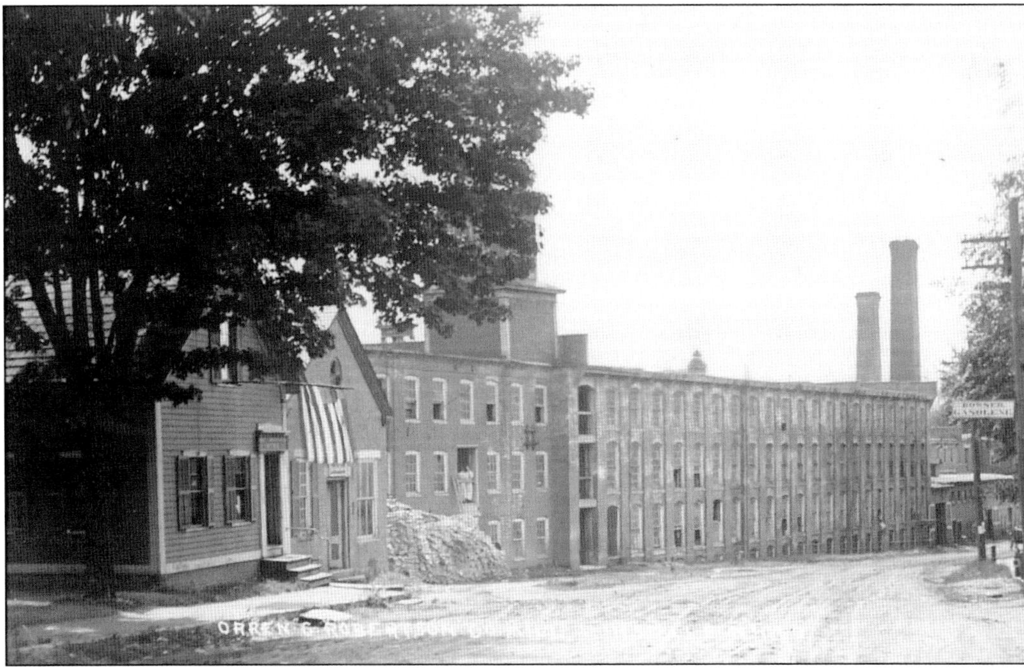

The Orren C. Robertson Company paper mill was located across the street from Bowser Gasoline in 1918, when the influenza epidemic was rampant.

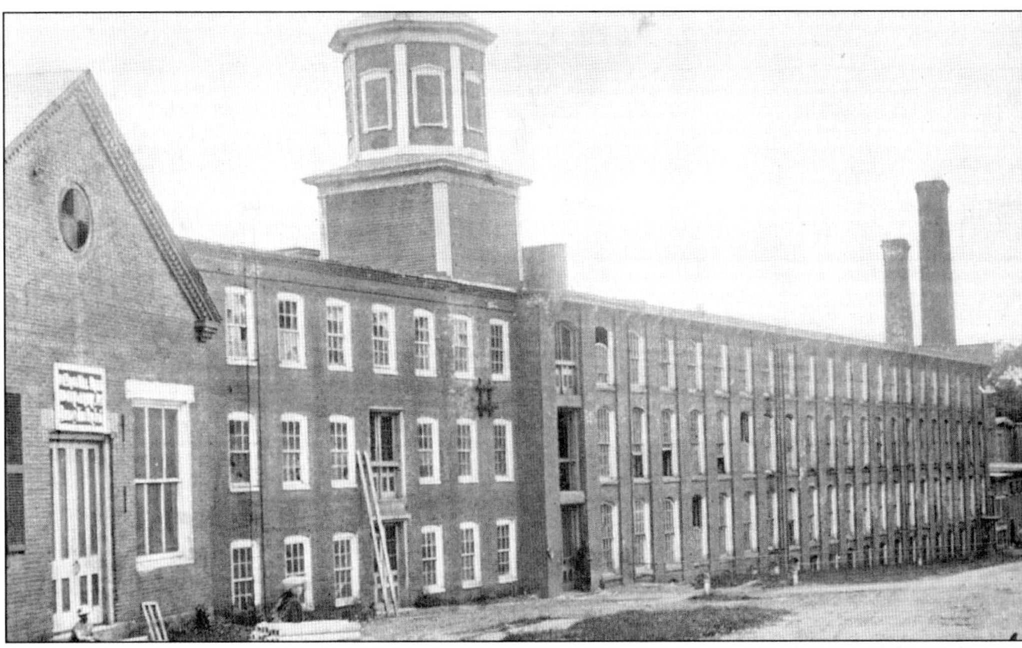

The Orren C. Robertson Company owned one of the mills that sat on the banks of the Ashuelot. For many years it sat derelict, a reminder of the ecological disaster threatened by the aging mills. This picture was taken in 1923.

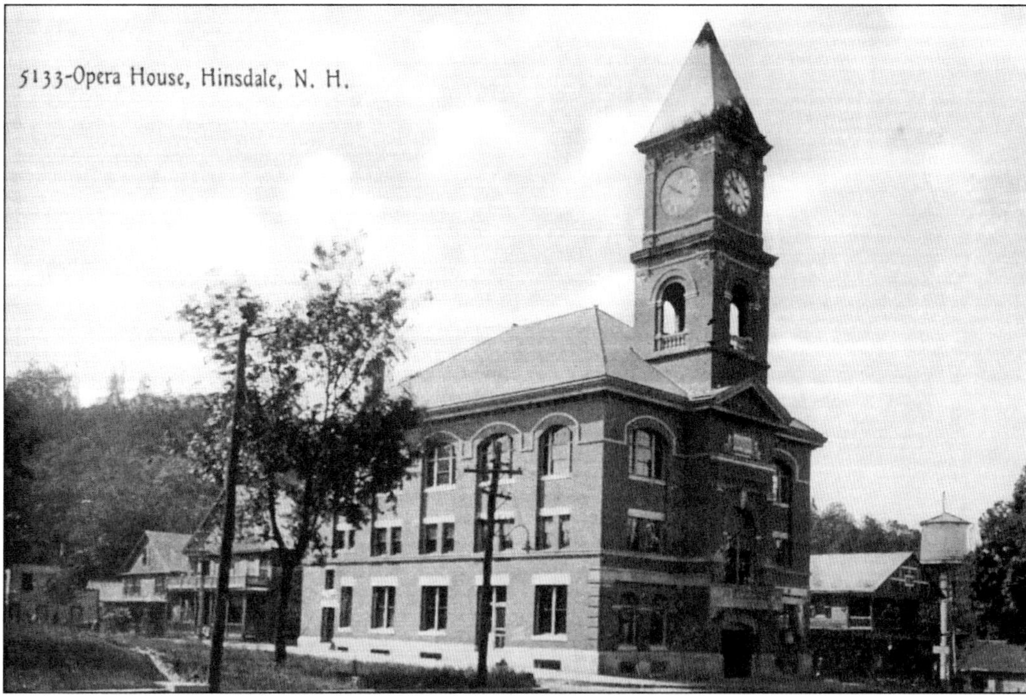

Opera houses were the first buildings in town that traveling entertainers visited. Operas, plays, and vaudeville variety shows were performed in the opera house. The building also served other functions, as it operated both as the town hall and a site for voting.

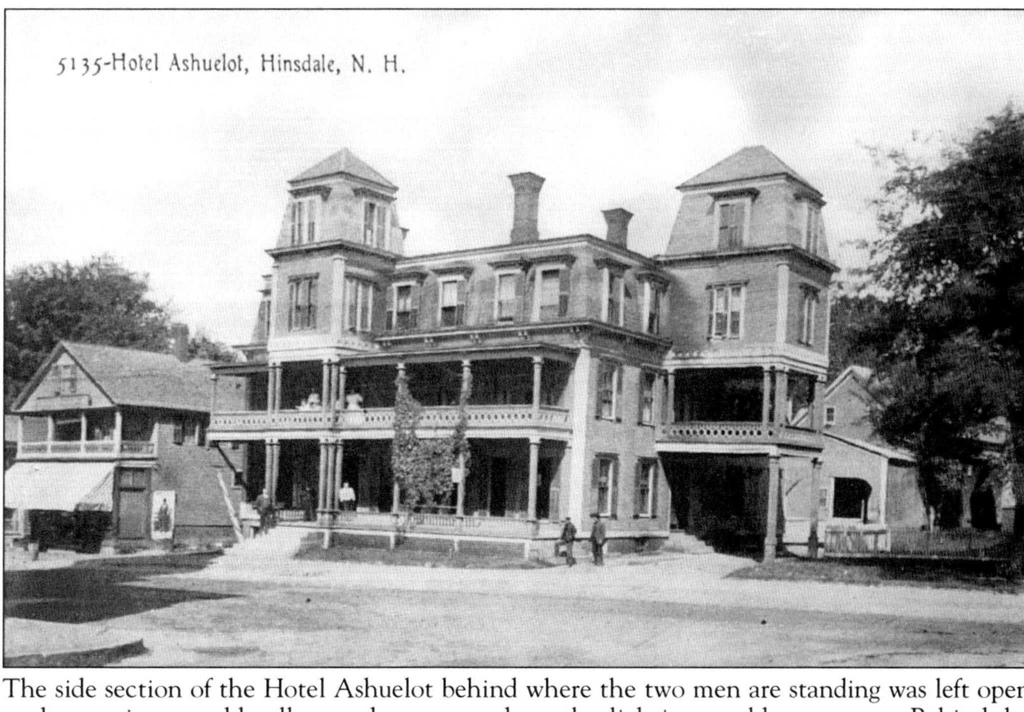

The side section of the Hotel Ashuelot behind where the two men are standing was left open so that carriages could pull up under cover and people alighting would not get wet. Behind the hotel is the stable where the horses were kept.

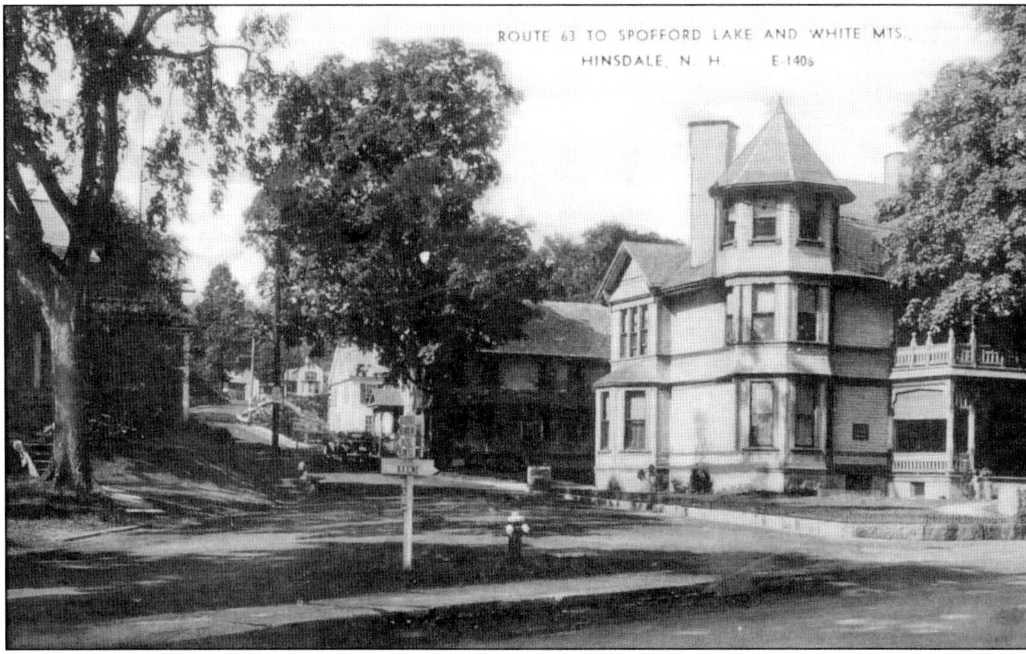

Large Victorian homes were a mark of prestige and affluence, and were usually situated on the main streets in town. This one was located on Route 63 heading toward Spofford Lake.

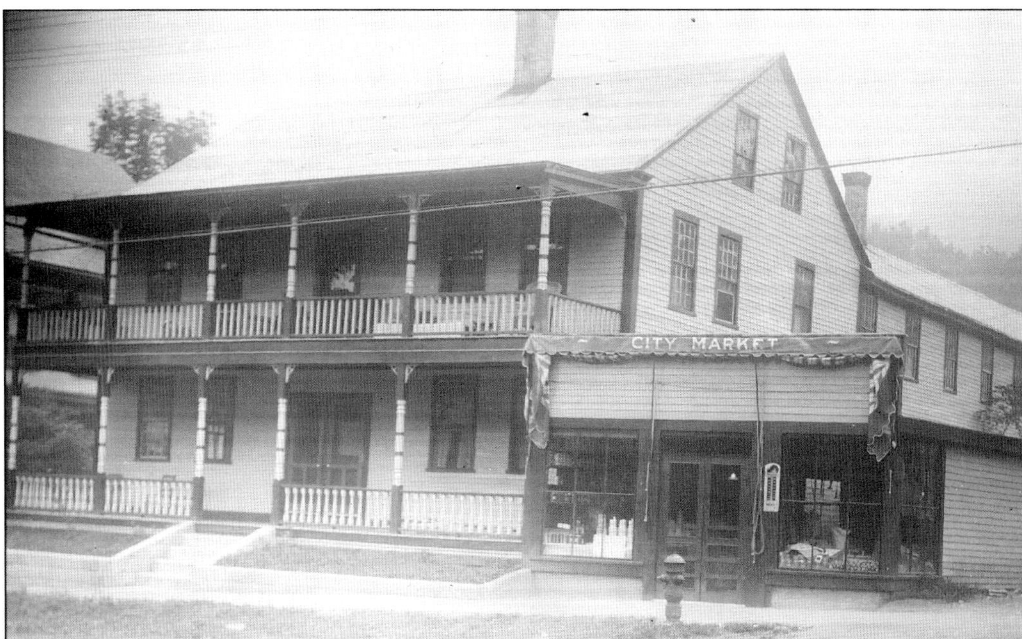

The city market was the forerunner of the modern-day grocery store. Vegetables, fruit, meat, soap, candy, flour, and all necessary items were available here when this picture was taken in 1915.

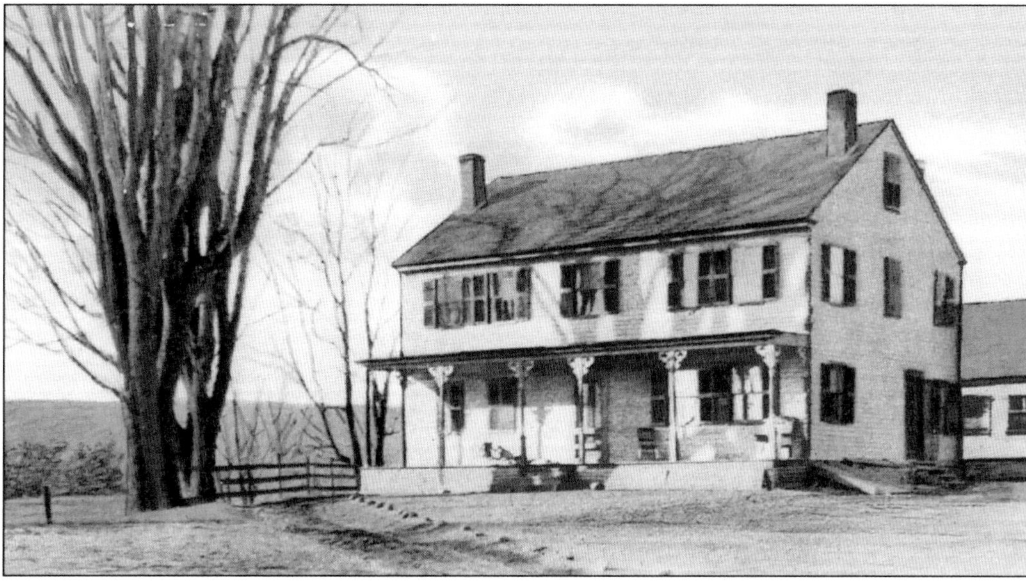

The Old River Tavern was near the Fort Hill station. The tavern was not like a modern bar, but rather was a place where people could stop and have a meal and a drink. Many taverns put up boarders or casual overnight guests. Much socializing took place in taverns such as this.

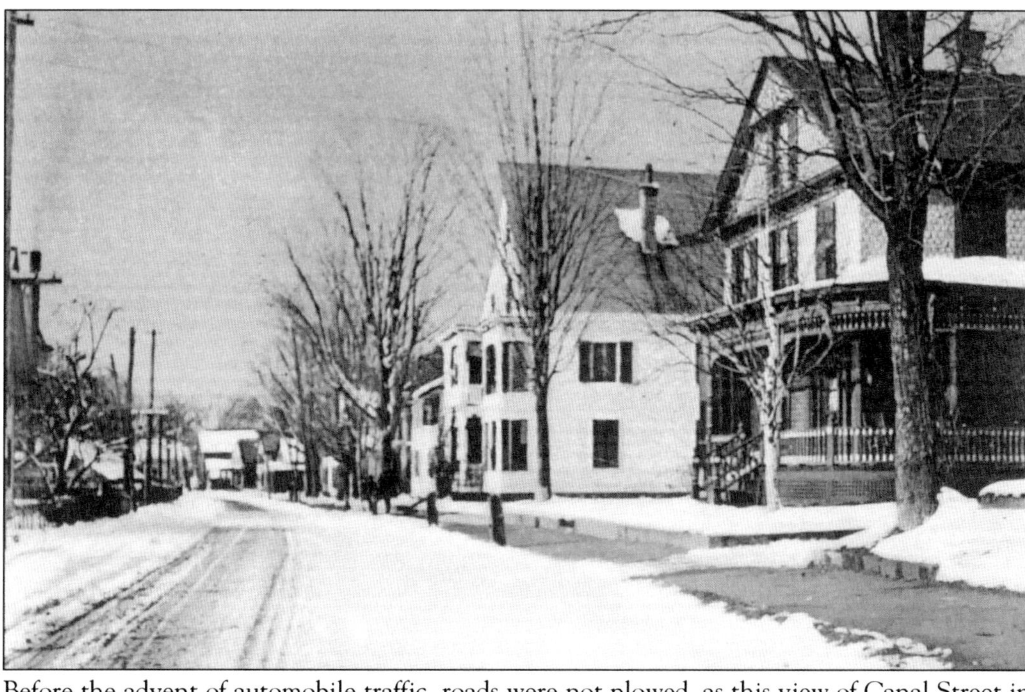

Before the advent of automobile traffic, roads were not plowed, as this view of Canal Street in the winter demonstrates; carriages and sleighs made their own paths and shovels were used by residents to clear paths and walks.

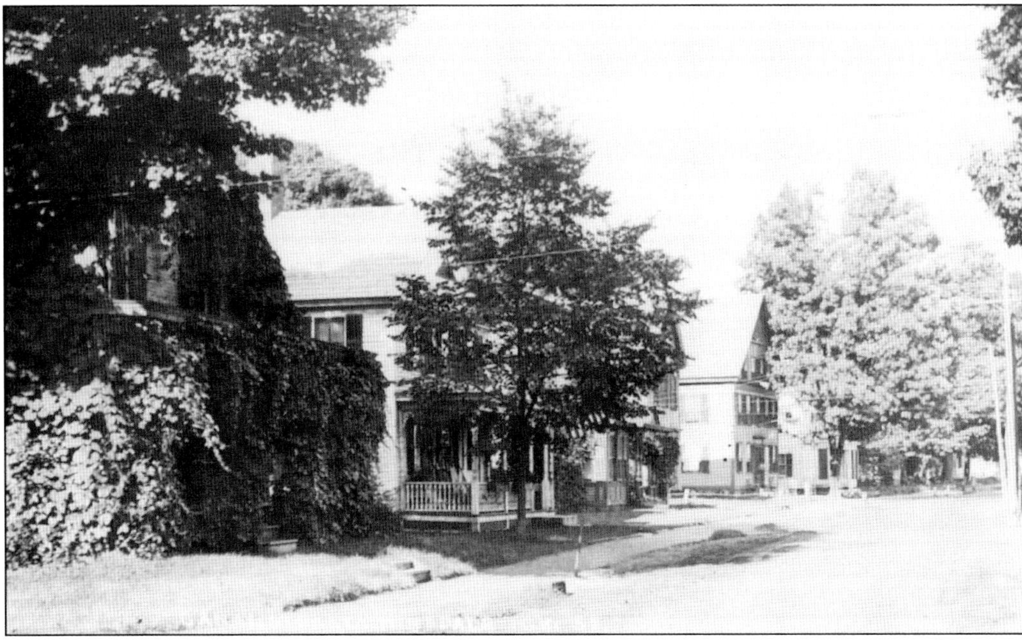

This view of Canal Street illustrates the importance of trees and vines as a means of keeping homes cool during the summer.

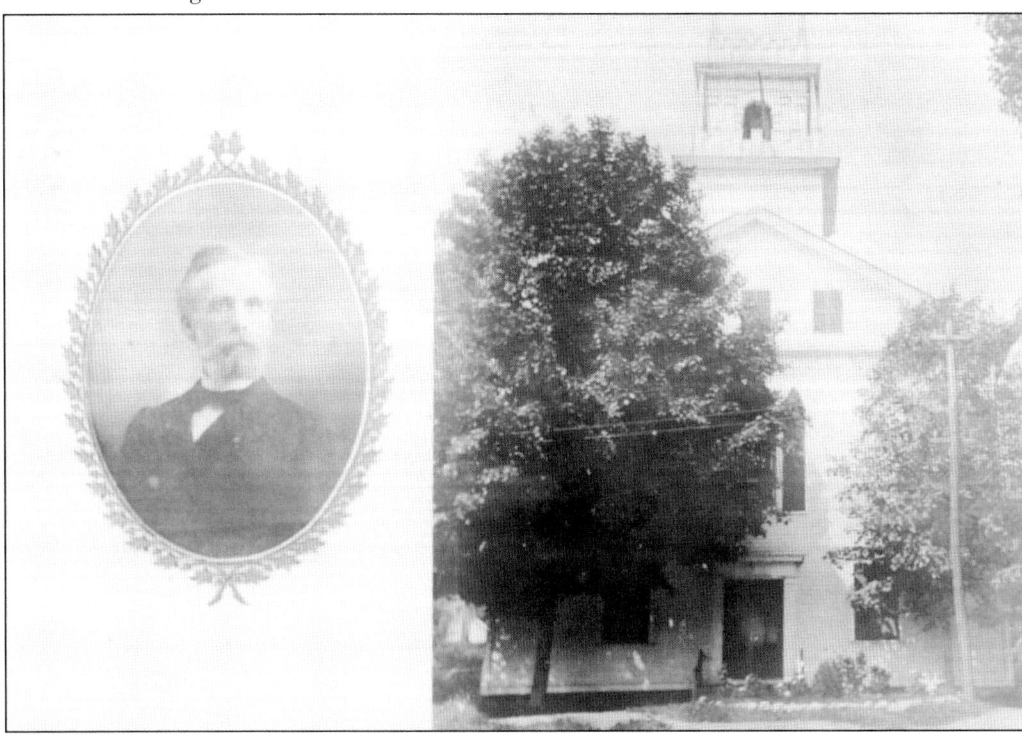

The Universalist church appears here alongside a cameo photograph of the pastor at the time, Reverend W.R. Trickey. Built in 1839–40, the church was sold to the Masonic order in 1934. This postcard was sent as a valentine on February 14, 1906. The church fair and festival were held on February 15 and 16.

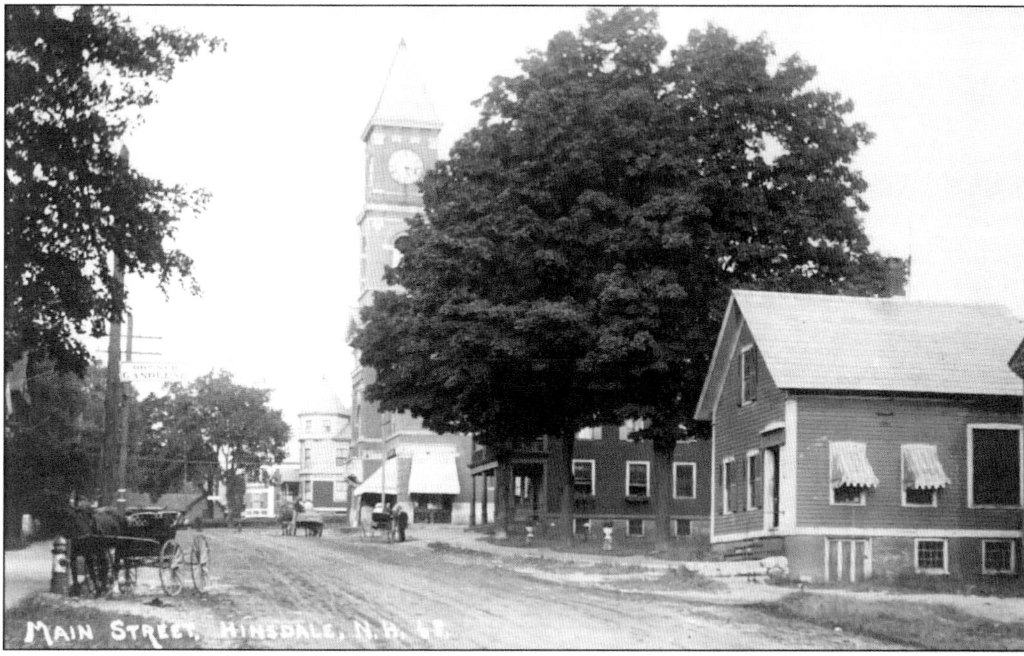

Main Street was the most important section of town. In 1918 the carriage was still the dominant mode of transportation, but already there was a gas station—Bower's.

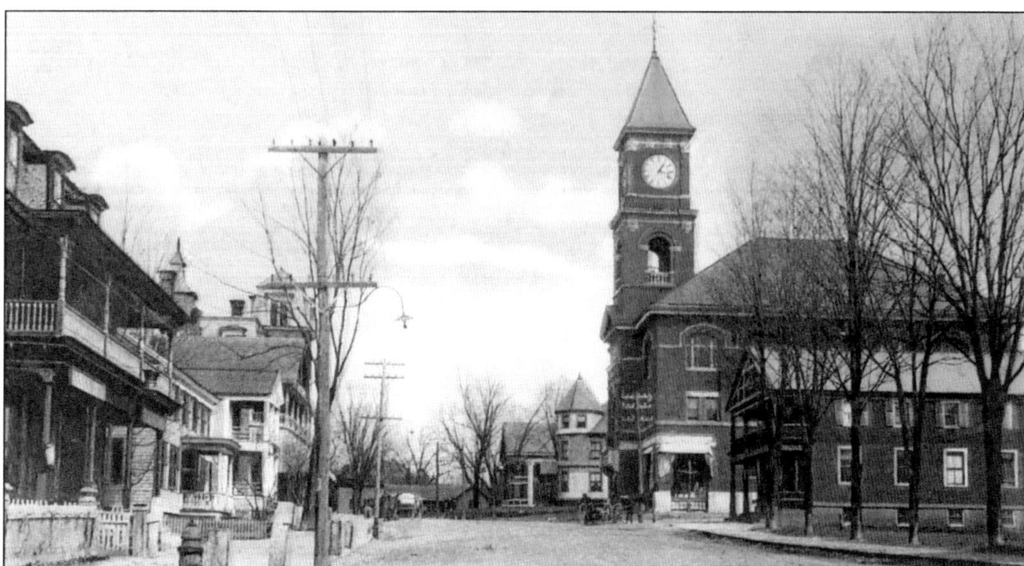

At the time this photograph of Main Street as taken, Hinsdale had both electricity and telephone service. It also still had hitching posts for horses.

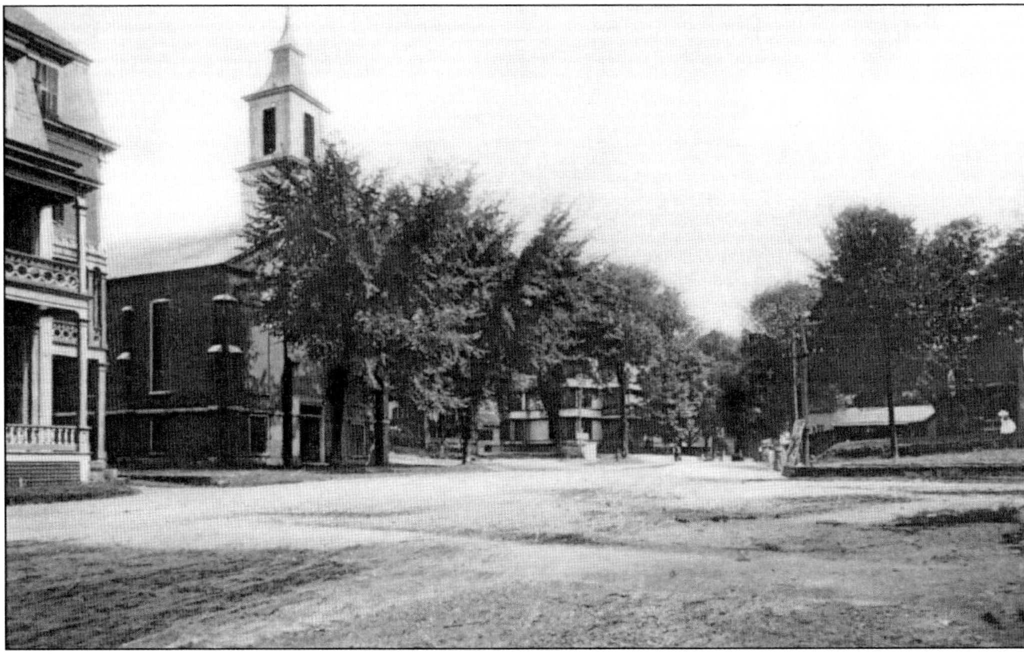

The main street was always the widest in town. Still unpaved and uneven in this shot, it was sufficient for the transportation that traversed it.

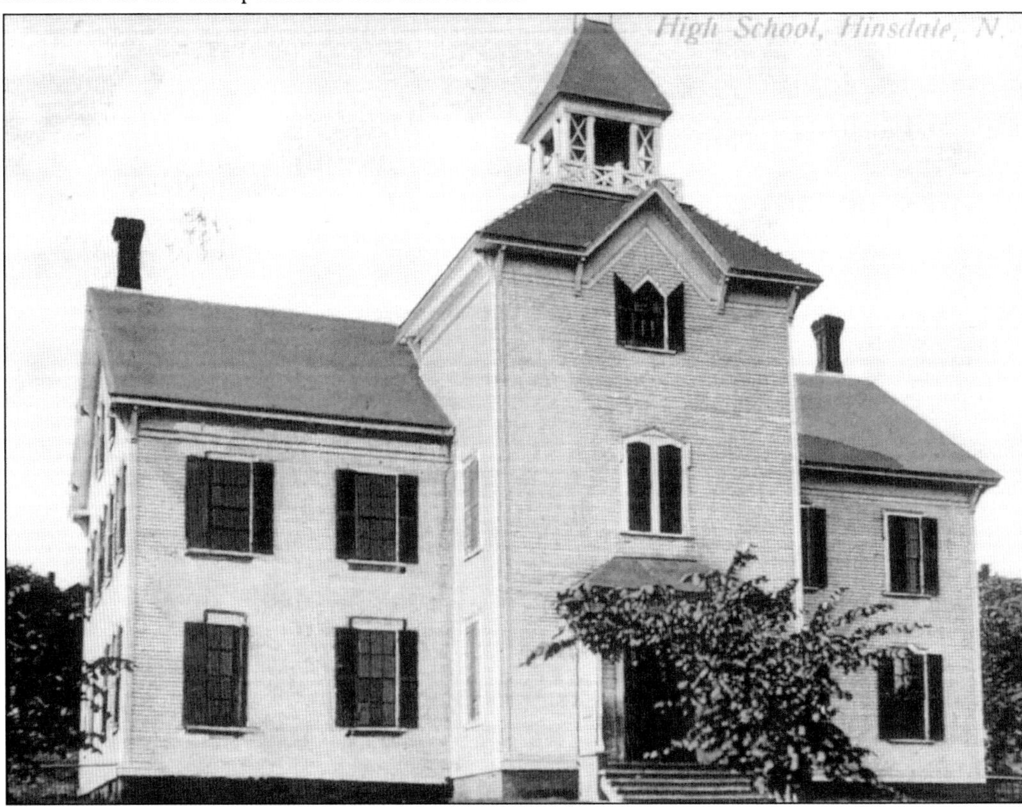

The high school was built on Brattleboro Street in 1878.

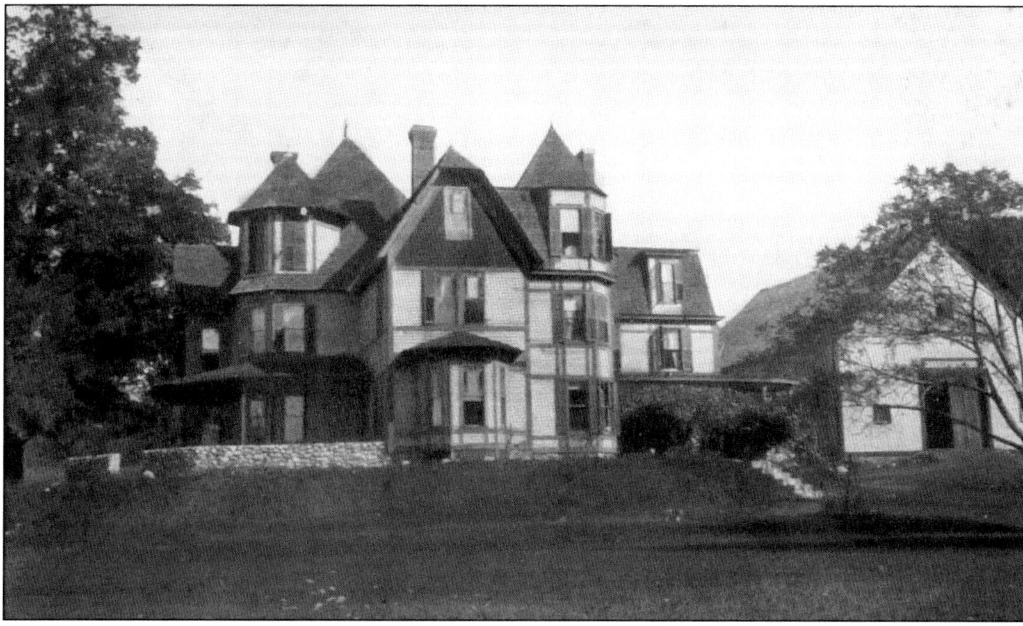

Building like Mountainside, a beautiful gothic pile with stables behind it, often became multi-family homes and professional offices later on.

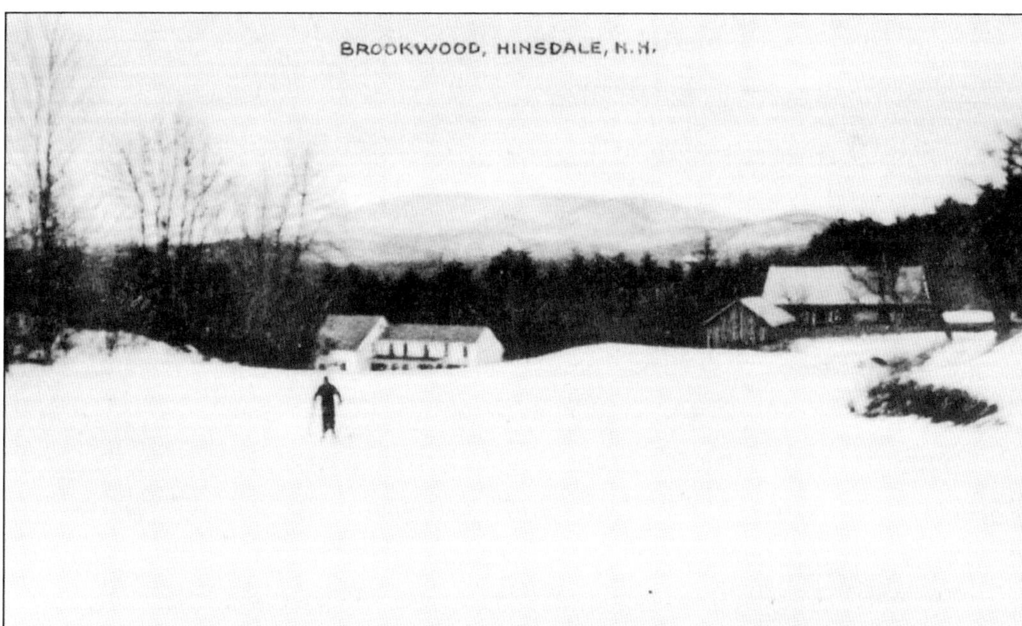

Skiing and snowshoeing were a way of life in snow-laden New England, and especially in Brookwood. Note the mountain in the background and the height of the snowdrifts.

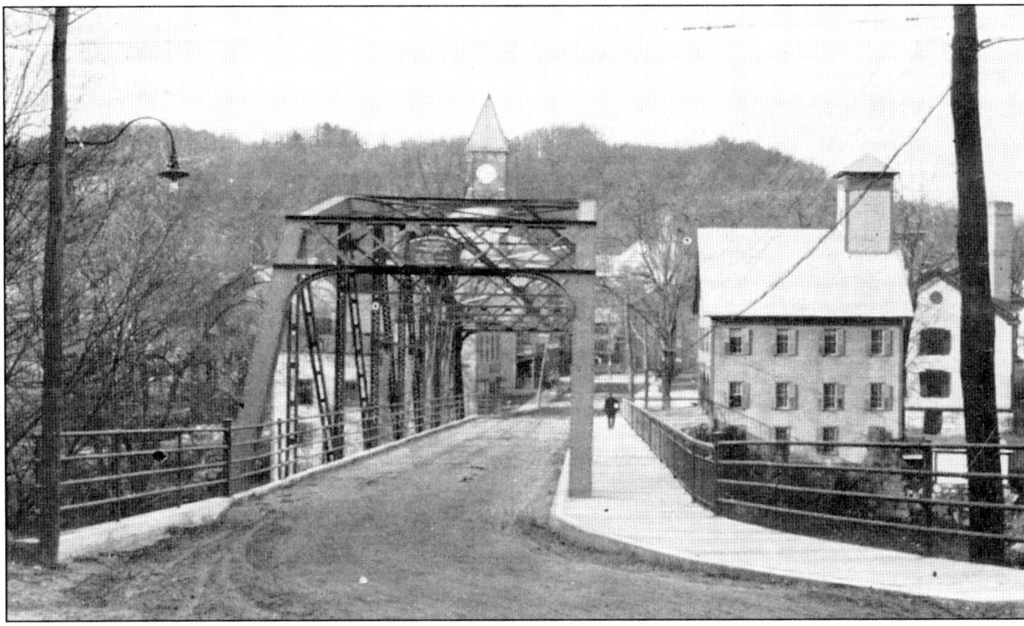

The new iron bridge and Depot Street are featured in this view.

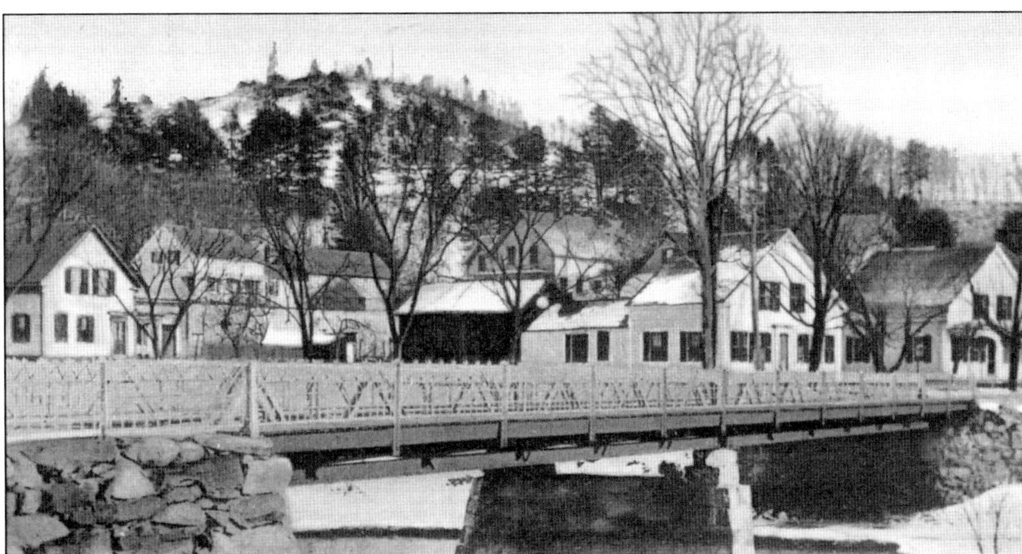

The Northfield Street Bridge is shown here with the town in the background in 1908. The bridge was built in 1892 and replaced by a concrete structure in 1940.

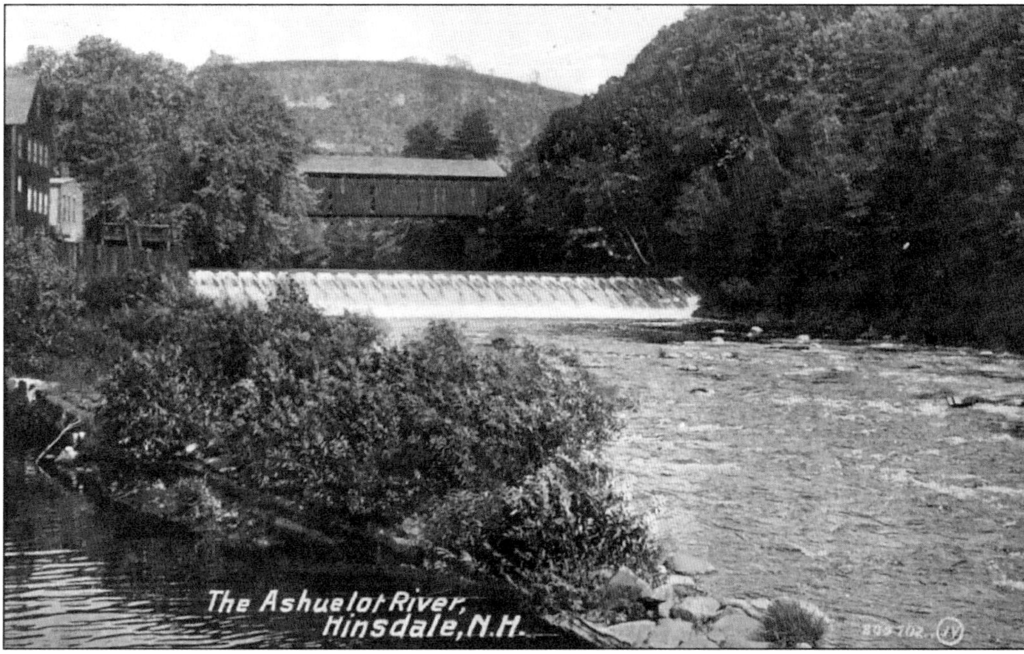

The Ashuelot River, the covered bridge, and the dam appear here as they looked in 1908.

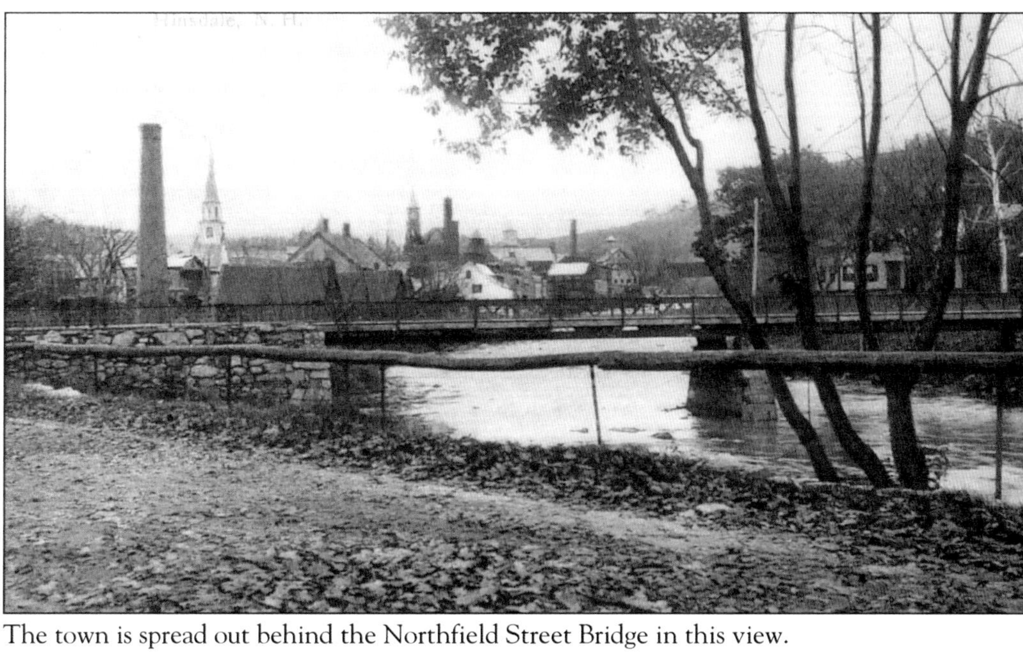
The town is spread out behind the Northfield Street Bridge in this view.

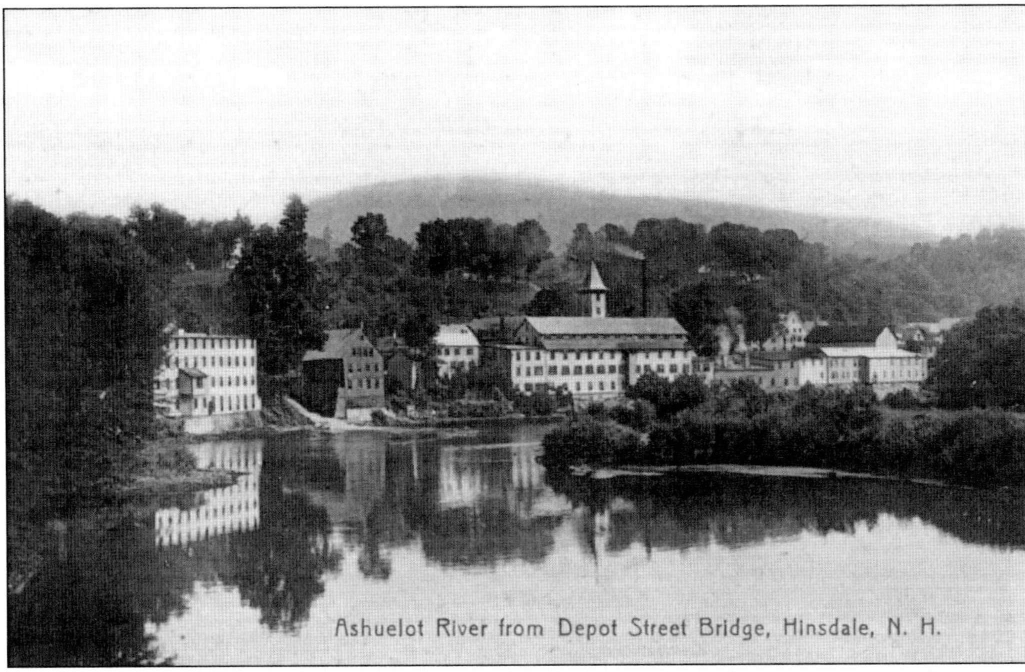

The Ashuelot River is shown here from the Depot Street Bridge. This is a picture-perfect image of a mill town: serene and affluent.

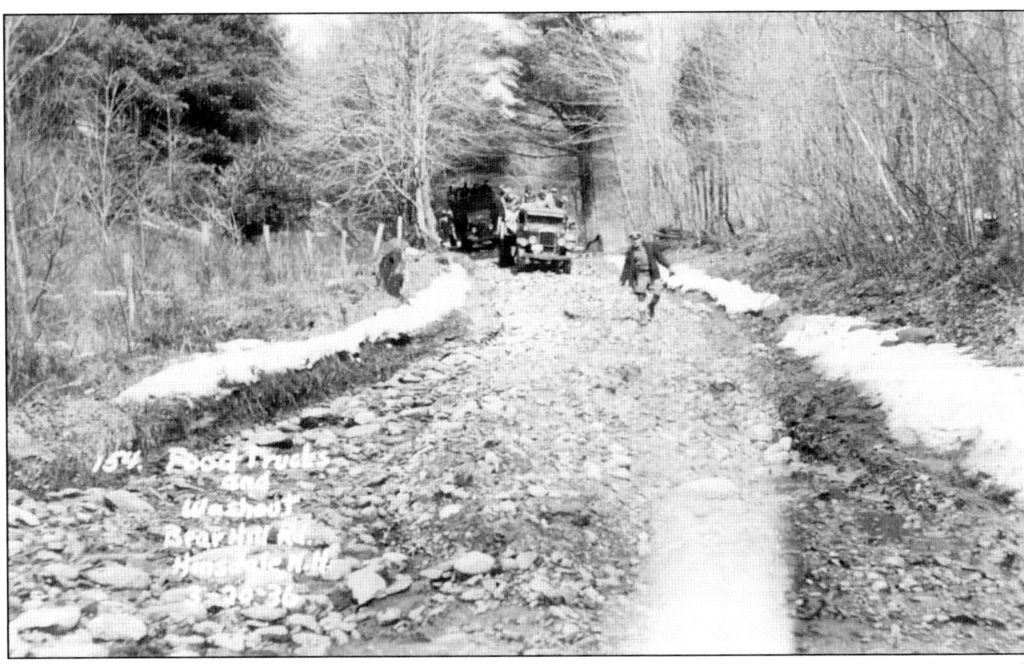

The 1936 flood affected all of southwest New Hampshire. Bear Hill Road is shown here with the flood trucks; the entire road was washed away. Peoples' homes and public buildings were flooded, and residents were forced to use rowboats for transportation on the streets.

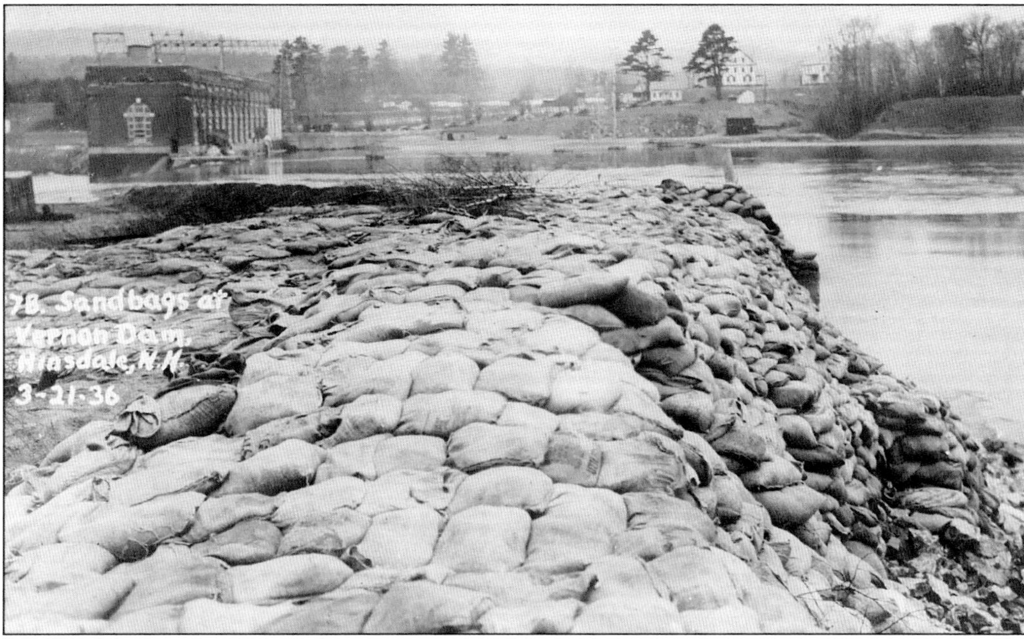

Sandbags were used at the Vernon Dam during the 1936 flood.

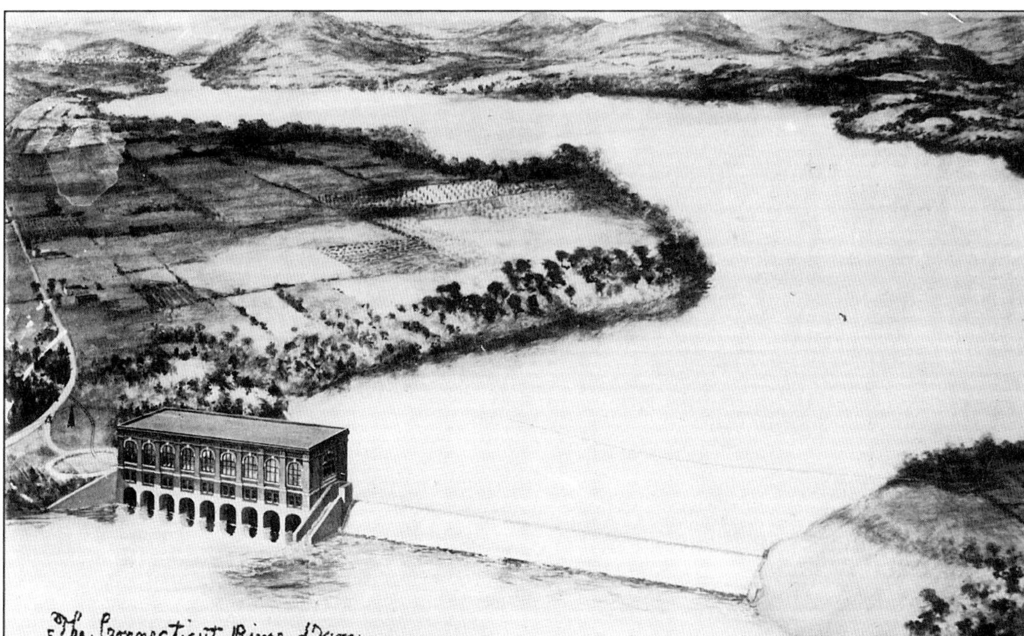

The Connecticut River Dam fronts Vernon, Vermont, on one side and Hinsdale, New Hampshire, on the other.

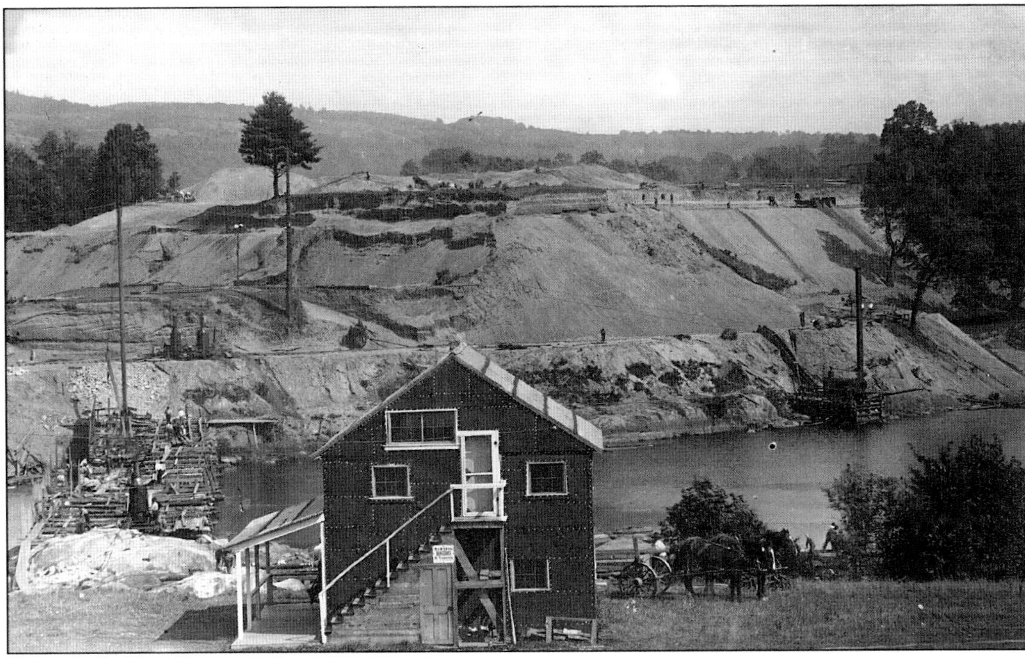

The building of the dam was important not only because it provided employment for residents but because of the excitement it bought to the town. The dam's progress was watched and commented on daily. The sign on the dam site offices says: "Warning Danger."

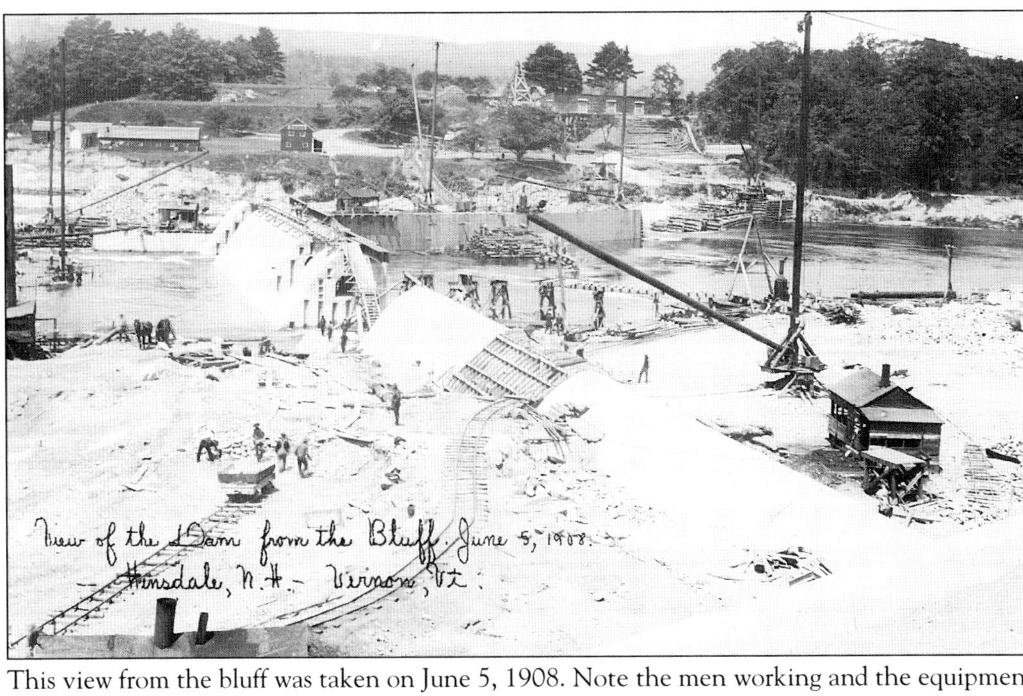

This view from the bluff was taken on June 5, 1908. Note the men working and the equipment they are using.

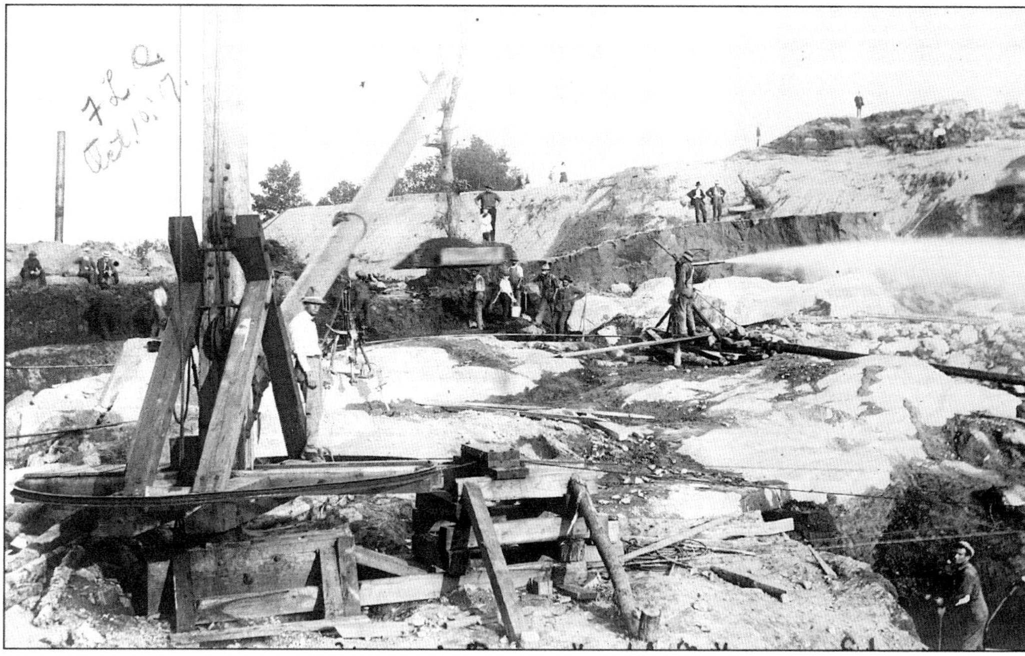

Two supervisors stand on the ridge overseeing the construction of the dam on September 15, 1907.

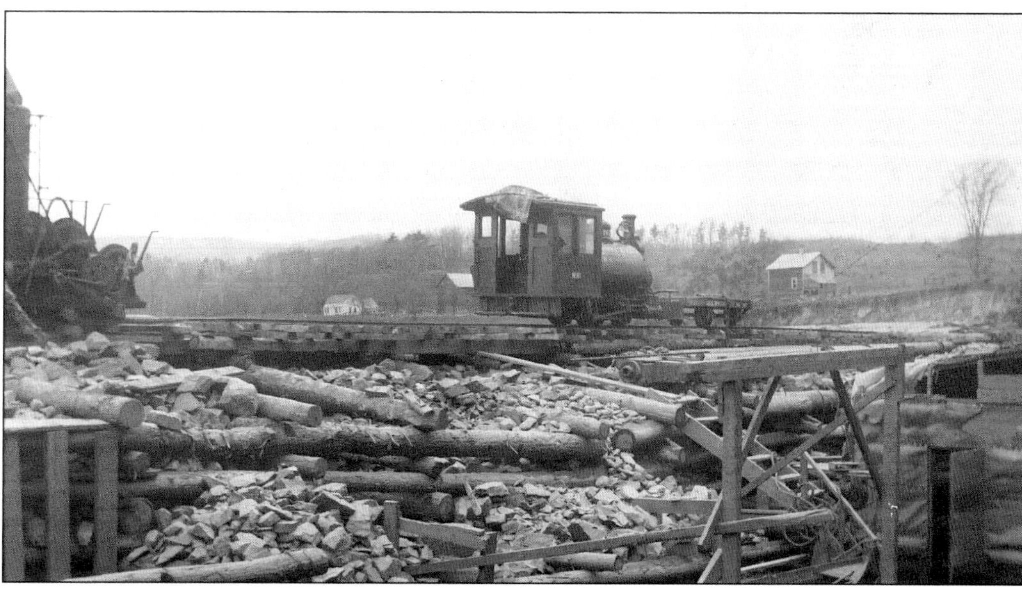

Engines were used to tow cars loaded with building materials to the site.

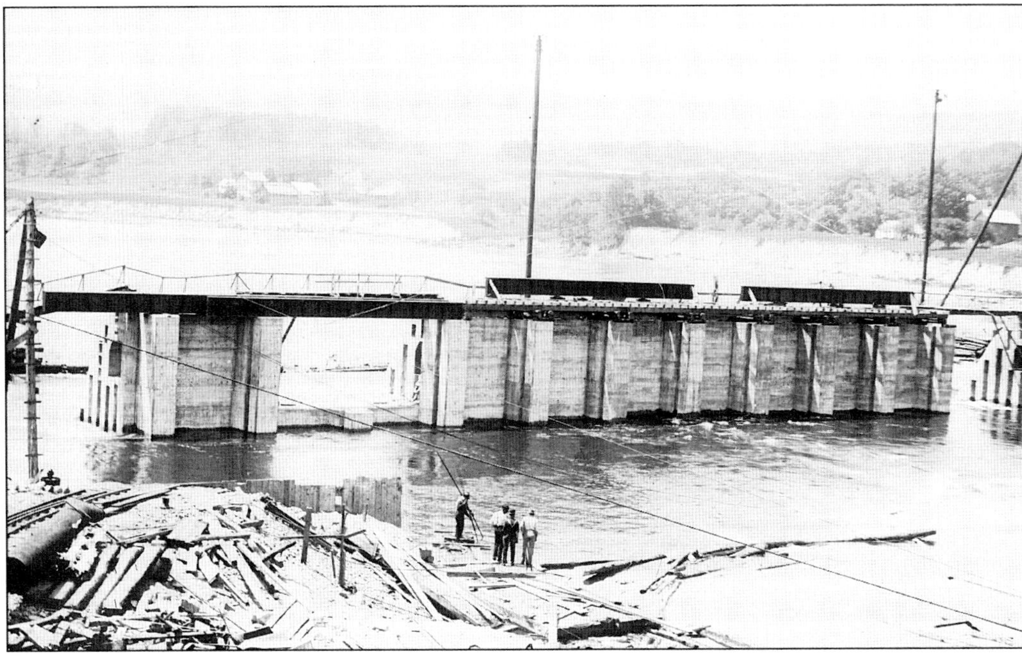

Workers on the dam congregated on June 5, 1908, near a huge pile of building materials.

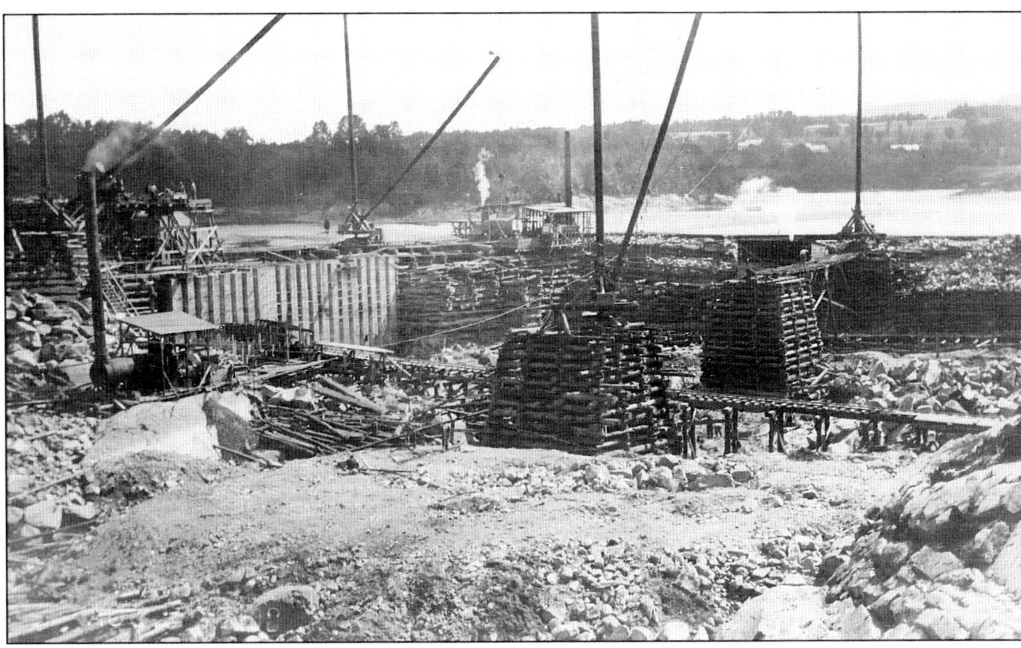

Work on the dam continued for two years.

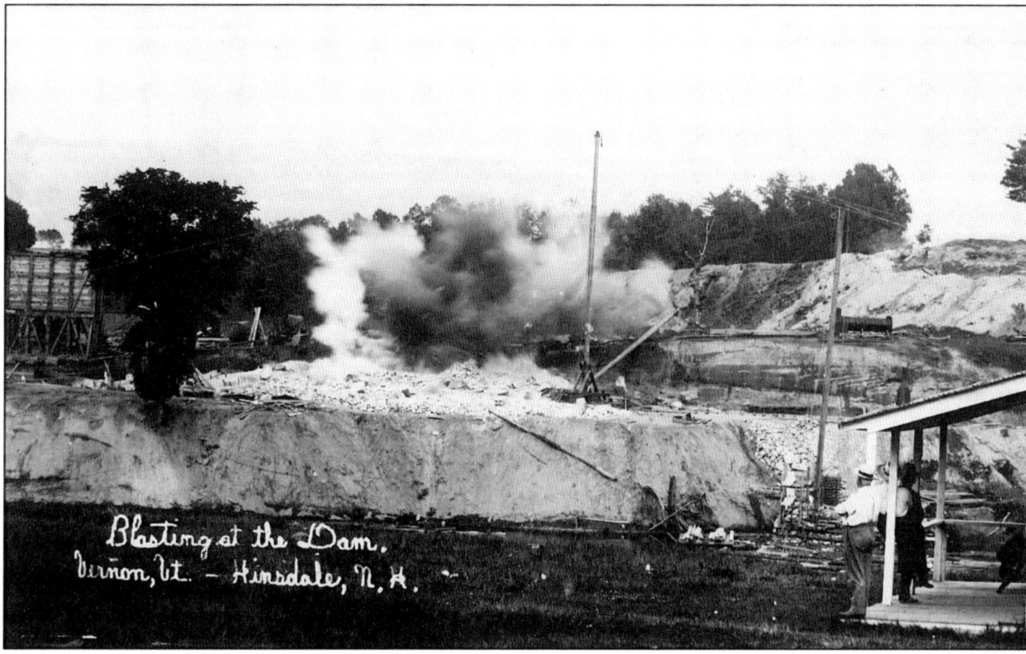

Blasting took place at the dam between the river and the foreman's office.

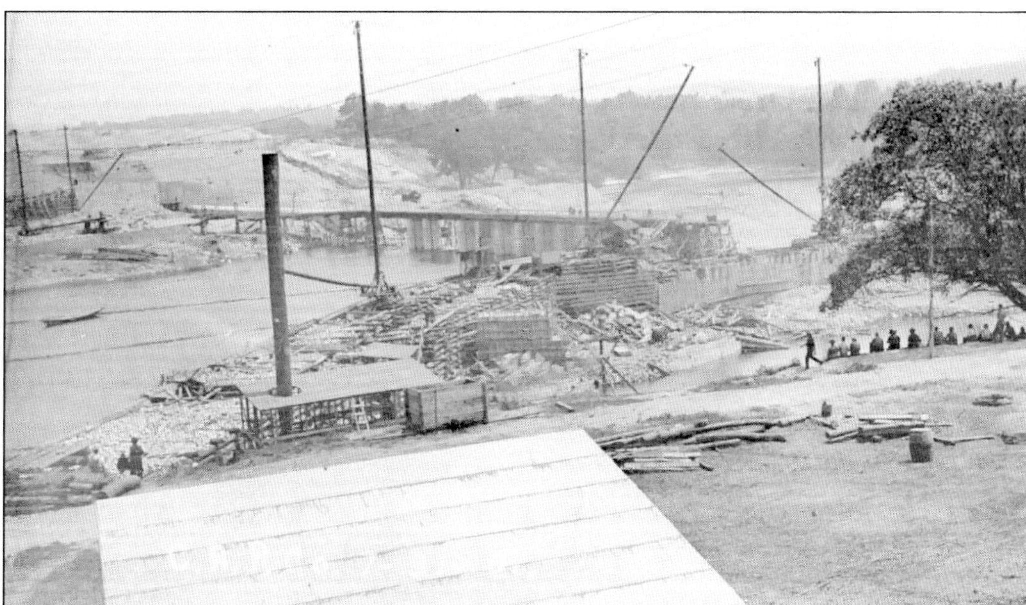

Employees of the CRP Company (responsible for constructing the dam) are shown here taking lunch under a tree on September 31, 1908.

EPILOGUE

Southwest New Hampshire consists of Swanzey, Winchester, Ashuelot, Richmond, Fitzwilliam, and Hinsdale. Situated on the borders of Vermont and Massachusetts and separated from the eastern part of the state by poor east-west roads, the area has taken on a personality very different from the rest of the state. The region has produced soldiers from pre-Revolutionary war times to the present. Its cultural life has been sustained by churches and social organizations. Its economic life was once agrarian, but became industrial and now relies mainly on small entrepreneurial businesses like garden centers, antique shops, and boutiques. It has known Indian wars, influenza epidemics, floods, loss of industry, depressions, and world wars, and yet through it all, with the strength of some of its rugged characters, the area has held its own. The entire region has grown slowly, like an oak tree, and only the future will see its fruition. The influence of the "Old Homestead" mentality cannot be overemphasized when one considers the hearty individuality of this area.

Many historic buildings are still standing in southwest New Hampshire, and with the arrival of new people into the area many of these old homes are being restored. Historical societies like the Swanzey Museum are researching and preserving the documentation that represents the history of the region. Parades, celebrations, and baseball games were special situations worth preserving for posterity. The social history of any area is revealed in the economic and cultural influences captured in print and on film. What an area does with those influences is dependent on the honesty, intelligence, and foresight of the ruling generation, and only through reflection on these types of artifacts can one properly evaluate the progress of the area over the years. It is my hope that this book will assist in the preservation of such valuable vestiges of the past.